MONTANA'S
BEST FISHING WATERS™

170 Detailed Maps of 34 of the Best Rivers, Streams, and Lakes

BEST FISHING WATERS™

Wilderness
Adventures
Press, Inc.™

Belgrade, Montana

© 2006 Text, Wilderness Adventures Press, Inc.™
Cover photograph (Rock Creek) © 2006 Chuck Robins

Maps, book and cover design © 2006 Wilderness Adventures Press, Inc.™
Best Fishing Waters™

Published by Wilderness Adventures Press, Inc.™
45 Buckskin Road
Belgrade, MT 59714
866-400-2012
Website: www.wildadvpress.com
Email: books@wildadvpress.com

First Edition

Printed in Singapore

ISBN 9-781932-09824-2 (1-932098-24-0)

TABLE OF CONTENTS

WATERS

FEATURED WATERS

1. Beaverhead River
2. Big Hole River
3. Bighorn River
4. Big Spring Creek
5. Bitterroot River
6. Blackfeet Lakes
7. Blackfoot River
8. Boulder River
9. Clark Canyon Reservoir
10. Clark Fork River
11. Flathead River
12. Middle Fork Flathead River
13. North Fork Flathead River
14. South Fork Flathead River
15. Gallatin River
16. Glacier National Park
17. Georgetown Lake
18. Hebgen and Quake Lake
19. Jefferson River
20. Kootenai River
21. Madison River
22. Missouri River
23. Rattlesnake Creek
24. Rock Creek
25. Rock Creek, Tributary of Clark Fork of the Yellowstone River
26. Rosebud Creek
27. Ruby River
28. Shields River
29. Smith River
30. Stillwater River
31. Swan River
32. Tongue River
33. Yaak River
34. Yellowstone River

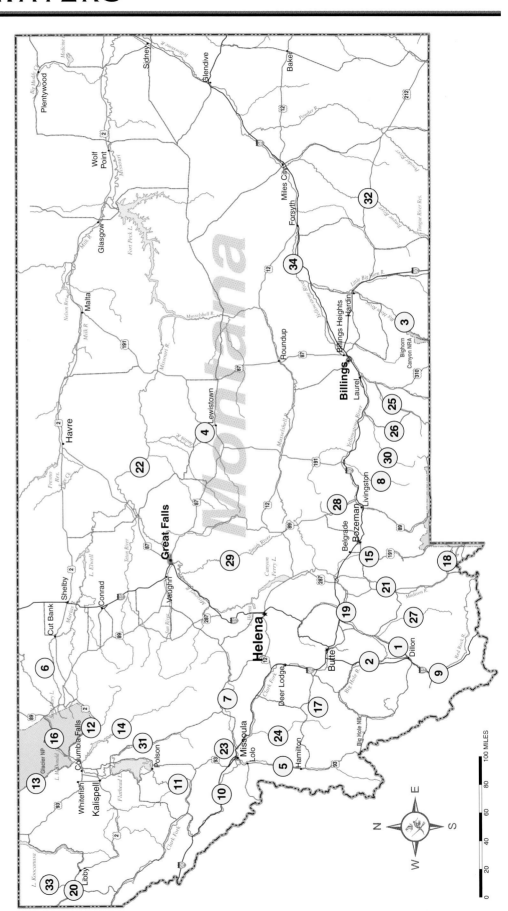

INTRODUCTION AND ACKNOWLEDGEMENTS

Montana hosts some of the most sought-after fisheries in the world. In a state where trout are king you have a chance of hooking up with seven different species of them alone, not to mention burbot, grayling, kokanee salmon, and more than ten different species of warmwater fish. You can fish for tiny cutthroats in a high mountain stream one day and find yourself hooked up with a giant northern pike the next. You can bump elbows with fly fishers in the upper Madison or be the only soul for miles on the lower Missouri. Finally you can spend months, maybe years, fishing the Yellowstone, Clark Fork, Flathead, or Missouri Rivers and never see the same water twice. *Montana's Best Fishing Waters* is the fourth book in our great map book series. Chris Camuto of Gray's Sporting Journal wrote of our first book, *Colorado's Best Fishing Waters*, "This book has by far the clearest road and river maps I've ever seen in a guide book, all in a decent scale so that you can get on good water, off state highways and local roads, with a minimum of fuss and second guessing."

This comprehensive map book contains 170 full-page maps and covers 34 rivers, lakes, and streams. Our maps are based on the U.S. Geological Survey maps and include a wealth of useful angling information, along with an overview of the fishing opportunities and the fish found in each water. Access points are clearly indicated, along with boat ramps and campgrounds. Most access points have corresponding GPS coordinates. We also show roads, trails, and public access in the National Forest and State Lands. The information in this book enables you to get to many overlooked areas and waters that result in a better overall angling experience. Each of the waters has an overview map showing the entire river. Then we break the river down into more detailed maps, each showing a smaller section of the river; giving you a more comprehensive view than you will find in other map books.

The waters are listed in alphabetical order for easy reference without the need to consult an index. As with anywhere you fish, always make sure you have a copy of the most current regulations. Copies are available at most sporting goods shops or online at http://fwp.mt.gov.

We would like to extend a special thanks to Chuck Robbins, author of our *Flyfisher's Guide to Montana*, who has helped us extensively in the research for this book, especially the lower Yellowstone and Missouri Rivers. The *Flyfisher's Guide to Montana* is the perfect companion book to this mapbook. We would also like to thank Chris Francis for his help on the Ruby and Beaverhead Rivers, and Jack (John) Angle for his help on the Upper Yellowstone River. If there are any mistakes in the maps it is our fault, not theirs.

MONTANA RESOURCES

FWP Headquarters
Phone: (406) 444-2535
Fax: (406) 444-4952
1420 E 6th Ave.
P.O. Box 200701
Helena, MT 59620-0701
http://fwp.state.mt.us

FWP Region 1 Headquarters
490 North Meridian Road
Kalispell, MT 59901
Phone: (406) 752-5501
Fax: (406) 257-0349
E-mail: fwprg12@mt.gov

FWP Region 2 Office
3201 Spurgin Road
Missoula, MT 59804
Phone: (406) 542-5500
Fax: (406) 542-5529
E-mail: fwprg22@mt.gov

FWP Region 3 Office
1400 South 19th
Bozeman, MT 59718
Phone: (406) 994-4042
Phone: (406) 994-4043
Fax: (406) 994-4090
E-mail: fwprg3@mt.gov

FWP Region 4 Office
4600 Giant Springs Road
Great Falls, MT 59405
Phone: (406) 454-5840
Fax: (406) 761-8477
E-mail: fwprg42@mt.gov

FWP Region 5 Office
2300 Lake Elmo Drive
Billings, MT 59105
Phone: (406) 247-2940
Fax: (406) 248-5026
E-mail: fwprg52@mt.gov

FWP Region 6 Headquarters
Route 1-4210
Glasgow, MT 59230
Phone: (406) 228-3700
Fax: (406) 228-8161
E-mail: fwprg62@mt.gov

FWP Region 7 Headquarters
Industrial Site West
Miles City, MT 59301
Phone: (406) 234-0900
Fax: (406) 234-4368
E-mail: fwprg72@mt.gov

LEGEND

———	Interstate	State - Public Land		Marina / Moorage	
═══	Primary Highway	Indian Reservation		Picnic Area	
———	Road or Street	National Forest		Airport	
·········	Trails	BLM - Public Land		Rapids	
+—+—+	Railroad	Boat Launch		Locale	
15	Interstate Route	Campsite		Danger	
86	State Route	RV Access		GPS Coordinates	
287	U.S. Route	Fishing Access		Red / Blue Ribbon Water	

Trout
Salmon
Grayling
Whitefish
Burbot
Warmwater

Easily flip through the pages to locate the species you wish to target. Our new fish indicators tell you with the flip of a page what kind of fish are primarily targeted in that particular stream. A blue fish indicates trout, a red fish a salmon. A gray fish is for grayling, and the white is for mountain whitefish. Finally the green fish indicator is for burbot and the orange is for warm water species. These fish indicators are not suggesting quality of fishing, or that there are not other species in the stream. They are simply a guide to help you find the type of fish you would like to hook up with. Overview maps contain more specifics on which species are hosted by that stream. Read more on the stream maps themselves to learn about the quality of fishing and access provided.

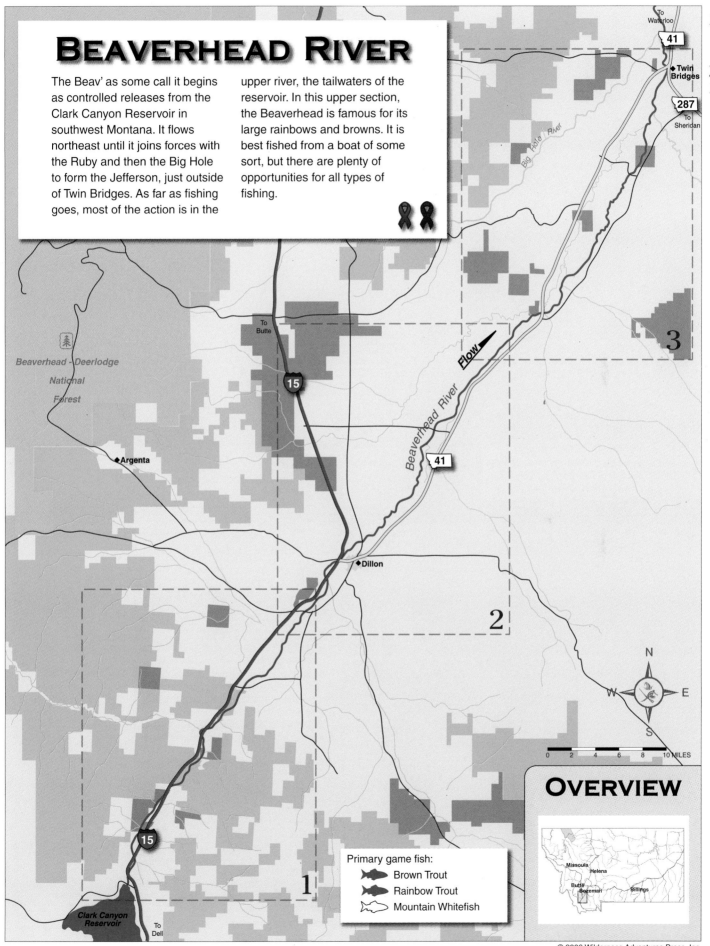

BEAVERHEAD RIVER

The Beav' as some call it begins as controlled releases from the Clark Canyon Reservoir in southwest Montana. It flows northeast until it joins forces with the Ruby and then the Big Hole to form the Jefferson, just outside of Twin Bridges. As far as fishing goes, most of the action is in the upper river, the tailwaters of the reservoir. In this upper section, the Beaverhead is famous for its large rainbows and browns. It is best fished from a boat of some sort, but there are plenty of opportunities for all types of fishing.

OVERVIEW

Primary game fish:
- Brown Trout
- Rainbow Trout
- Mountain Whitefish

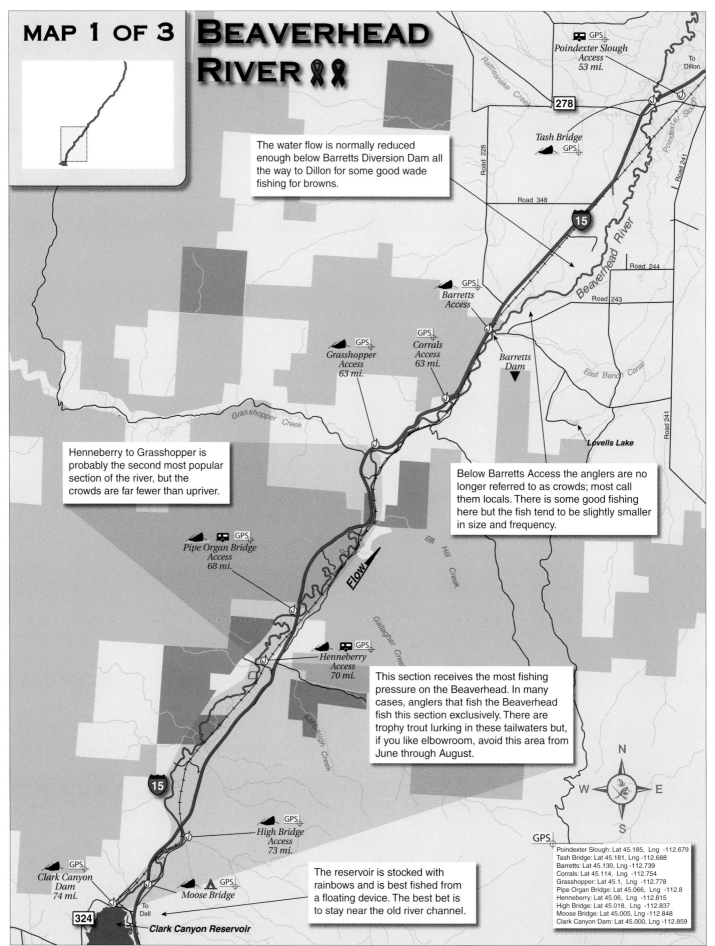

MAP 1 OF 3 BEAVERHEAD RIVER

The water flow is normally reduced enough below Barretts Diversion Dam all the way to Dillon for some good wade fishing for browns.

To Dillon

Poindexter Slough Access 53 mi.

Road 228

278

Tash Bridge GPS

Road 348

15

Barretts Access GPS

Road 244

Road 243

Grasshopper Access 63 mi. GPS

Corrals Access 63 mi. GPS

Barretts Dam

East Bench Canal

Rattlesnake Creek

Poindexter Slough

Road 241

Beaverhead River

Lovells Lake

Grasshopper Creek

Henneberry to Grasshopper is probably the second most popular section of the river, but the crowds are far fewer than upriver.

Below Barretts Access the anglers are no longer referred to as crowds; most call them locals. There is some good fishing here but the fish tend to be slightly smaller in size and frequency.

BM Hill Creek

Pipe Organ Bridge Access 68 mi. GPS

Flow

Gallagher Creek

Henneberry Access 70 mi. GPS

This section receives the most fishing pressure on the Beaverhead. In many cases, anglers that fish the Beaverhead fish this section exclusively. There are trophy trout lurking in these tailwaters but, if you like elbowroom, avoid this area from June through August.

Ashbaugh Creek

15

N
W · E
S

High Bridge Access 73 mi. GPS

Clark Canyon Dam 74 mi. GPS

Moose Bridge GPS

The reservoir is stocked with rainbows and is best fished from a floating device. The best bet is to stay near the old river channel.

GPS

Poindexter Slough: Lat 45.185, Lng -112.679
Tash Bridge: Lat 45.181, Lng -112.688
Barretts: Lat 45.130, Lng -112.739
Corrals: Lat 45.114, Lng -112.754
Grasshopper: Lat 45.1, Lng -112.778
Pipe Organ Bridge: Lat 45.066, Lng -112.8
Henneberry: Lat 45.06, Lng -112.815
High Bridge: Lat 45.018, Lng -112.837
Moose Bridge: Lat 45.005, Lng -112.848
Clark Canyon Dam: Lat 45.000, Lng -112.859

324

To Dell

Clark Canyon Reservoir

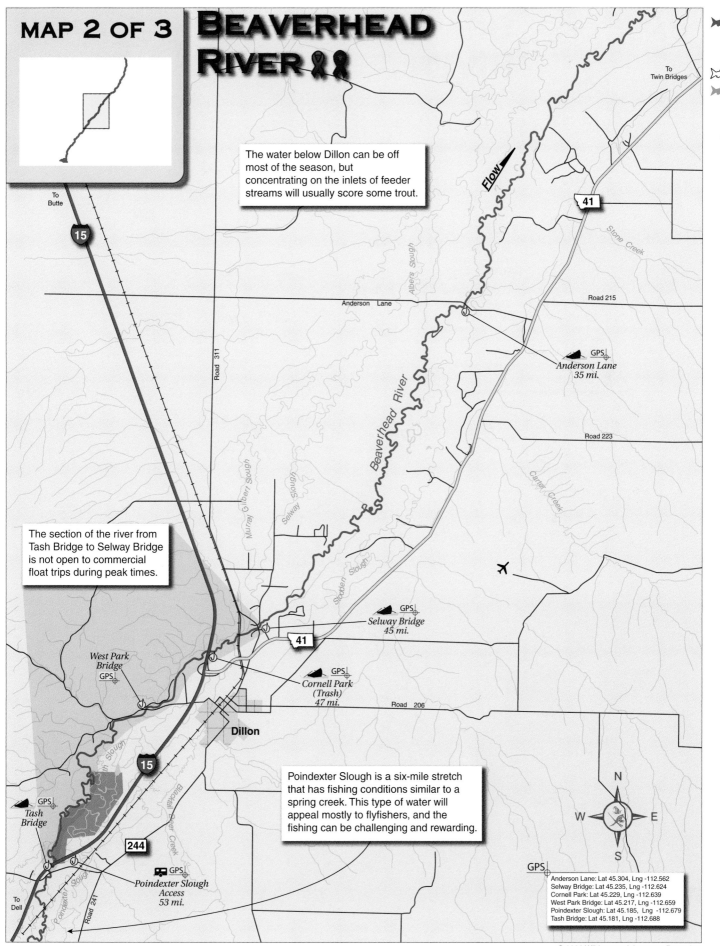

MAP 2 OF 3
BEAVERHEAD RIVER

The water below Dillon can be off most of the season, but concentrating on the inlets of feeder streams will usually score some trout.

The section of the river from Tash Bridge to Selway Bridge is not open to commercial float trips during peak times.

Poindexter Slough is a six-mile stretch that has fishing conditions similar to a spring creek. This type of water will appeal mostly to flyfishers, and the fishing can be challenging and rewarding.

To Butte

To Twin Bridges

Flow

Anderson Lane

Beaverhead River

Road 215

Road 223

Stone Creek

Carter Creek

Albers Slough

GPS
Anderson Lane
35 mi.

Murray Gilbert Slough

Selway Slough

Stodden Slough

GPS
Selway Bridge
45 mi.

GPS
Cornell Park
(Trash)
47 mi.

Road 206

West Park
Bridge
GPS

Dillon

GPS
Tash
Bridge

Blacktail Deer Creek

Poindexter Slough

GPS
Poindexter Slough
Access
53 mi.

To Dell

Road 241

Road 311

N
W E
S

GPS

Anderson Lane: Lat 45.304, Lng -112.562
Selway Bridge: Lat 45.235, Lng -112.624
Cornell Park: Lat 45.229, Lng -112.639
West Park Bridge: Lat 45.217, Lng -112.659
Poindexter Slough: Lat 45.185, Lng -112.679
Tash Bridge: Lat 45.181, Lng -112.688

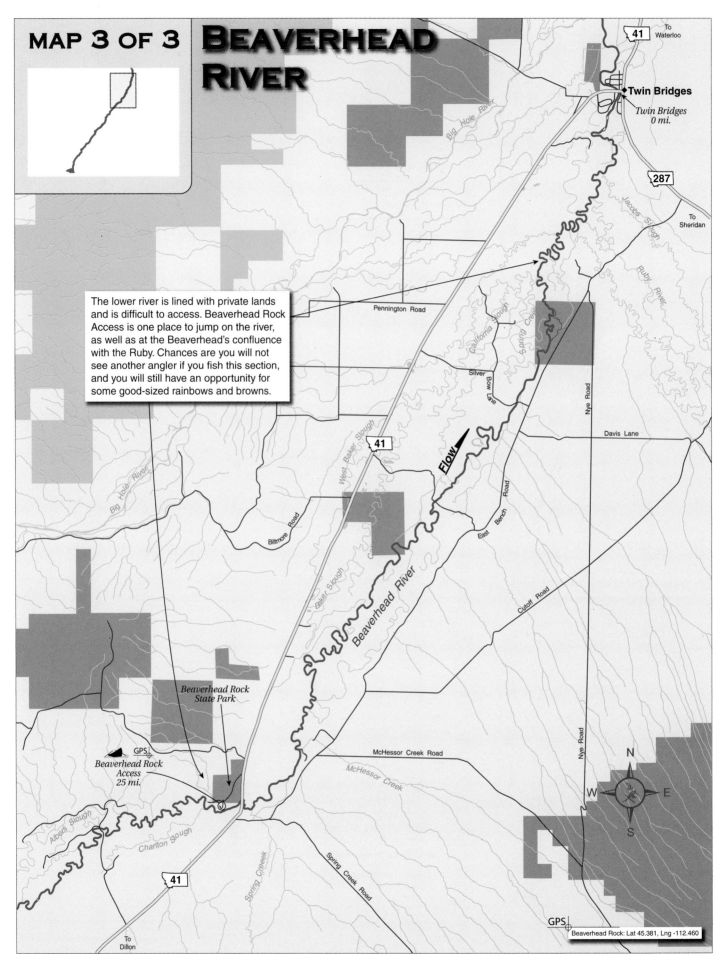

MAP 3 OF 3

BEAVERHEAD RIVER

41 To Waterloo

◆ **Twin Bridges**

Twin Bridges 0 mi.

287

To Sheridan

Big Hole River

Jacobs Slough

Ruby River

Pennington Road

California Slough

Spring Creek

Silver Bow Lane

Nye Road

Davis Lane

The lower river is lined with private lands and is difficult to access. Beaverhead Rock Access is one place to jump on the river, as well as at the Beaverhead's confluence with the Ruby. Chances are you will not see another angler if you fish this section, and you will still have an opportunity for some good-sized rainbows and browns.

41

Flow

West Baker Slough

East Bench Road

Cutoff Road

Big Hole River

Biltmore Road

Baker Slough

Beaverhead River

Beaverhead Rock State Park

Nye Road

GPS

Beaverhead Rock Access 25 mi.

McHessor Creek Road

McHessor Creek

N

W   E

S

Albers Slough

Charlton Slough

Spring Creek

Spring Creek Road

41

GPS

Beaverhead Rock: Lat 45.381, Lng -112.460

To Dillon

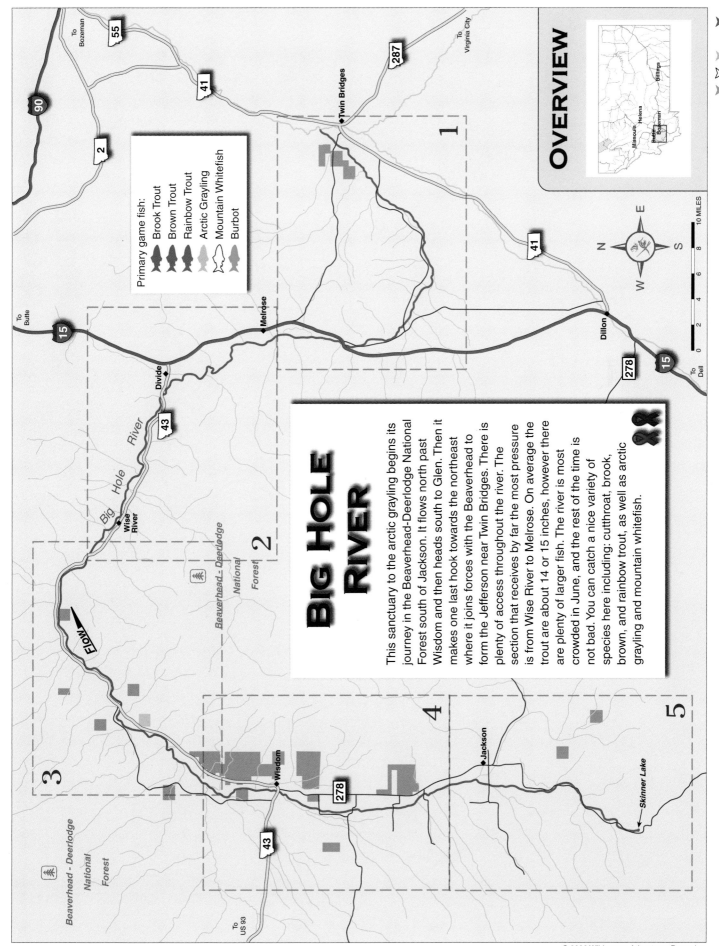

OVERVIEW

Primary game fish:
Brook Trout
Brown Trout
Rainbow Trout
Arctic Grayling
Mountain Whitefish
Burbot

BIG HOLE RIVER

This sanctuary to the arctic grayling begins its journey in the Beaverhead-Deerlodge National Forest south of Jackson. It flows north past Wisdom and then heads south to Glen. Then it makes one last hook towards the northeast where it joins forces with the Beaverhead to form the Jefferson near Twin Bridges. There is plenty of access throughout the river. The section that receives by far the most pressure is from Wise River to Melrose. On average the trout are about 14 or 15 inches, however there are plenty of larger fish. The river is most crowded in June, and the rest of the time is not bad. You can catch a nice variety of species here including: cutthroat, brook, brown, and rainbow trout, as well as arctic grayling and mountain whitefish.

To Bozeman

55

41

287

To Virginia City

Twin Bridges

1

90

2

To Butte

15

Melrose

41

Dillon

278

15

To Dell

Divide

43

Big Hole River

Wise River

FLOW

Beaverhead - Deerlodge National Forest

2

Beaverhead - Deerlodge National Forest

3

Wisdom

278

43

4

Jackson

Skinner Lake

5

To US 93

N E S W

10 MILES
0 2 4 6 8

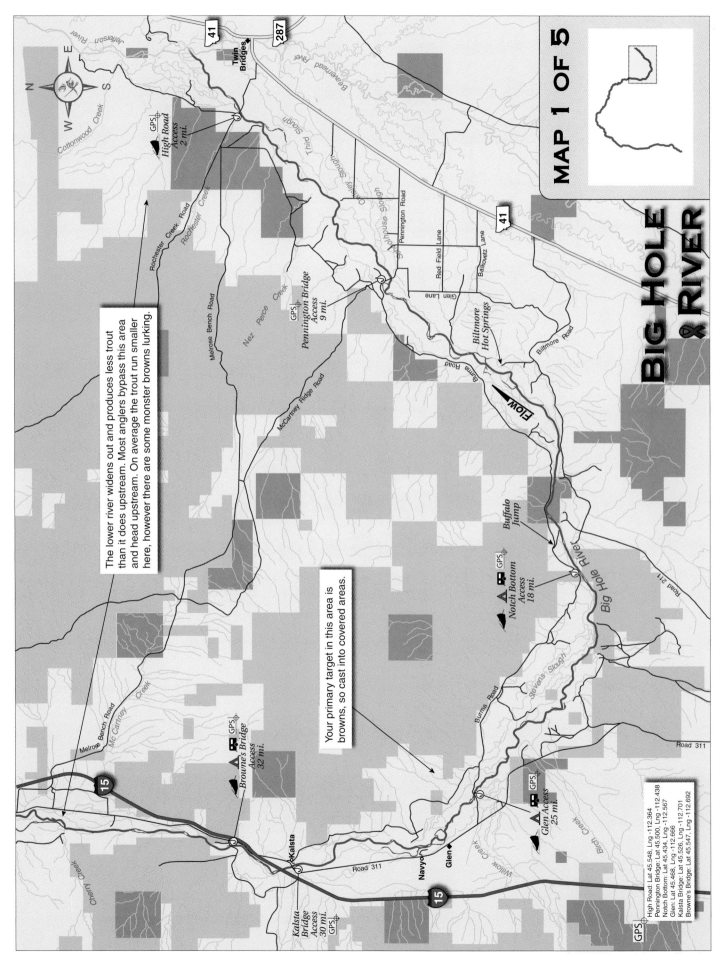

MAP 1 OF 5

BIG HOLE RIVER

The lower river widens out and produces less trout than it does upstream. Most anglers bypass this area and head upstream. On average the trout run smaller here, however there are some monster browns lurking.

Your primary target in this area is browns, so cast into covered areas.

High Road Access 2 mi.

Pennington Bridge Access 9 mi.

Notch Bottom Access 18 mi.

Browne's Bridge Access 32 mi.

Glen Access 25 mi.

Kalsta Bridge Access 30 mi.

GPS
High Road: Lat 45.548, Lng -112.364
Pennington Bridge: Lat 45.500, Lng -112.438
Notch Bottom: Lat 45.434, Lng -112.567
Glen: Lat 45.468, Lng -112.666
Kalsta Bridge: Lat 45.526, Lng -112.701
Browne's Bridge: Lat 45.547, Lng -112.692

Flow

Twin Bridges

Biltmore Hot Springs

Buffalo Jump

Glen

Navyo

Kalsta

Melrose

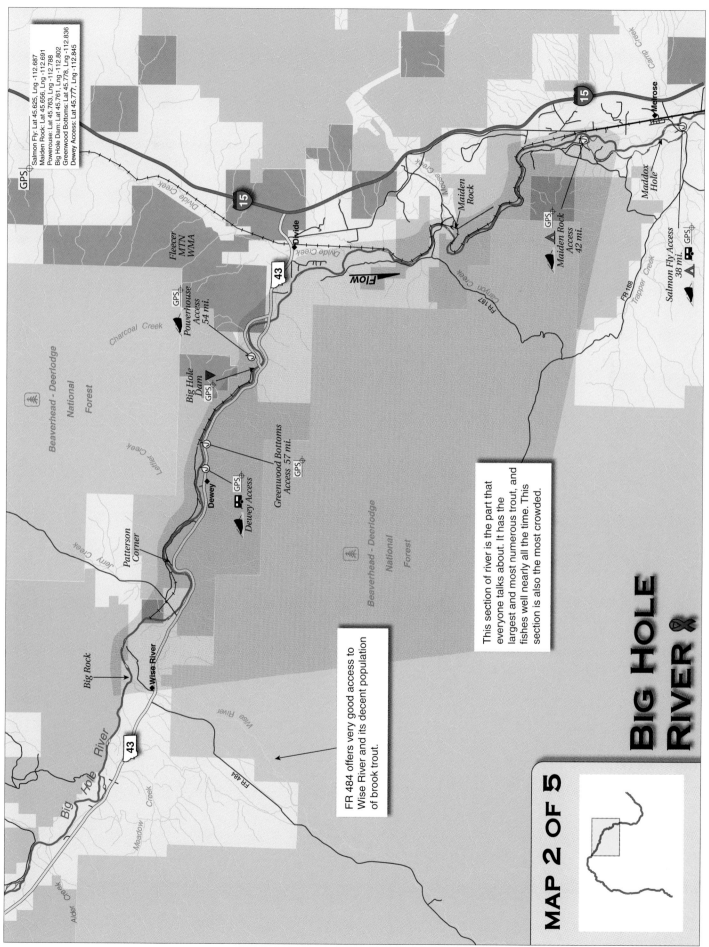

Salmon Fly: Lat 45.625, Lng -112.687
Maiden Rock: Lat 45.656, Lng -112.691
Powerouse: Lat 45.763, Lng -112.788
Big Hole Dam: Lat 45.761, Lng -112.802
Greenwood Bottoms: Lat 45.778, Lng -112.836
Dewey Access: Lat 45.777, Lng -112.845

GPS

15

Melrose

Maddox
Hole

Maiden
Rock

Maiden Rock
Access
42 mi.

Salmon Fly Access
38 mi.

FR 188

Trapper Creek

Canyon Creek

FR 187

Moose Creek

Divide Creek

Divide

15

Flow

43

Fleecer
MTN
WMA

GPS

Powerhouse
Access
54 mi.

Charcoal Creek

Big Hole
Dam

GPS

Beaverhead - Deerlodge

National

Forest

Lanier Creek

Greenwood Bottoms
Access 57 mi.

GPS

Dewey

GPS

Dewey Access

Beaverhead - Deerlodge

National

Forest

This section of river is the part that
everyone talks about. It has the
largest and most numerous trout, and
fishes well nearly all the time. This
section is also the most crowded.

Patterson
Corner

Jerry Creek

Big Rock

Wise River

Wise River

43

FR 484

Meadow Creek

Big Hole River

Alder Creek

FR 484 offers very good access to
Wise River and its decent population
of brook trout.

BIG HOLE
RIVER

MAP 2 OF 5

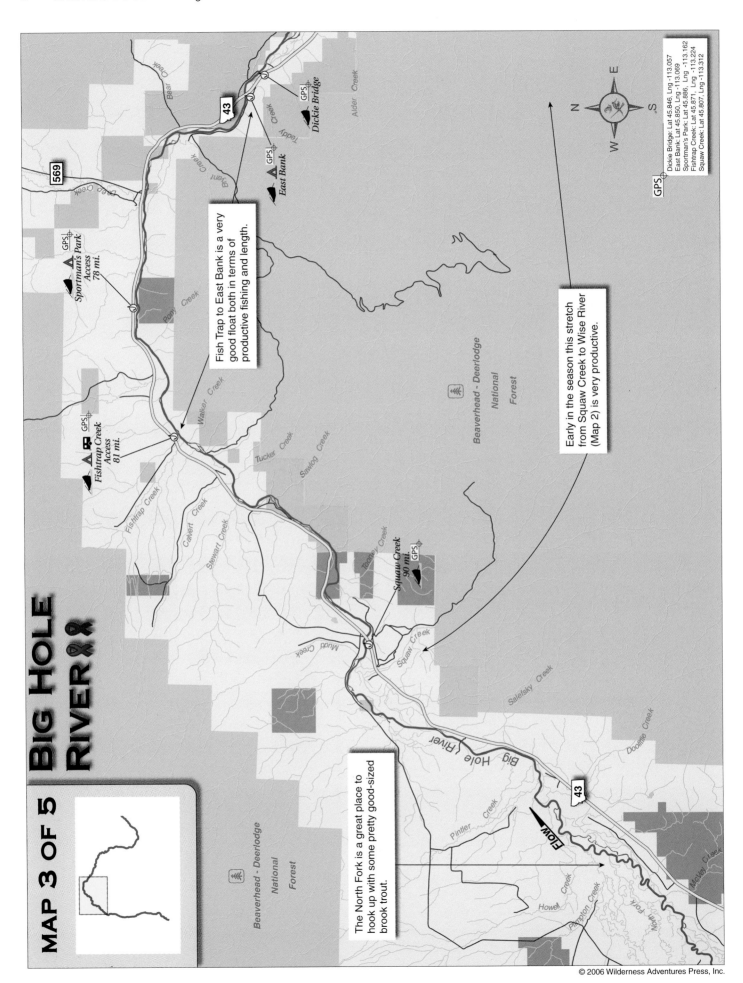

MAP 3 OF 5

BIG HOLE RIVER

Beaverhead - Deerlodge National Forest

The North Fork is a great place to hook up with some pretty good-sized brook trout.

Early in the season this stretch from Squaw Creek to Wise River (Map 2) is very productive.

Fish Trap to East Bank is a very good float both in terms of productive fishing and length.

Sportsman's Park Access 78 mi.

Fishtrap Creek Access 81 mi.

Squaw Creek 90 mi.

East Bank

Dickie Bridge

GPS
Dickie Bridge: Lat 45.846, Lng -113.057
East Bank: Lat 45.850, Lng -113.069
Sportman's Park: Lat 45.886, Lng -113.162
Fishtrap Creek: Lat 45.871, Lng -113.224
Squaw Creek: Lat 45.807, Lng -113.312

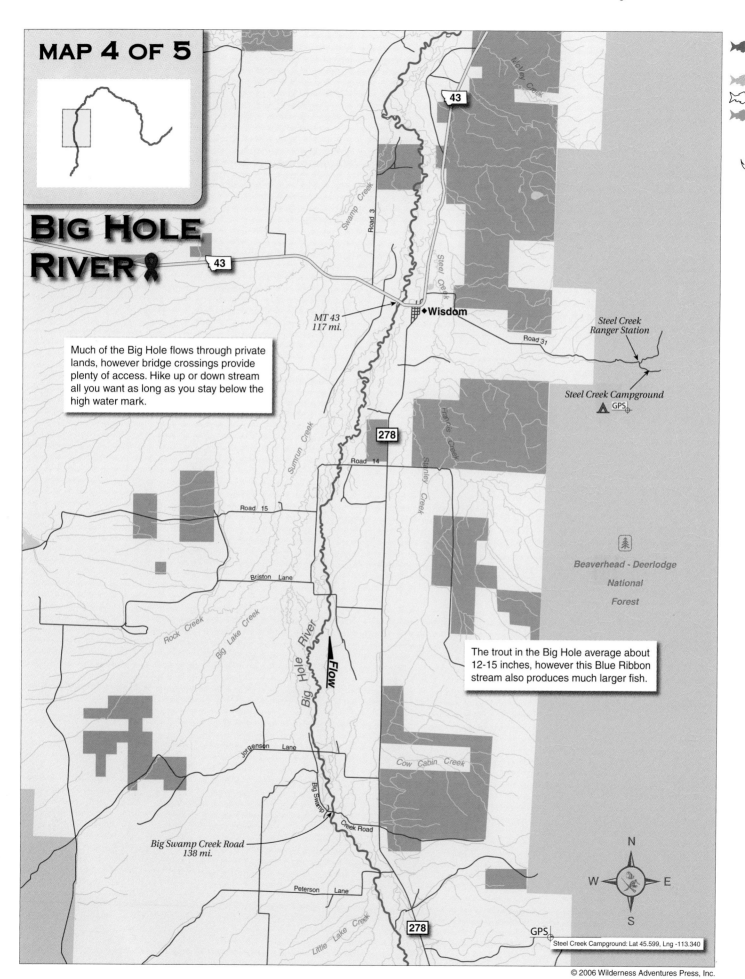

MAP 4 OF 5

BIG HOLE RIVER

43

MT 43
117 mi.

◆**Wisdom**

Swamp Creek

Road 3

Steel Creek

43

Steel Creek
Ranger Station

Road 31

Steel Creek Campground
⛺ GPS

Much of the Big Hole flows through private
lands, however bridge crossings provide
plenty of access. Hike up or down stream
all you want as long as you stay below the
high water mark.

Sumrun Creek

278

Road 14

Fravis Creek

Stanley Creek

Road 15

Beaverhead - Deerlodge

National

Forest

Briston Lane

Rock Creek

Big Lake Creek

Big Hole River

Flow

The trout in the Big Hole average about
12-15 inches, however this Blue Ribbon
stream also produces much larger fish.

Jorgenson Lane

Cow Cabin Creek

Big Swamp

Creek Road

Big Swamp Creek Road
138 mi.

Peterson Lane

Little Lake Creek

278

GPS

N
W ⊕ E
S

Steel Creek Campground: Lat 45.599, Lng -113.340

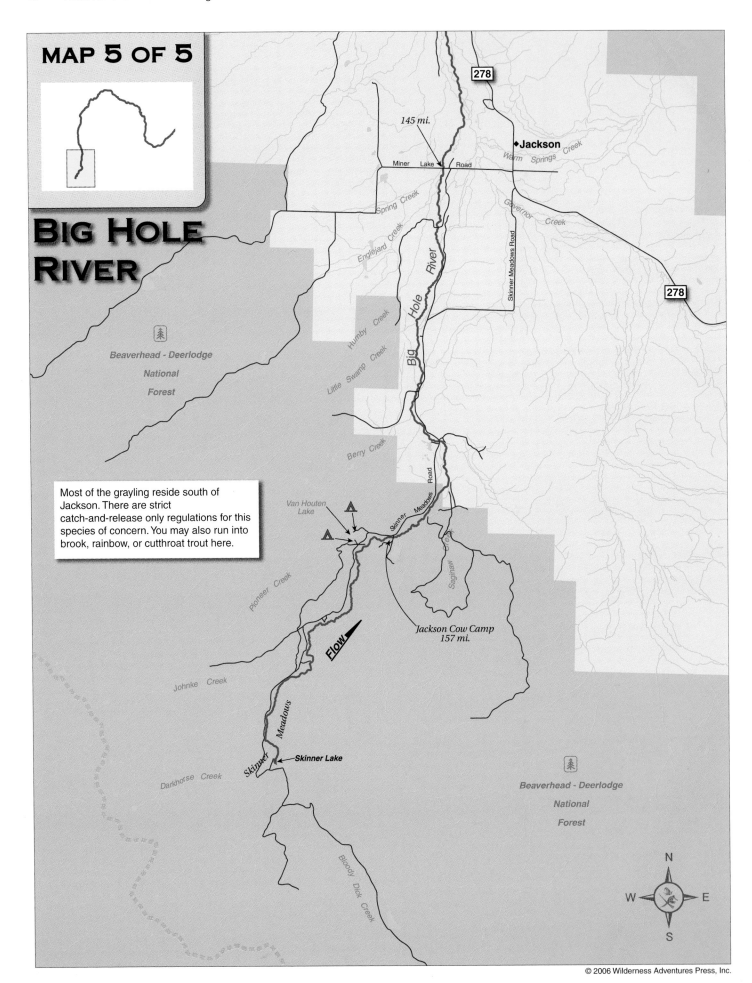

MAP 5 OF 5

BIG HOLE RIVER

278

145 mi.

◆Jackson

Miner   Lake   Road

Warm   Springs   Creek

Spring Creek

Englejard Creek

Governor   Creek

Skinner Meadows Road

278

Beaverhead - Deerlodge

National

Forest

Humby Creek

Little   Swamp   Creek

Big   Hole   River

Berry Creek

Most of the grayling reside south of Jackson. There are strict catch-and-release only regulations for this species of concern. You may also run into brook, rainbow, or cutthroat trout here.

Van Houten Lake

Skinner   Meadows   Road

Saginaw   Creek

Pioneer   Creek

Flow

Jackson Cow Camp
157 mi.

Johnke   Creek

Skinner   Meadows

Skinner ← Skinner Lake

Darkhorse   Creek

Beaverhead - Deerlodge

National

Forest

Bloody   Dick   Creek

N
W   E
S

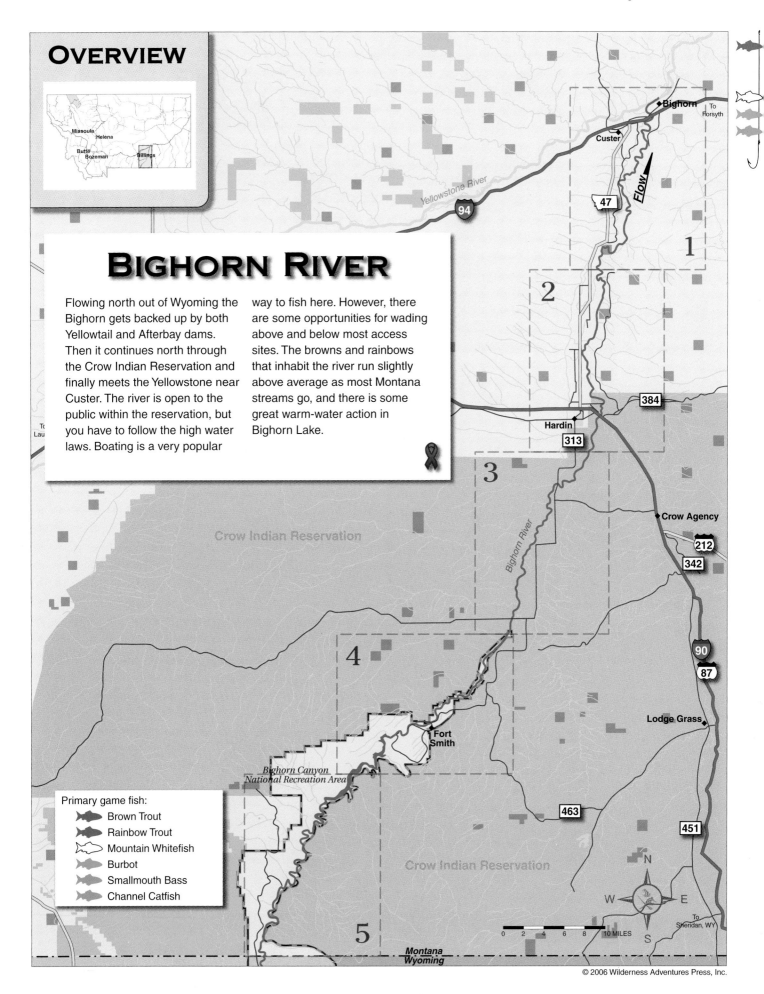

OVERVIEW

BIGHORN RIVER

Flowing north out of Wyoming the Bighorn gets backed up by both Yellowtail and Afterbay dams. Then it continues north through the Crow Indian Reservation and finally meets the Yellowstone near Custer. The river is open to the public within the reservation, but you have to follow the high water laws. Boating is a very popular way to fish here. However, there are some opportunities for wading above and below most access sites. The browns and rainbows that inhabit the river run slightly above average as most Montana streams go, and there is some great warm-water action in Bighorn Lake.

Primary game fish:
- Brown Trout
- Rainbow Trout
- Mountain Whitefish
- Burbot
- Smallmouth Bass
- Channel Catfish

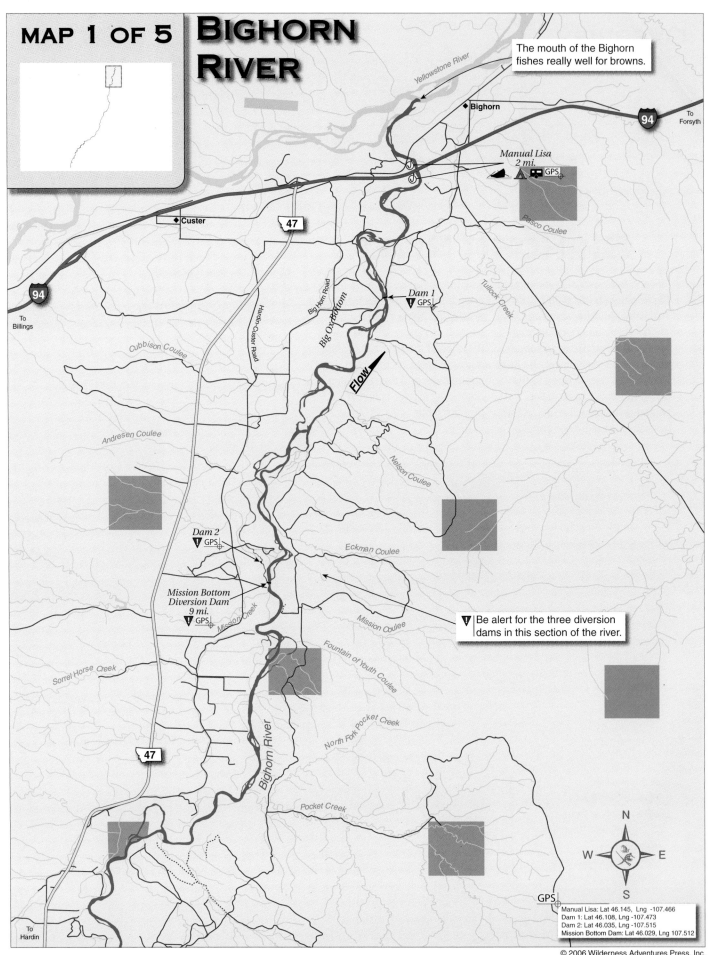

MAP 1 OF 5

BIGHORN RIVER

The mouth of the Bighorn fishes really well for browns.

To Forsyth

◆ Bighorn

94

Yellowstone River

Manual Lisa 2 mi. GPS

Pasco Coulee

◆ Custer

47

94

To Billings

Big Horn Road

Big Ox Bottom

Hardin-Custer Road

Dam 1 GPS

Tullock Creek

Cubbison Coulee

Flow

Nelson Coulee

Andresen Coulee

Eckman Coulee

Dam 2 GPS

Mission Bottom Diversion Dam 9 mi. GPS

Mission Creek

Mission Coulee

Be alert for the three diversion dams in this section of the river.

Sorrel Horse Creek

Fountain of Youth Coulee

North Fork Pocket Creek

47

Bighorn River

Pocket Creek

N
W   E
S

To Hardin

GPS

Manual Lisa: Lat 46.145, Lng -107.466
Dam 1: Lat 46.108, Lng -107.473
Dam 2: Lat 46.035, Lng -107.515
Mission Bottom Dam: Lat 46.029, Lng 107.512

© 2006 Wilderness Adventures Press, Inc.

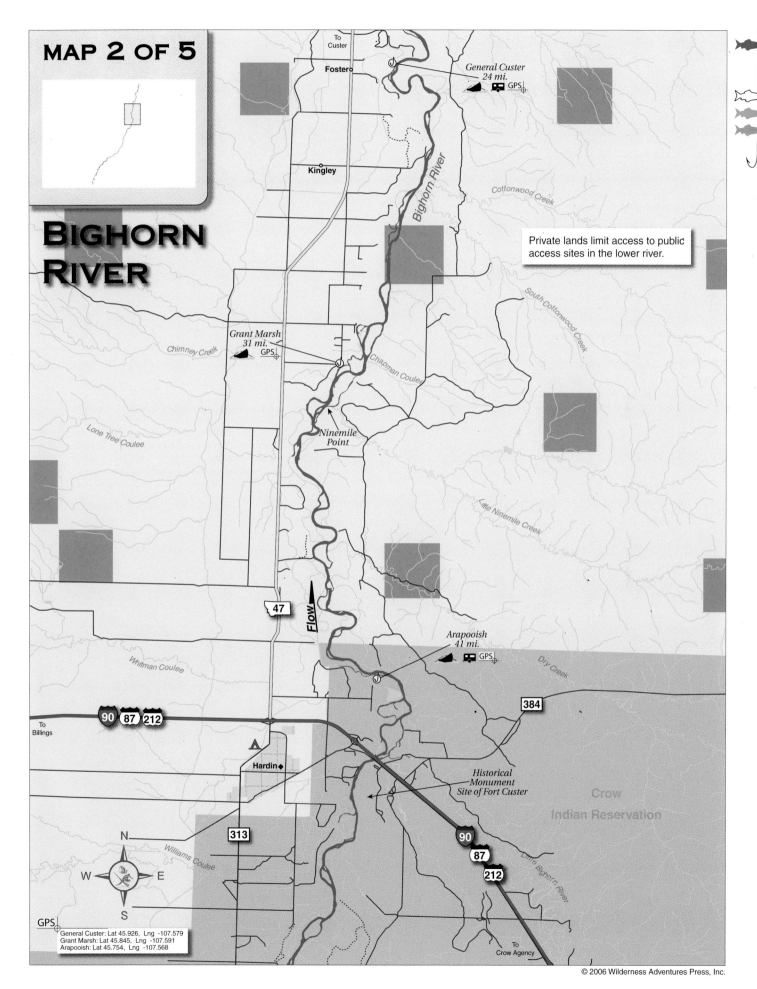

MAP 2 OF 5

BIGHORN
RIVER

To
Custer

Fostero

General Custer
24 mi.
GPS

Kingley

Bighorn River

Cottonwood Creek

Private lands limit access to public
access sites in the lower river.

South Cottonwood Creek

Grant Marsh
31 mi.
GPS

Chimney Creek

Chapman Coulee

Ninemile
Point

Lone Tree Coulee

Late Ninemile Creek

Flow

47

Arapooish
41 mi.
GPS

Whitman Coulee

Dry Creek

384

90 87 212

To
Billings

Historical
Monument
Site of Fort Custer

Crow
Indian Reservation

Hardin

90

N

87

313

Little Bighorn River

212

Williams Coulee

W   E

S

GPS

General Custer: Lat 45.926, Lng -107.579
Grant Marsh: Lat 45.845, Lng -107.591
Arapooish: Lat 45.754, Lng -107.568

To
Crow Agency

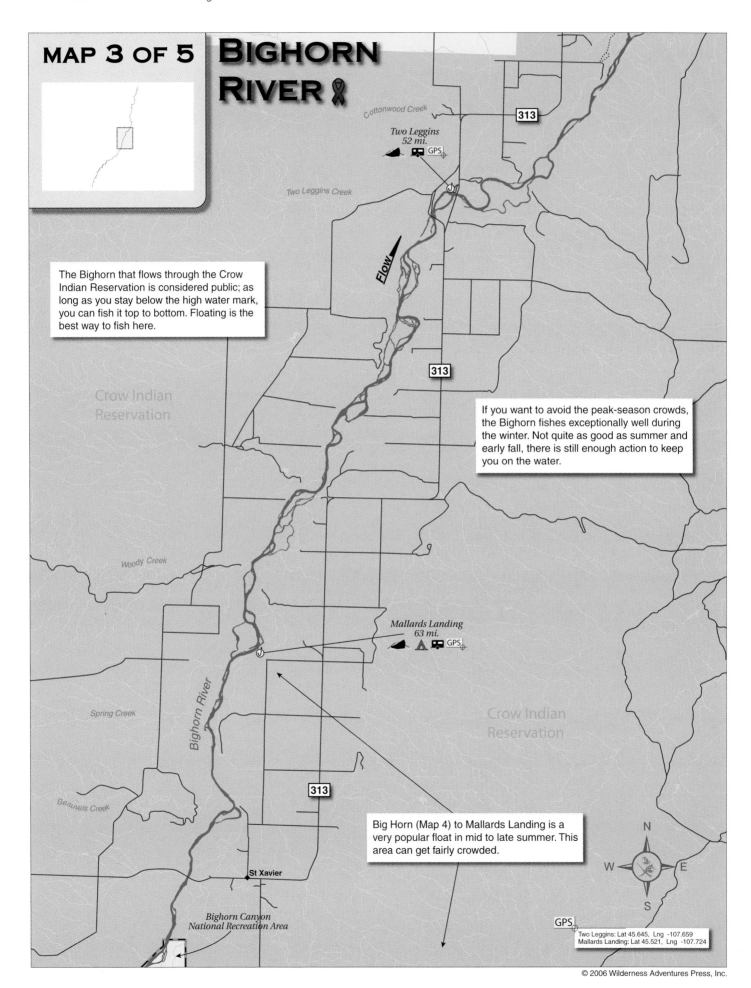

MAP 3 OF 5

BIGHORN RIVER

Cottonwood Creek

313

Two Leggins
52 mi.
GPS

Two Leggins Creek

Flow

The Bighorn that flows through the Crow Indian Reservation is considered public; as long as you stay below the high water mark, you can fish it top to bottom. Floating is the best way to fish here.

313

Crow Indian Reservation

If you want to avoid the peak-season crowds, the Bighorn fishes exceptionally well during the winter. Not quite as good as summer and early fall, there is still enough action to keep you on the water.

Woody Creek

Mallards Landing
63 mi.
GPS

Bighorn River

Crow Indian Reservation

Spring Creek

313

Beauveis Creek

Big Horn (Map 4) to Mallards Landing is a very popular float in mid to late summer. This area can get fairly crowded.

N
W   E
S

St Xavier

Bighorn Canyon
National Recreation Area

GPS

Two Leggins: Lat 45.645, Lng -107.659
Mallards Landing: Lat 45.521, Lng -107.724

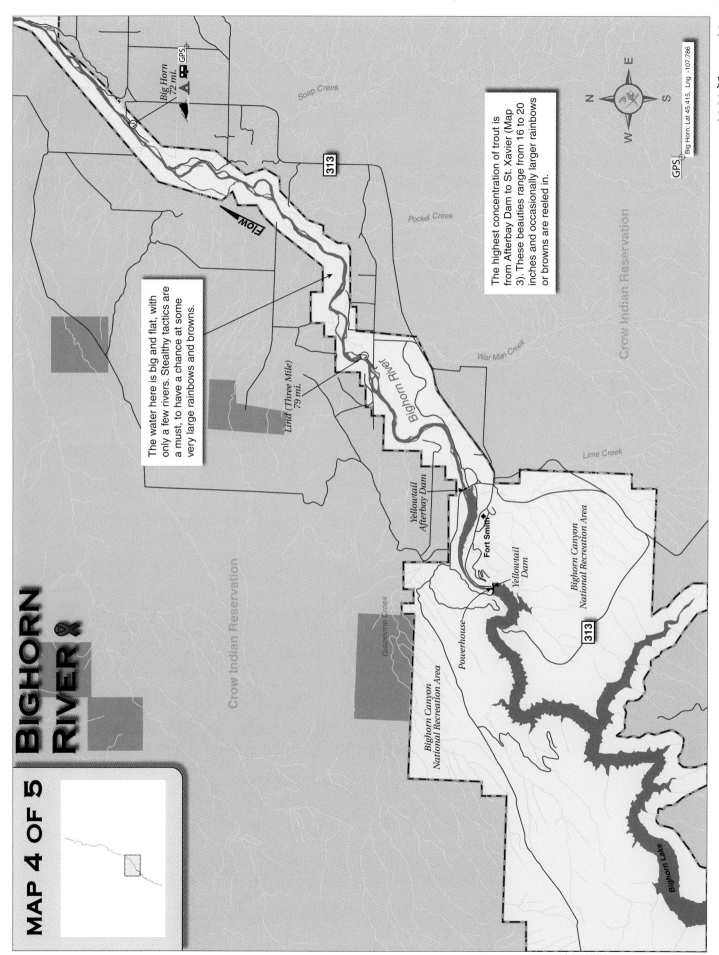

MAP 4 OF 5

BIGHORN
RIVER

The water here is big and flat, with only a few rivers. Stealthy tactics are a must, to have a chance at some very large rainbows and browns.

The highest concentration of trout is from Afterbay Dam to St. Xavier (Map 3). These beauties range from 16 to 20 inches and occasionally larger rainbows or browns are reeled in.

Big Horn: Lat 45.415, Lng -107.786

GPS

Big Horn
72 mi.

313

Soap Creek

Pocket Creek

Flow

Lind (Three Mile)
79 mi.

Bighorn River

War Man Creek

Crow Indian Reservation

Crow Indian Reservation

Lime Creek

Yellowtail
Afterbay Dam

Fort Smith

Yellowtail
Dam

Powerhouse

Grapevine Creek

Bighorn Canyon
National Recreation Area

Bighorn Canyon
National Recreation Area

313

Bighorn Lake

N
W E
S

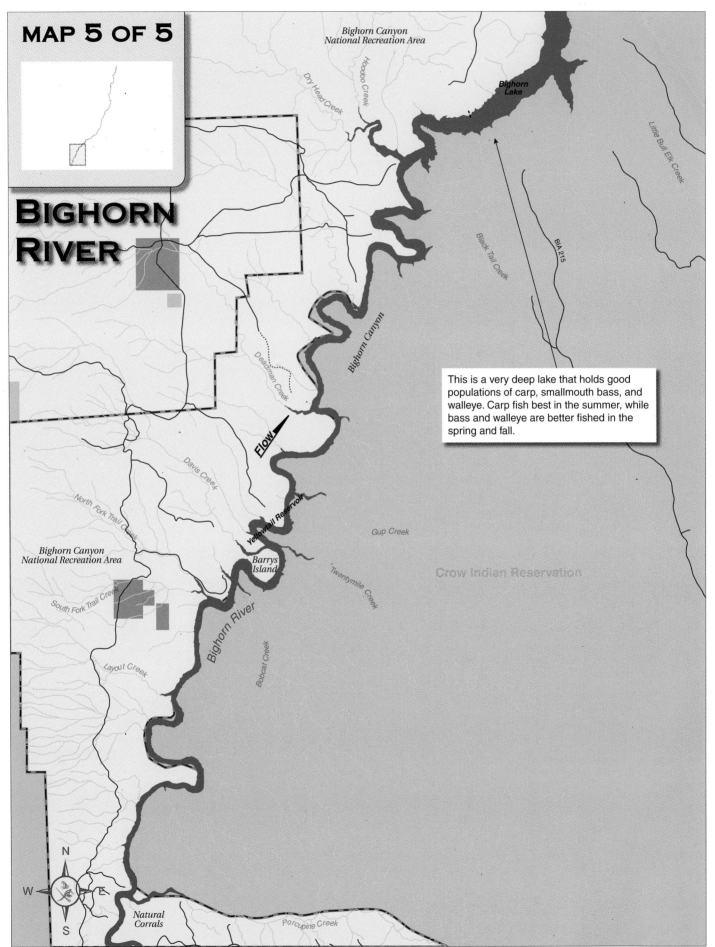

MAP 5 OF 5

BIGHORN RIVER

Bighorn Canyon
National Recreation Area

Hoodoo Creek

Dry Head Creek

Bighorn Lake

Little Bull Elk Creek

Black Tail Creek

BIA 215

Bighorn Canyon

Deadman Creek

Flow

This is a very deep lake that holds good
populations of carp, smallmouth bass, and
walleye. Carp fish best in the summer, while
bass and walleye are better fished in the
spring and fall.

Davis Creek

North Fork Trail Creek

Yellowtail Reservoir

Gup Creek

Bighorn Canyon
National Recreation Area

Barrys
Island

Crow Indian Reservation

South Fork Trail Creek

Twentymile Creek

Bighorn River

Layout Creek

Bobcat Creek

N
W   E
S

Natural
Corrals

Porcupine Creek

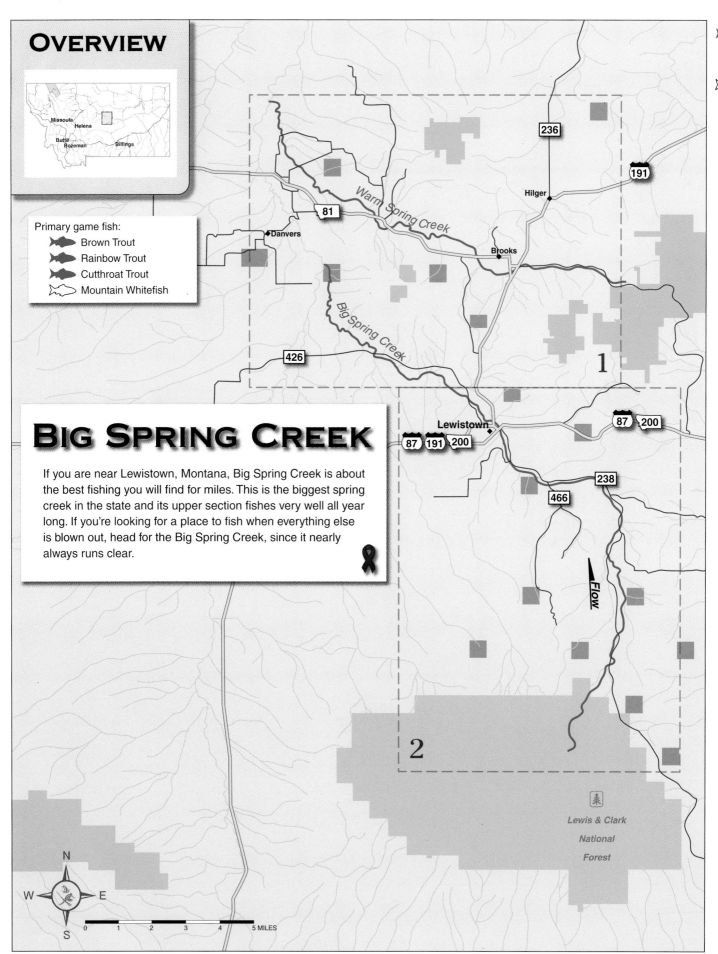

OVERVIEW

Primary game fish:
- Brown Trout
- Rainbow Trout
- Cutthroat Trout
- Mountain Whitefish

BIG SPRING CREEK

If you are near Lewistown, Montana, Big Spring Creek is about the best fishing you will find for miles. This is the biggest spring creek in the state and its upper section fishes very well all year long. If you're looking for a place to fish when everything else is blown out, head for the Big Spring Creek, since it nearly always runs clear.

Lewis & Clark National Forest

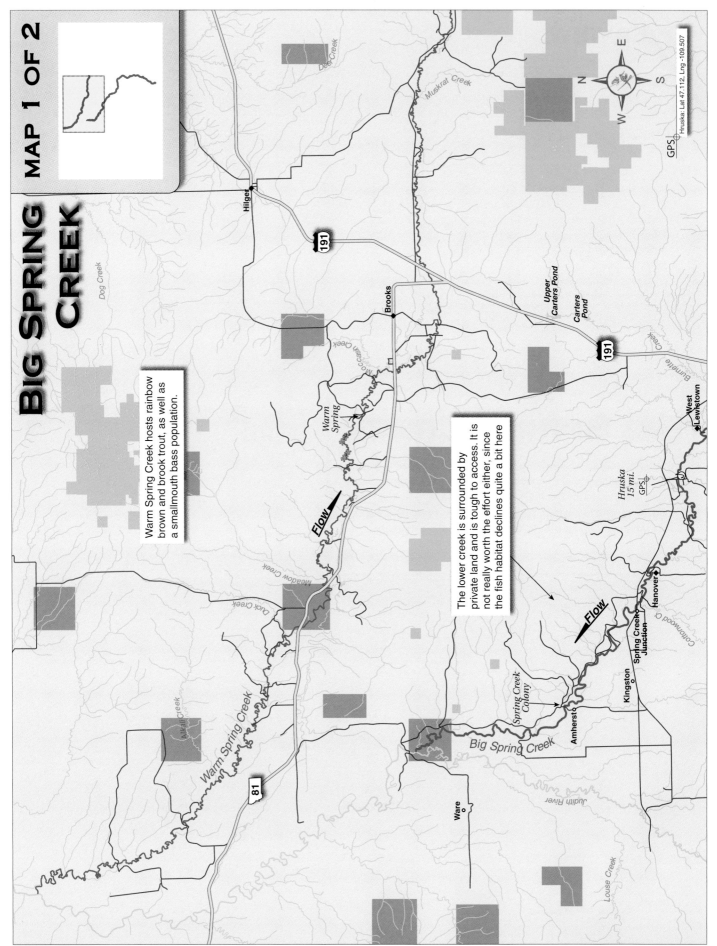

BIG SPRING CREEK

MAP 1 OF 2

Warm Spring Creek hosts rainbow brown and brook trout, as well as a smallmouth bass population.

The lower creek is surrounded by private land and is tough to access. It is not really worth the effort either, since the fish habitat declines quite a bit here

GPS Hruska: Lat 47.112, Lng -109.507

Deer Creek

Muskrat Creek

Hilger

191

Dog Creek

Brooks

Upper Carters Pond

Carters Pond

191

Burnette Creek

West Lewistown

Warm Spring

Moccasin Creek

Flow

Meadow Creek

Duck Creek

Hruska 15 mi.

GPS

Hanover

Cottonwood C.

Flow

Spring Creek Junction

Kingston

Alkali Creek

Warm Spring Creek

81

Spring Creek Colony

Amherst

Big Spring Creek

Ware

Judith River

Louse Creek

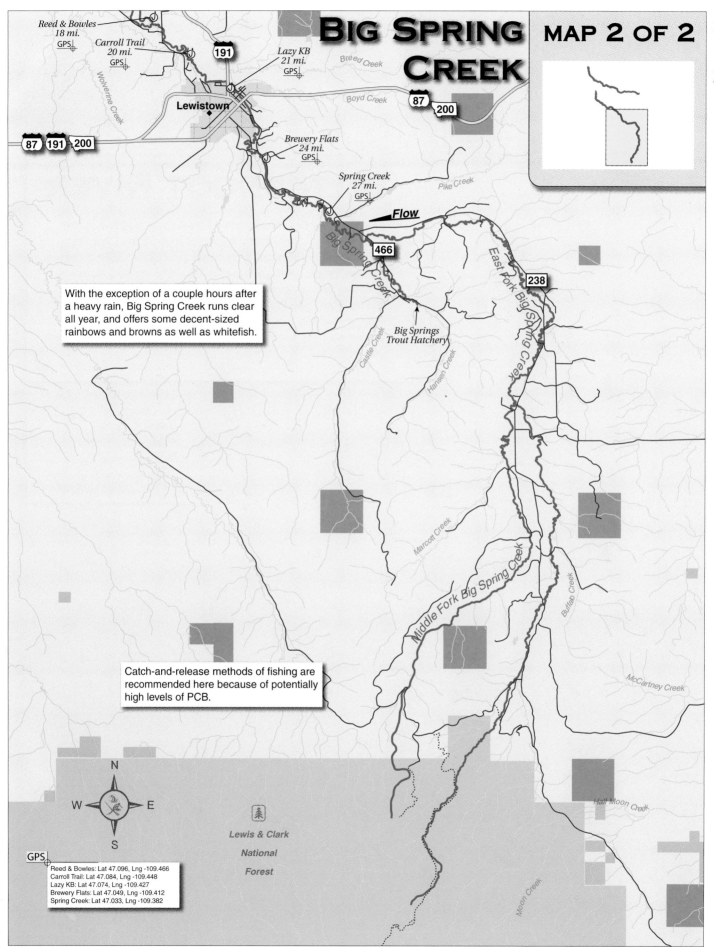

BIG SPRING CREEK

MAP 2 OF 2

Reed & Bowles
18 mi.
GPS

Carroll Trail
20 mi.
GPS

Lazy KB
21 mi.
GPS

Breed Creek

191

Lewistown

Boyd Creek

87
200

87 191 200

Brewery Flats
24 mi.
GPS

Spring Creek
27 mi.
GPS

Pike Creek

Flow

Wolverine Creek

Big Spring Creek

466

East Fork Big Spring Creek

238

Big Springs
Trout Hatchery

Castle Creek

Hansen Creek

With the exception of a couple hours after a heavy rain, Big Spring Creek runs clear all year, and offers some decent-sized rainbows and browns as well as whitefish.

Marcott Creek

Middle Fork Big Spring Creek

Buffalo Creek

McCartney Creek

Catch-and-release methods of fishing are recommended here because of potentially high levels of PCB.

Half Moon Creek

Moon Creek

N
W   E
S

Lewis & Clark

National

Forest

GPS
Reed & Bowles: Lat 47.096, Lng -109.466
Carroll Trail: Lat 47.084, Lng -109.448
Lazy KB: Lat 47.074, Lng -109.427
Brewery Flats: Lat 47.049, Lng -109.412
Spring Creek: Lat 47.033, Lng -109.382

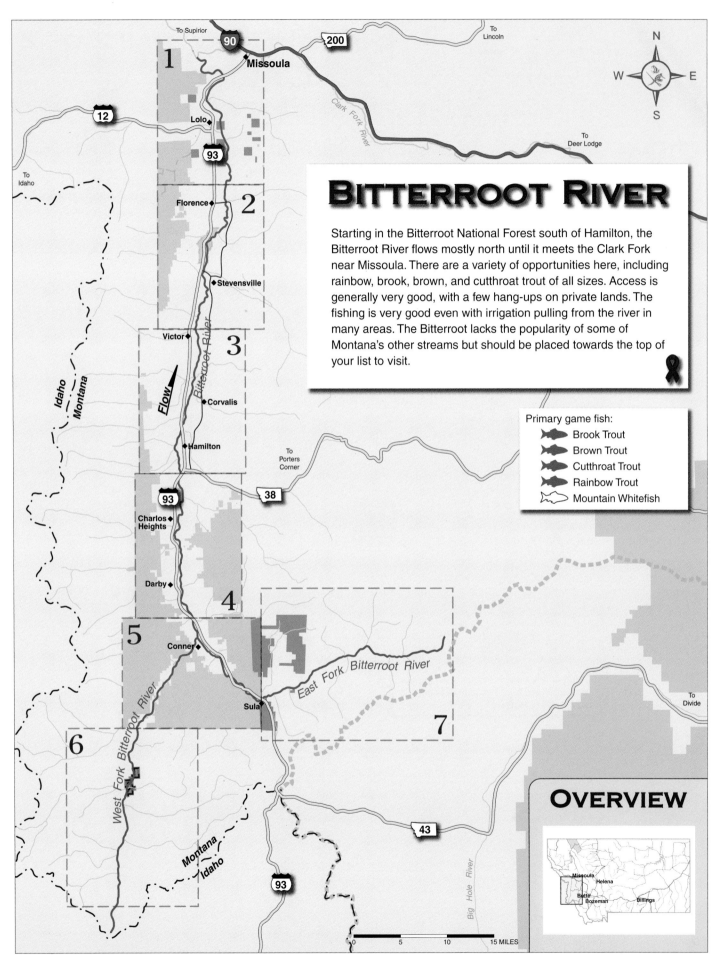

BITTERROOT RIVER

Starting in the Bitterroot National Forest south of Hamilton, the Bitterroot River flows mostly north until it meets the Clark Fork near Missoula. There are a variety of opportunities here, including rainbow, brook, brown, and cutthroat trout of all sizes. Access is generally very good, with a few hang-ups on private lands. The fishing is very good even with irrigation pulling from the river in many areas. The Bitterroot lacks the popularity of some of Montana's other streams but should be placed towards the top of your list to visit.

Primary game fish:
- Brook Trout
- Brown Trout
- Cutthroat Trout
- Rainbow Trout
- Mountain Whitefish

OVERVIEW

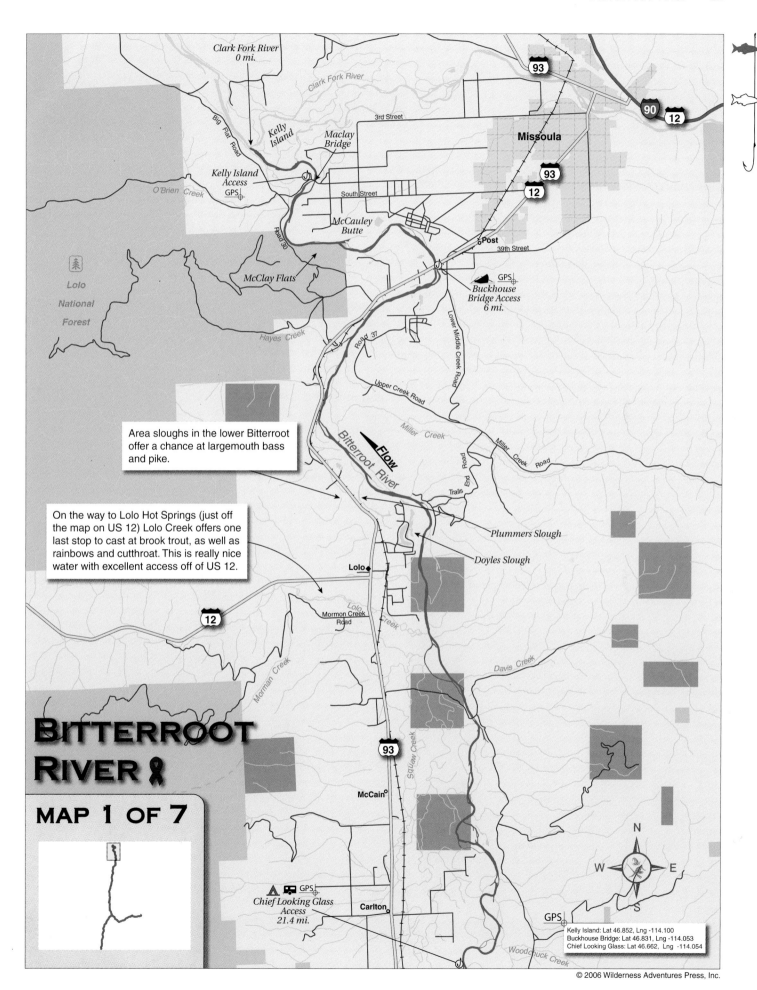

Clark Fork River
0 mi.

Clark Fork River

93

Missoula

90   12

3rd Street

Kelly
Island

Maclay
Bridge

93

Kelly Island
Access
GPS

12

O'Brien Creek

Road 30

South Street

Post

39th Street

McCauley
Butte

GPS

Buckhouse
Bridge Access
6 mi.

Lolo
National
Forest

McClay Flats

Hayes Creek

Road 37

Lower Middle Creek Road

Upper Creek Road

Miller Creek

Area sloughs in the lower Bitterroot
offer a chance at largemouth bass
and pike.

Flow

Bitterroot River

Miller Creek Road

Trails End Road

On the way to Lolo Hot Springs (just off
the map on US 12) Lolo Creek offers one
last stop to cast at brook trout, as well as
rainbows and cutthroat. This is really nice
water with excellent access off of US 12.

Plummers Slough

Doyles Slough

Lolo

12

Lolo Creek

Mormon Creek
Road

Davis Creek

Morman Creek

**BITTERROOT
RIVER**

93

Squaw Creek

MAP 1 OF 7

McCain

N

W   E

S

GPS

Chief Looking Glass
Access
21.4 mi.

Carlton

GPS

Kelly Island: Lat 46.852, Lng -114.100
Buckhouse Bridge: Lat 46.831, Lng -114.053
Chief Looking Glass: Lat 46.662, Lng -114.054

Woodchuck Creek

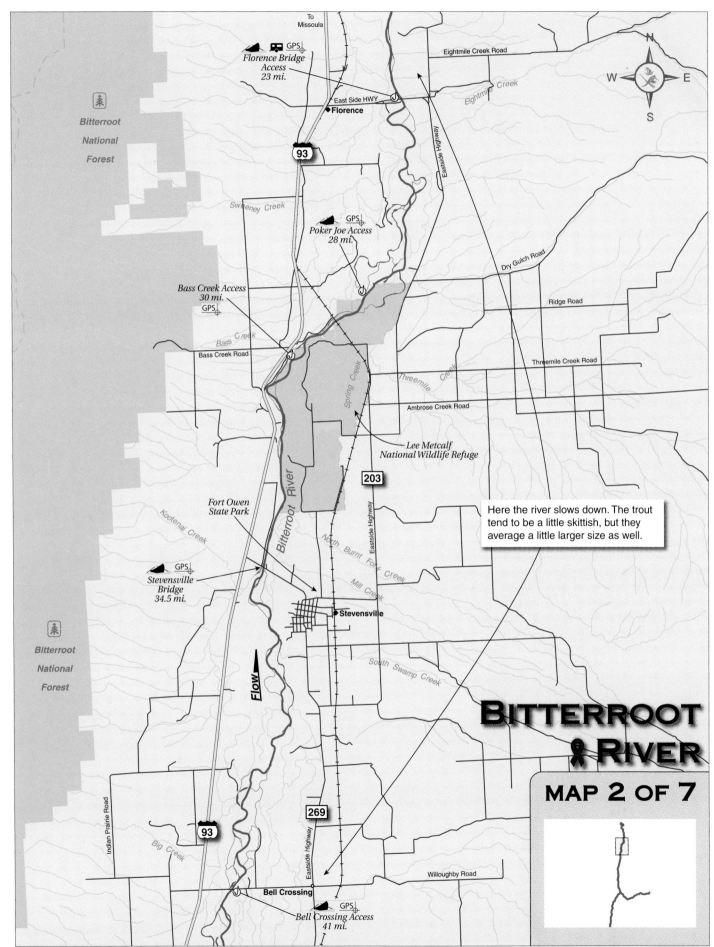

Florence Bridge
Access
23 mi.

East Side HWY

Florence

93

Bitterroot
National
Forest

Sweeney Creek

Eightmile Creek Road

Eightmile Creek

Poker Joe Access
28 mi.

Dry Gulch Road

Ridge Road

Bass Creek Access
30 mi.
GPS

Bass Creek

Bass Creek Road

Spring Creek

Threemile Creek

Threemile Creek Road

Ambrose Creek Road

Lee Metcalf
National Wildlife Refuge

203

Here the river slows down. The trout
tend to be a little skittish, but they
average a little larger size as well.

Fort Owen
State Park

Kootenai Creek

Bitterroot River

Stevensville
Bridge
34.5 mi.

North Burnt Fork Creek

Mill Creek

Stevensville

Eastside Highway

FLOW

South Swamp Creek

Bitterroot
National
Forest

Indian Prairie Road

93

Big Creek

269

Eastside Highway

BITTERROOT
RIVER

MAP 2 OF 7

Willoughby Road

Bell Crossing

Bell Crossing Access
41 mi.

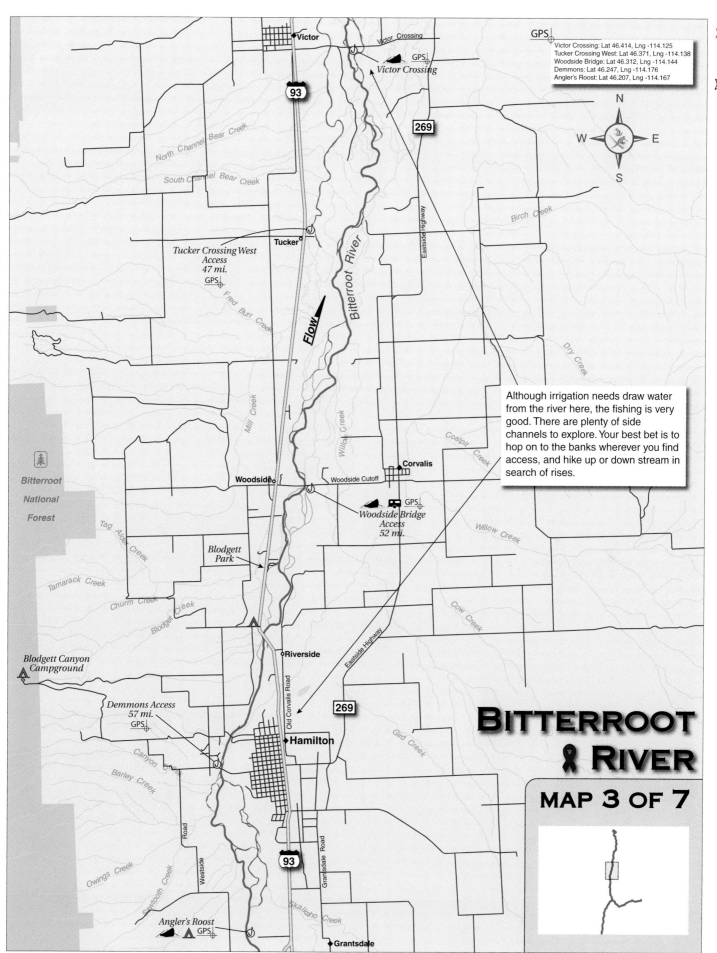

GPS

Victor Crossing: Lat 46.414, Lng -114.125
Tucker Crossing West: Lat 46.371, Lng -114.138
Woodside Bridge: Lat 46.312, Lng -114.144
Demmons: Lat 46.247, Lng -114.176
Angler's Roost: Lat 46.207, Lng -114.167

Victor

Victor Crossing

93

269

N
W   E
S

Tucker

Tucker Crossing West
Access
47 mi.
GPS

Flow

Bitterroot River

Eastside Highway

Birch Creek

North Channel Bear Creek

South Channel Bear Creek

Fred Burr Creek

Dry Creek

Mill Creek

Willow Creek

Coalpit Creek

Corvalis

Woodside   Woodside Cutoff

Woodside Bridge
Access
52 mi.   GPS

Willow Creek

Although irrigation needs draw water
from the river here, the fishing is very
good. There are plenty of side
channels to explore. Your best bet is to
hop on to the banks wherever you find
access, and hike up or down stream in
search of rises.

Bitterroot
National
Forest

Tag Alder Creek

Blodgett
Park

Blodgett Creek

Tamarack Creek

Churm Creek

Cow Creek

Blodgett Canyon
Campground

Riverside

Old Corvalis Road

Eastside Highway

269

Demmons Access
57 mi.
GPS

Gird Creek

Canyon Creek

Barley Creek

Hamilton

**BITTERROOT
RIVER**

MAP 3 OF 7

Owings Creek

Sawtooth Creek

Westside Road

Road

Grantsdale Road

93

Skalkaho Creek

Angler's Roost   GPS

Grantsdale

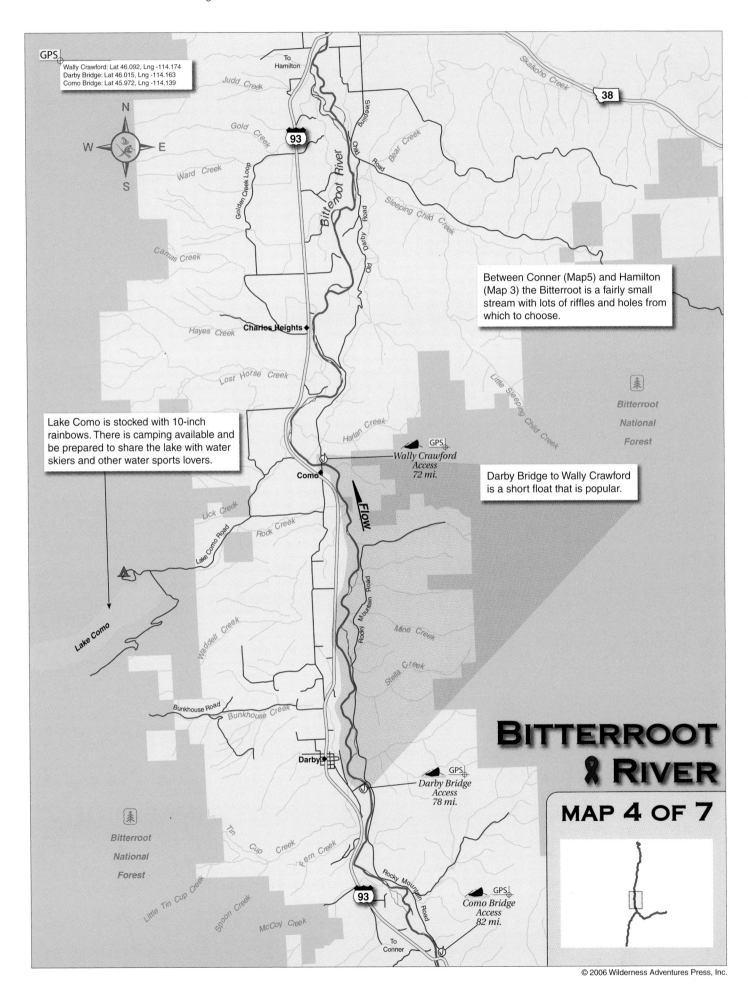

GPS
Wally Crawford: Lat 46.092, Lng -114.174
Darby Bridge: Lat 46.015, Lng -114.163
Como Bridge: Lat 45.972, Lng -114.139

N
W   E
S

To
Hamilton

Judd Creek

Gold Creek

93

Ward Creek

Golden Creek Loop

Bitterroot River

Camas Creek

Skalkaho Creek

38

Bear Creek

Sleeping Child Road

Old Darby Road

Sleeping Child Creek

Between Conner (Map5) and Hamilton
(Map 3) the Bitterroot is a fairly small
stream with lots of riffles and holes from
which to choose.

Hayes Creek   Charles Heights ◆

Lost Horse Creek

Little Sleeping Child Creek

Bitterroot

National

Forest

Lake Como is stocked with 10-inch
rainbows. There is camping available and
be prepared to share the lake with water
skiers and other water sports lovers.

Harlan Creek

GPS
Wally Crawford
Access
72 mi.

Darby Bridge to Wally Crawford
is a short float that is popular.

Como ◆

Flow

Lick Creek

Rock Creek

Lake Como Road

Lake Como

Waddell Creek

Rocky Mountain Road

Mine Creek

Stella Creek

Bunkhouse Road

Bunkhouse Creek

Darby

GPS
Darby Bridge
Access
78 mi.

Bitterroot

National

Forest

Tin Cup Creek

Little Tin Cup Creek

Spoon Creek

Fern Creek

McCoy Creek

93

Rocky Mountain Road

GPS
Como Bridge
Access
82 mi.

To
Conner

BITTERROOT
🎗 RIVER

MAP 4 OF 7

© 2006 Wilderness Adventures Press, Inc.

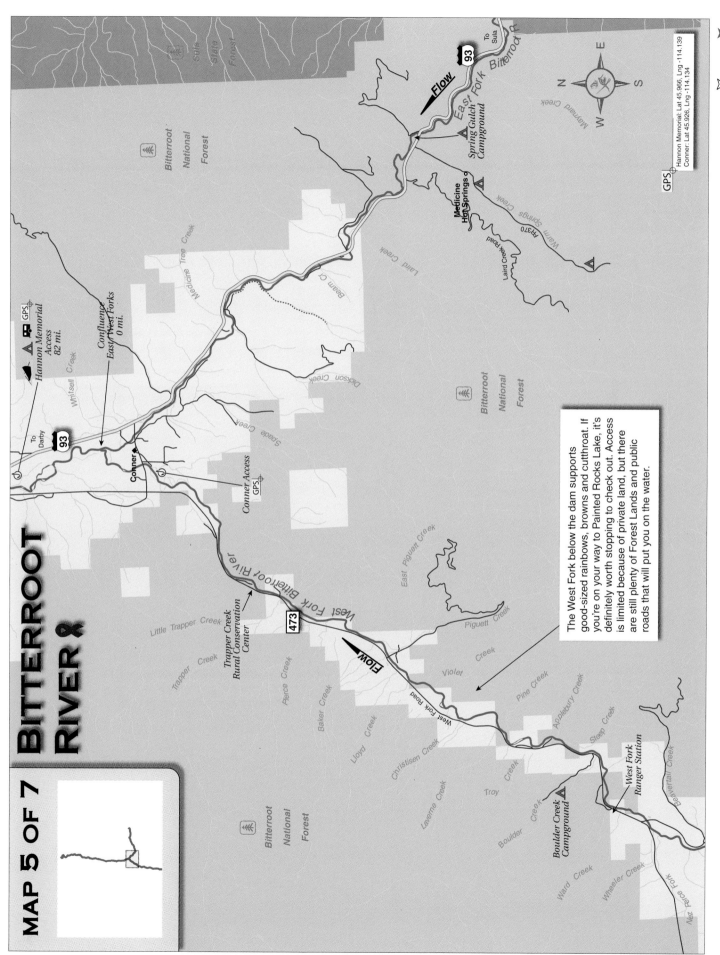

Hannon Memorial: Lat 45.966, Lng -114.139
Conner: Lat 45.926, Lng -114.134

GPS

MAP 5 OF 7

BITTERROOT
RIVER ⅜

To Sula

93

Flow

East Fork Bitterroot R.

Maynard Creek

N E S W

Spring Gulch
Campground

Medicine
Hot Springs

GPS

Warm Springs Creek

FR370
Laird Creek Road

Bitterroot
National
Forest

Laird Creek

Bitterroot
National
Forest

Medicine Tree Creek

Beam Cr.

Dickson Creek

GPS
Hannon Memorial
Access
82 mi.

Whitsell Creek

To Darby

93

Confluence
East/West Forks
0 mi.

Spade Creek

Conner

Conner Access
GPS

East Piguett Creek

The West Fork below the dam supports good-sized rainbows, browns and cutthroat. If you're on your way to Painted Rocks Lake, it's definitely worth stopping to check out. Access is limited because of private land, but there are still plenty of Forest Lands and public roads that will put you on the water.

Little Trapper Creek

Trapper Creek
Rural Conservation
Center

West Fork Bitterroot River

473

Piguett Creek

Creek

Violet

Pine Creek

Appleberry Creek

Trapper Creek

Pierce Creek

Baker Creek

Flow

West Fork Road

Lloyd Creek

Christisen Creek

Creek

Steep Creek

West Fork
Ranger Station

Beavertail Creek

Bitterroot
National
Forest

Laverne Creek

Troy

Boulder

Boulder Creek
Campground

Ward Creek

Wheeler Creek

Nez Perce Fork

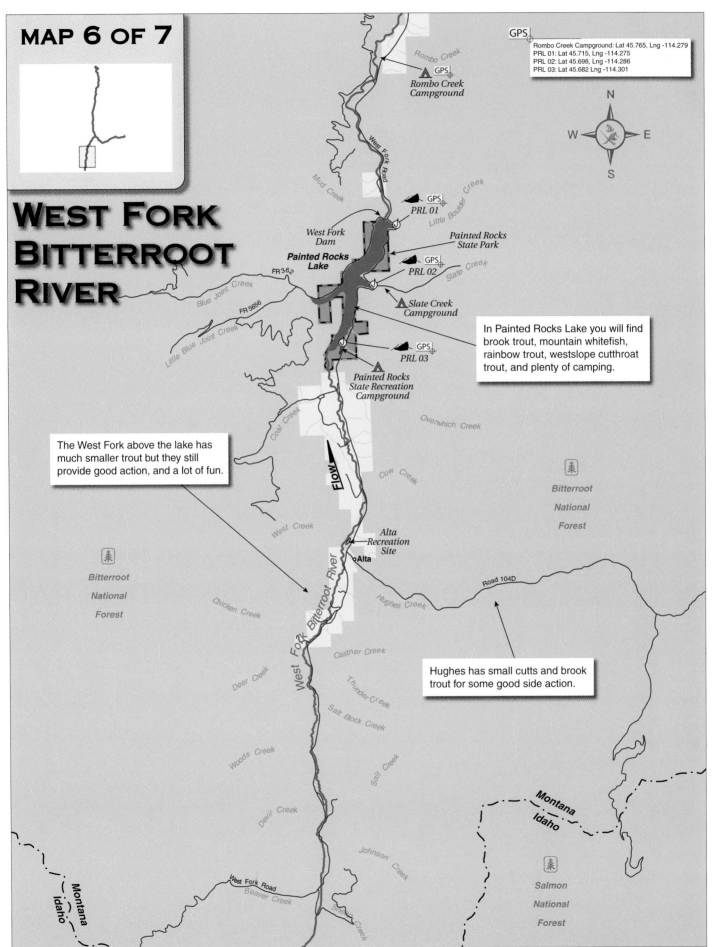

MAP 6 OF 7

WEST FORK BITTERROOT RIVER

Rombo Creek Campground: Lat 45.765, Lng -114.279
PRL 01: Lat 45.715, Lng -114.275
PRL 02: Lat 45.698, Lng -114.286
PRL 03: Lat 45.682 Lng -114.301

Rombo Creek

GPS

Rombo Creek Campground

West Fork Road

Mud Creek

GPS
PRL 01

Little Boulder Creek

West Fork Dam

Painted Rocks Lake

Painted Rocks State Park

FR 362

GPS
PRL 02

Slate Creek

Blue Joint Creek

FR 5656

Slate Creek Campground

Little Blue Joint Creek

GPS
PRL 03

In Painted Rocks Lake you will find brook trout, mountain whitefish, rainbow trout, westslope cutthroat trout, and plenty of camping.

Painted Rocks State Recreation Campground

Coal Creek

Overwhich Creek

The West Fork above the lake has much smaller trout but they still provide good action, and a lot of fun.

FLOW

Cow Creek

West Creek

Bitterroot National Forest

Alta Recreation Site

Alta

Bitterroot National Forest

Chicken Creek

Hughes Creek

Road 104D

West Fork Bitterroot River

Castner Creek

Hughes has small cutts and brook trout for some good side action.

Deer Creek

Thunder Creek

Salt Block Creek

Salt Creek

Woods Creek

Montana
Idaho

Devil Creek

Johnson Creek

Montana
Idaho

Salmon National Forest

West Fork Road

Beaver Creek

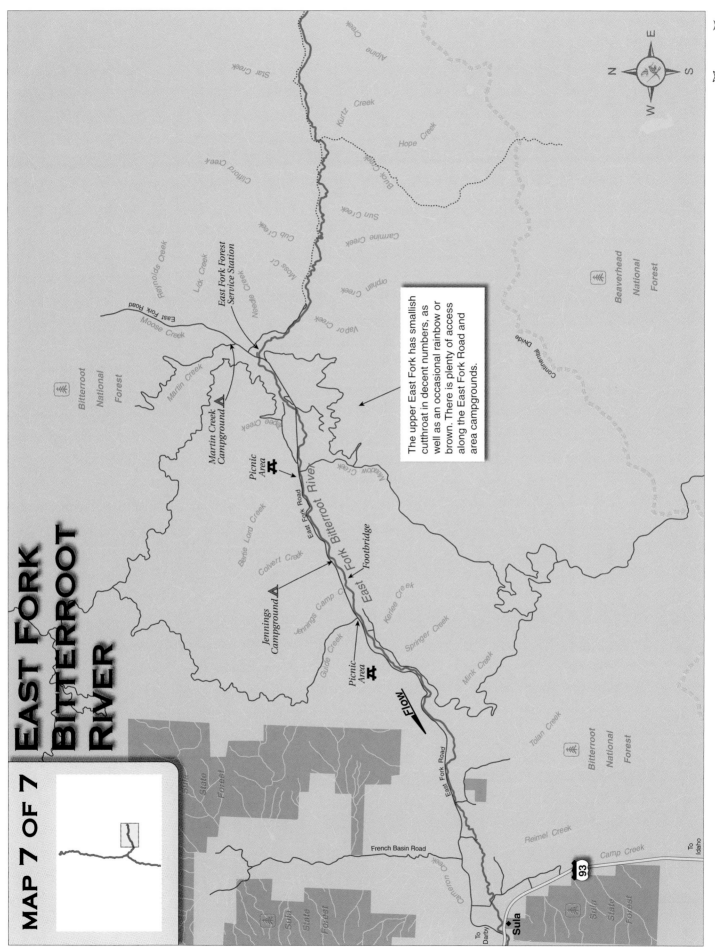

MAP 7 OF 7

EAST FORK
BITTERROOT
RIVER

The upper East Fork has smallish cutthroat in decent numbers, as well as an occasional rainbow or brown. There is plenty of access along the East Fork Road and area campgrounds.

East Fork Forest Service Station

Martin Creek Campground

Picnic Area

Jennings Campground

Footbridge

Picnic Area

FLOW

East Fork Road

East Fork Bitterroot River

Bitterroot National Forest

Beaverhead National Forest

Continental Divide

Sula State Forest

Bitterroot National Forest

Sula State Forest

French Basin Road

Sula

To Darby

To Idaho

93

© 2006 Wilderness Adventures Press, Inc.

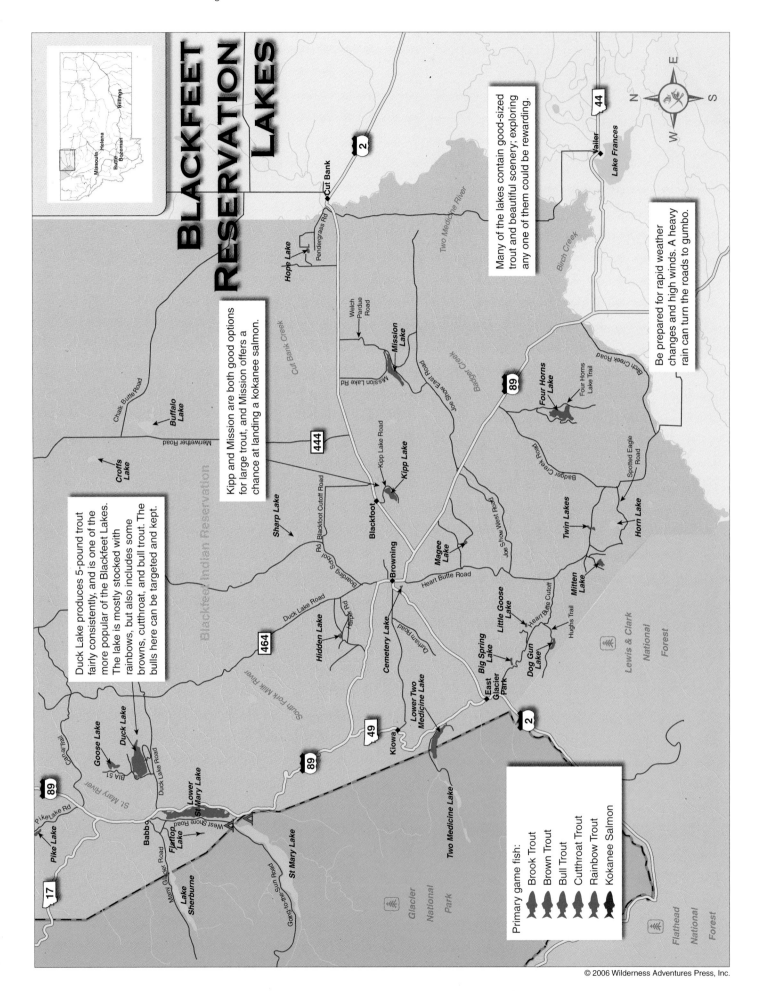

BLACKFEET RESERVATION LAKES

Many of the lakes contain good-sized trout and beautiful scenery; exploring any one of them could be rewarding.

Be prepared for rapid weather changes and high winds. A heavy rain can turn the roads to gumbo.

Kipp and Mission are both good options for large trout, and Mission offers a chance at landing a kokanee salmon.

Duck Lake produces 5-pound trout fairly consistently, and is one of the more popular of the Blackfeet Lakes. The lake is mostly stocked with rainbows, but also includes some browns, cutthroat, and bull trout. The bulls here can be targeted and kept.

Primary game fish:
- Brook Trout
- Brown Trout
- Bull Trout
- Cutthroat Trout
- Rainbow Trout
- Kokanee Salmon

© 2006 Wilderness Adventures Press, Inc.

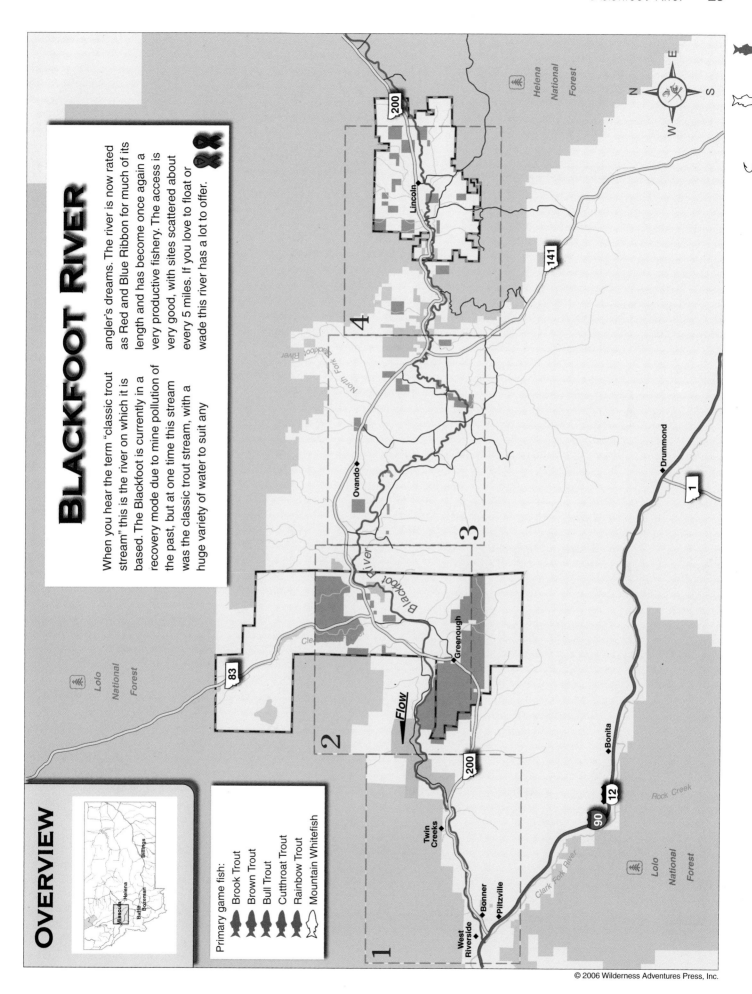

OVERVIEW

Primary game fish:
Brook Trout
Brown Trout
Bull Trout
Cutthroat Trout
Rainbow Trout
Mountain Whitefish

BLACKFOOT RIVER

When you hear the term "classic trout stream" this is the river on which it is based. The Blackfoot is currently in a recovery mode due to mine pollution of the past, but at one time this stream was the classic trout stream, with a huge variety of water to suit any angler's dreams. The river is now rated as Red and Blue Ribbon for much of its length and has become once again a very productive fishery. The access is very good, with sites scattered about every 5 miles. If you love to float or wade this river has a lot to offer.

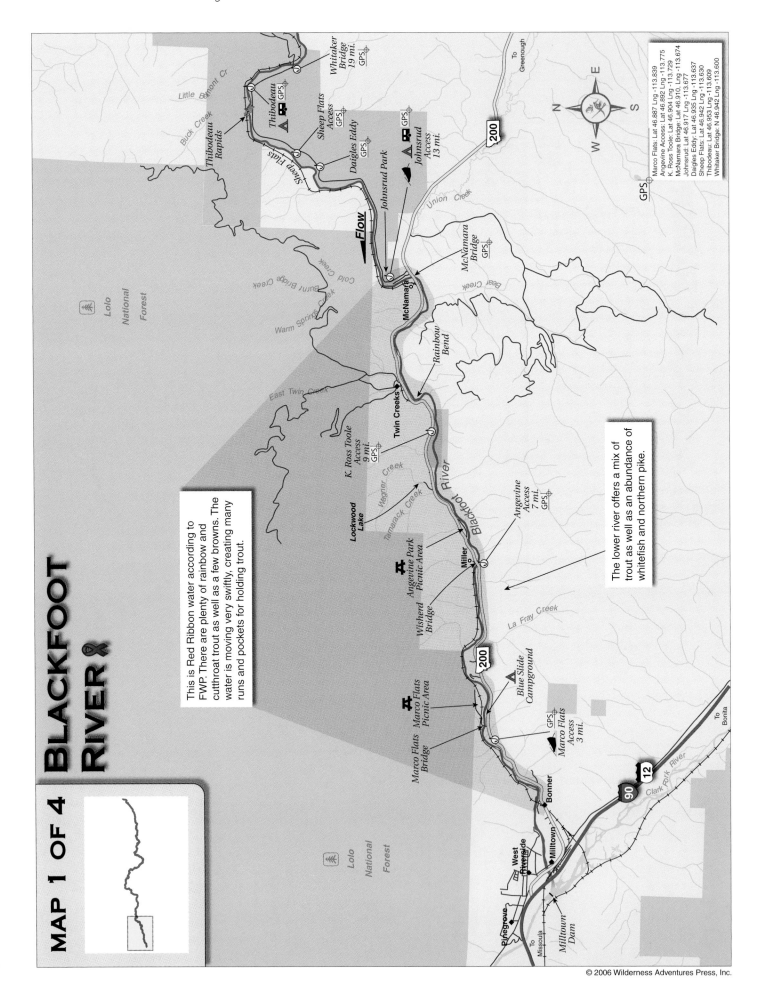

MAP 1 OF 4 BLACKFOOT RIVER

This is Red Ribbon water according to FWP. There are plenty of rainbow and cutthroat trout as well as a few browns. The water is moving very swiftly, creating many runs and pockets for holding trout.

The lower river offers a mix of trout as well as an abundance of whitefish and northern pike.

Marco Flats: Lat 46.887 Lng -113.839
Angevine Access: Lat 46.892 Lng -113.775
K. Ross Toole: Lat 46.904 Lng -113.729
McNamara Bridge: Lat 46.910, Lng -113.674
Johnsrud: Lat 46.917 Lng -113.677
Daigles Eddy: Lat 46.935 Lng -113.637
Sheep Flats: Lat 46.942 Lng -113.630
Thibodeau: Lat 46.953 Lng -113.609
Whitaker Bridge: N 46.942 Lng -113.600

Whitaker Bridge 19 mi. GPS

Thibodeau GPS

Thibodeau Rapids

Sheep Flats Access GPS

Daigles Eddy GPS

Johnsrud Park

Johnsrud Access 13 mi. GPS

To Greenough

200

Flow

Little Belmont Cr

Buck Creek

Sheep Flats

Cold Creek

Burnt Bridge Creek

Warm Springs Creek

Lolo National Forest

Union Creek

McNamara Bridge GPS

McNamara

Bear Creek

Rainbow Bend

East Twin Creek

Twin Creeks

K Ross Toole Access 9 mi. GPS

Wagner Creek

Lockwood Lake

Tamarack Creek

Angevine Park Picnic Area

Angevine Access 7 mi. GPS

Blackfoot River

Miller

Wisherd Bridge

La Fray Creek

200

Blue Slide Campground

Marco Flats Picnic Area

Marco Flats Bridge

GPS Marco Flats Access 3 mi.

Lolo National Forest

Bonner

West Riverside

Milltown

Milltown Dam

Pinegrove

To Missoula

To Bonita

90

12

Clark Fork River

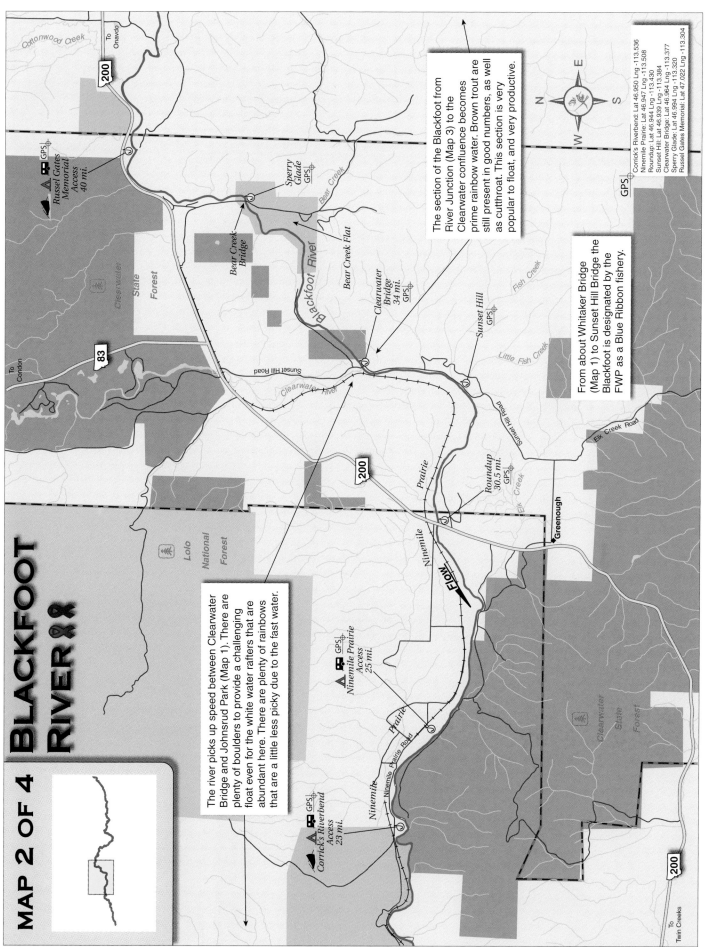

MAP 2 OF 4
BLACKFOOT RIVER

Blackfoot River

The river picks up speed between Clearwater Bridge and Johnsrud Park (Map 1). There are plenty of boulders to provide a challenging float even for the white water rafters that are abundant here. There are plenty of rainbows that are a little less picky due to the fast water.

The section of the Blackfoot from River Junction (Map 3) to the Clearwater confluence becomes prime rainbow water. Brown trout are still present in good numbers, as well as cutthroat. This section is very popular to float, and very productive.

From about Whitaker Bridge (Map 1) to Sunset Hill Bridge the Blackfoot is designated by the FWP as a Blue Ribbon fishery.

Corrick's Riverbend: Lat 46.950 Lng -113.536
Ninemile Prairie: Lat 46.947 Lng -113.508
Roundup: Lat 46.944 Lng -113.430
Sunset Hill: Lat 46.939 Lng -113.384
Clearwater Bridge: Lat 46.964 Lng -113.377
Sperry Glade: Lat 46.994 Lng -113.320
Russel Gates Memorial: Lat 47.022 Lng -113.304

GPS

N E W S

Russel Gates Memorial Access 40 mi.
Sperry Glade GPS
Bear Creek Bridge
Bear Creek
Bear Creek Flat
Clearwater State Forest
Clearwater Bridge 34 mi. GPS
Sunset Hill GPS
Fish Creek
Little Fish Creek
Sunset Hill Road
Clearwater River
Blackfoot River
To Condon
83
200
Prairie
Roundup 30.5 mi. GPS
Elk Creek
Elk Creek Road
Greenough
Ninemile
Ninemile Prairie Access 25 mi. GPS
Ninemile Prairie Road
Prairie
Ninemile
FLOW
Clearwater State Forest
Lolo National Forest
Corrick's Riverbend Access 23 mi. GPS
Cottonwood Creek
To Onavdo
200
200
To Twin Creeks

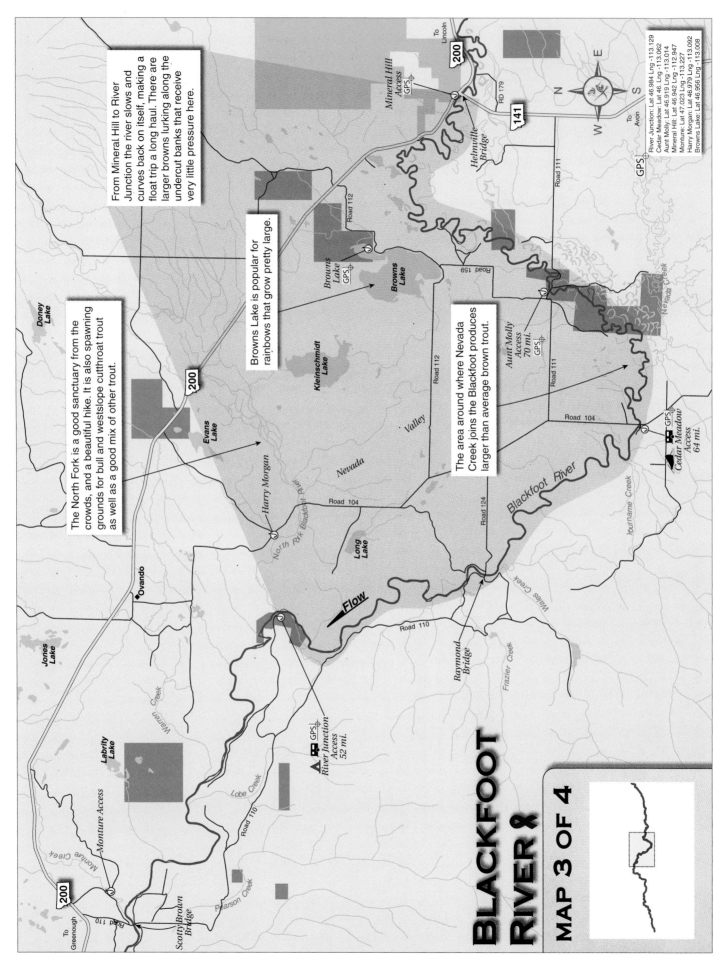

From Mineral Hill to River Junction the river slows and curves back on itself, making a float trip a long haul. There are larger browns lurking along the undercut banks that receive very little pressure here.

Browns Lake is popular for rainbows that grow pretty large.

The North Fork is a good sanctuary from the crowds, and a beautiful hike. It is also spawning grounds for bull and westslope cutthroat trout as well as a good mix of other trout.

The area around where Nevada Creek joins the Blackfoot produces larger than average brown trout.

River Junction: Lat 46.984 Lng -113.129
Cedar Meadow: Lat 46. Lng -113.062
Aunt Molly: Lat 46.919 Lng -113.014
Mineral Hill: Lat 46.942 Lng -112.947
Monture: Lat 47.023 Lng -113.227
Harry Morgan: Lat 46.979 Lng -113.092
Browns Lake: Lat 46.956 Lng -113.008

BLACKFOOT RIVER

MAP 3 OF 4

© 2006 Wilderness Adventures Press, Inc.

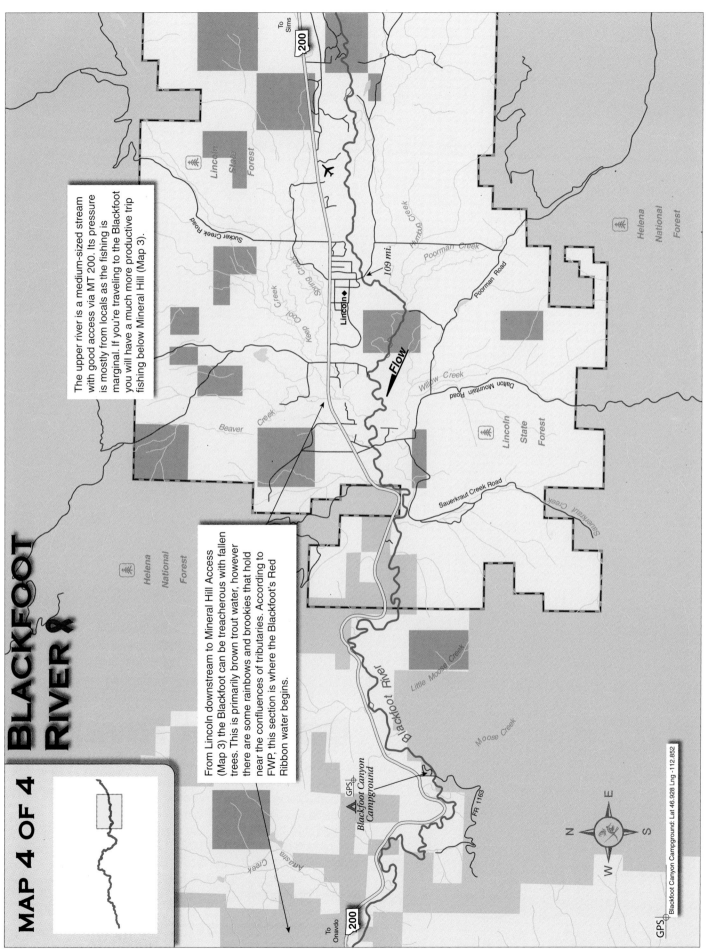

MAP 4 OF 4

BLACKFOOT RIVER

The upper river is a medium-sized stream with good access via MT 200. Its pressure is mostly from locals as the fishing is marginal. If you're traveling to the Blackfoot you will have a much more productive trip fishing below Mineral Hill (Map 3).

From Lincoln downstream to Mineral Hill Access (Map 3) the Blackfoot can be treacherous with fallen trees. This is primarily brown trout water, however there are some rainbows and brookies that hold near the confluences of tributaries. According to FWP, this section is where the Blackfoot's Red Ribbon water begins.

To Sims

200

Lincoln State Forest

Sucker Creek Road

Spring Creek

Keep Cool Creek

109 mi.

Lincoln

Pumpu Creek

Poorman Creek

Poorman Road

Helena National Forest

Flow

Willow Creek

Dalton Mountain Road

Lincoln State Forest

Beaver Creek

Sauerkraut Creek Road

Sauerkraut Creek

Helena National Forest

Little Moose Creek

Moose Creek

Blackfoot River

GPS

Blackfoot Canyon Campground

FR 1163

Artesia Creek

To Ovando

200

N E S W

GPS Blackfoot Canyon Campground: Lat 46.928 Lng -112.852

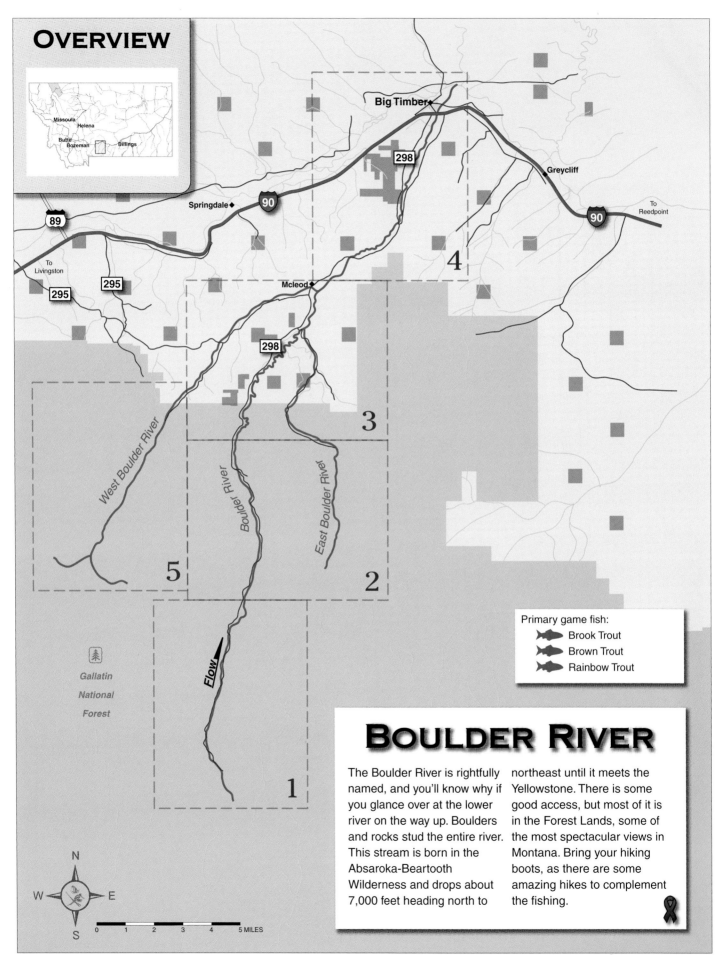

OVERVIEW

Missoula
Helena
Butte
Bozeman
Billings

Big Timber

298

90

Springdale

Greycliff

89

To
Reedpoint

90

To
Livingston

295

295

298

Mcleod

4

West Boulder River

Boulder River

East Boulder River

3

2

5

1

Flow

Gallatin

National

Forest

Primary game fish:
Brook Trout
Brown Trout
Rainbow Trout

N
W E
S

0   1   2   3   4   5 MILES

BOULDER RIVER

The Boulder River is rightfully named, and you'll know why if you glance over at the lower river on the way up. Boulders and rocks stud the entire river. This stream is born in the Absaroka-Beartooth Wilderness and drops about 7,000 feet heading north to northeast until it meets the Yellowstone. There is some good access, but most of it is in the Forest Lands, some of the most spectacular views in Montana. Bring your hiking boots, as there are some amazing hikes to complement the fishing.

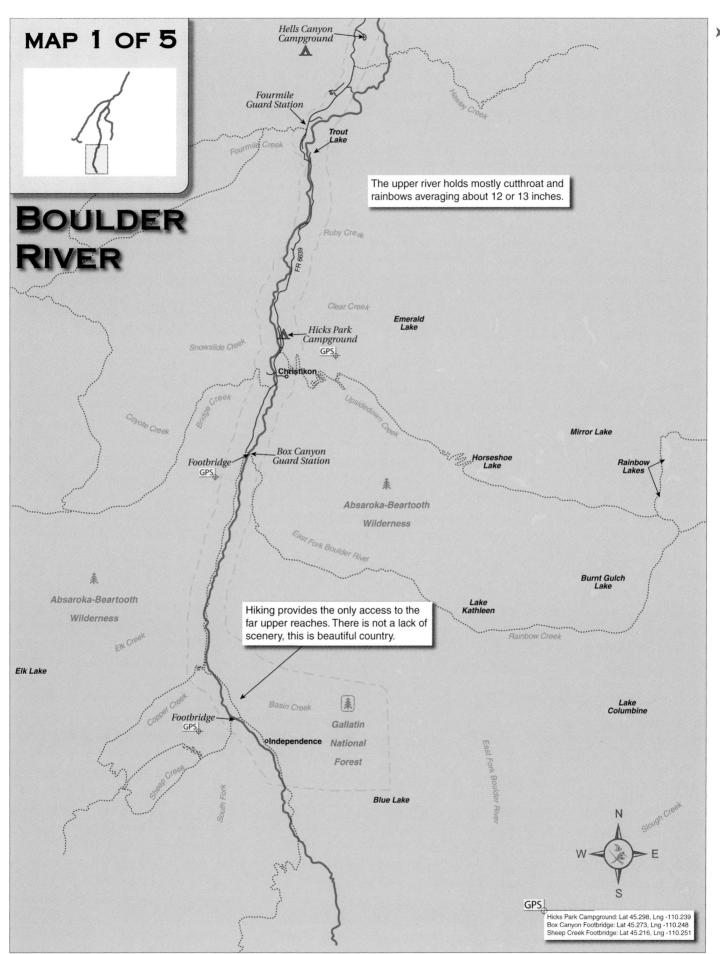

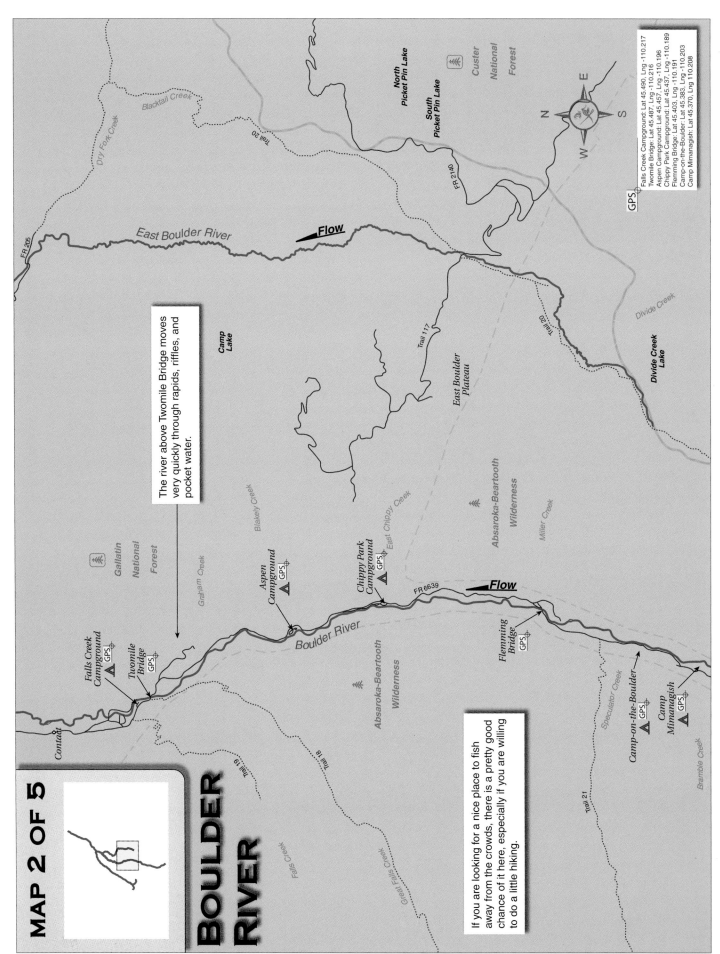

GPS

Falls Creek Campground: Lat 45.490, Lng -110.217
Twomile Bridge: Lat 45.487, Lng -110.216
Aspen Campground: Lat 45.457, Lng -110.196
Chippy Park Campground: Lat 45.437, Lng -110.189
Flemming Bridge: Lat 45.403, Lng -110.191
Camp-on-the-Boulder: Lat 45.383, Lng -110.203
Camp Mimanagish: Lat 45.370, Lng 110.208

The river above Twomile Bridge moves very quickly through rapids, riffles, and pocket water.

If you are looking for a nice place to fish away from the crowds, there is a pretty good chance of it here, especially if you are willing to do a little hiking.

MAP 2 OF 5

BOULDER RIVER

© 2006 Wilderness Adventures Press, Inc.

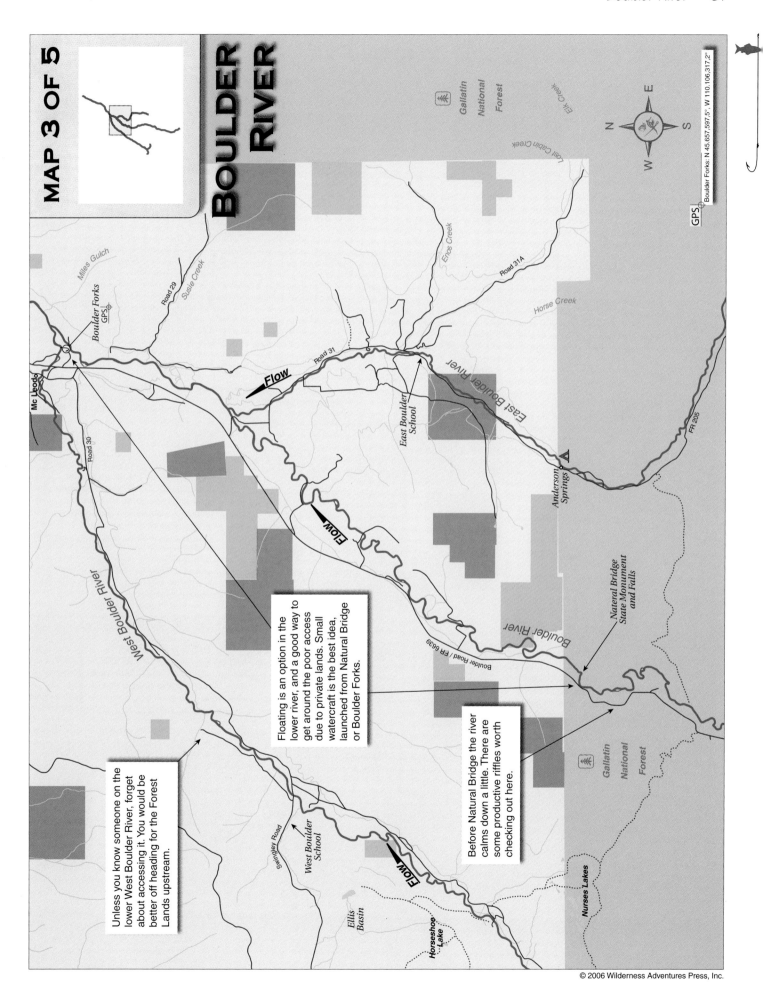

MAP 3 OF 5

BOULDER RIVER

Boulder Forks: N 45,657,597.5°, W 110,106,317.2°

GPS

Gallatin National Forest

Elk Creek

Lost Cabin Creek

Enos Creek

Road 31A

Horse Creek

Miles Gulch

Boulder Forks
GPS

Road 29

Susie Creek

Mc Leod

Road 30

Road 31

Flow

Flow

East Boulder School

East Boulder River

Anderson Springs

FR 205

West Boulder River

Natural Bridge State Monument and Falls

Boulder Road / FR 6639

Boulder River

Floating is an option in the lower river, and a good way to get around the poor access due to private lands. Small watercraft is the best idea, launched from Natural Bridge or Boulder Forks.

Unless you know someone on the lower West Boulder River, forget about accessing it. You would be better off heading for the Forest Lands upstream.

Before Natural Bridge the river calms down a little. There are some productive riffles worth checking out here.

Swingley Road

West Boulder School

Ellis Basin

Flow

Horseshoe Lake

Nurses Lakes

Gallatin National Forest

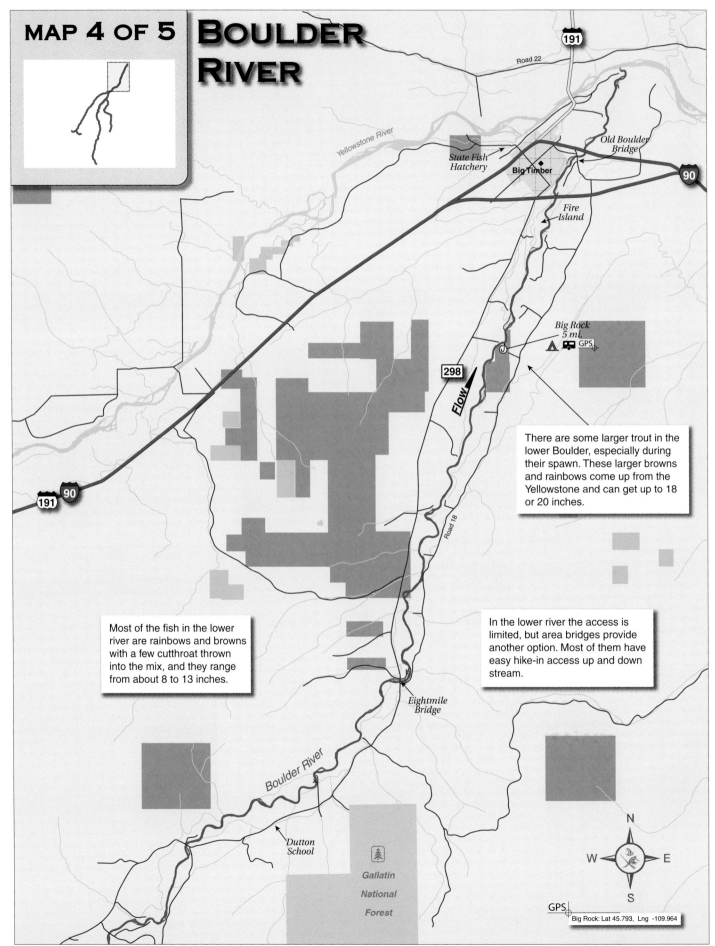

MAP 4 OF 5 **BOULDER RIVER**

Yellowstone River

State Fish Hatchery

Big Timber

Old Boulder Bridge

191

Road 22

90

Fire Island

Big Rock 5 mi.
GPS

191 90

298

Flow

Road 18

There are some larger trout in the lower Boulder, especially during their spawn. These larger browns and rainbows come up from the Yellowstone and can get up to 18 or 20 inches.

Most of the fish in the lower river are rainbows and browns with a few cutthroat thrown into the mix, and they range from about 8 to 13 inches.

In the lower river the access is limited, but area bridges provide another option. Most of them have easy hike-in access up and down stream.

Eightmile Bridge

Boulder River

Dutton School

Gallatin National Forest

N
W E
S

GPS
Big Rock: Lat 45.793, Lng -109.964

© 2006 Wilderness Adventures Press, Inc.

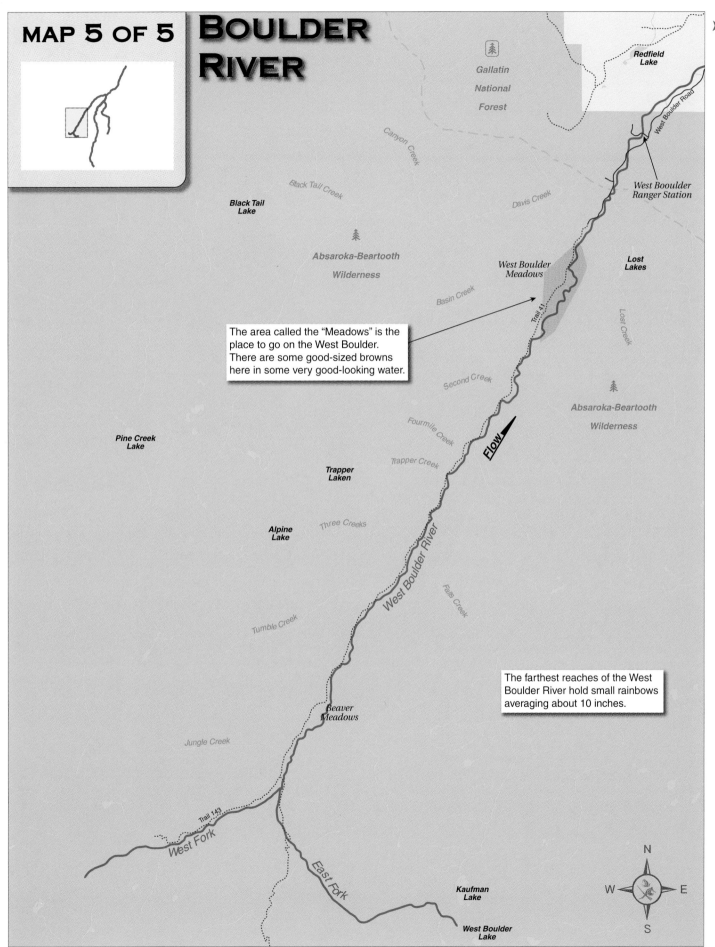

MAP 5 OF 5

BOULDER
RIVER

Gallatin

National

Forest

Redfield
Lake

West Boulder Road

West Booulder
Ranger Station

Canyon Creek

Black Tail Creek

Davis Creek

Black Tail
Lake

Absaroka-Beartooth

Wilderness

West Boulder
Meadows

Lost
Lakes

Basin Creek

Lost Creek

Trail 41

The area called the "Meadows" is the
place to go on the West Boulder.
There are some good-sized browns
here in some very good-looking water.

Second Creek

Absaroka-Beartooth

Wilderness

Fourmile Creek

Flow

Pine Creek
Lake

Trapper Creek

Trapper
Laken

Three Creeks

Alpine
Lake

West Boulder River

Falls Creek

Tumble Creek

The farthest reaches of the West
Boulder River hold small rainbows
averaging about 10 inches.

Beaver
Meadows

Jungle Creek

Trail 143

West Fork

East Fork

Kaufman
Lake

N

W   E

S

West Boulder
Lake

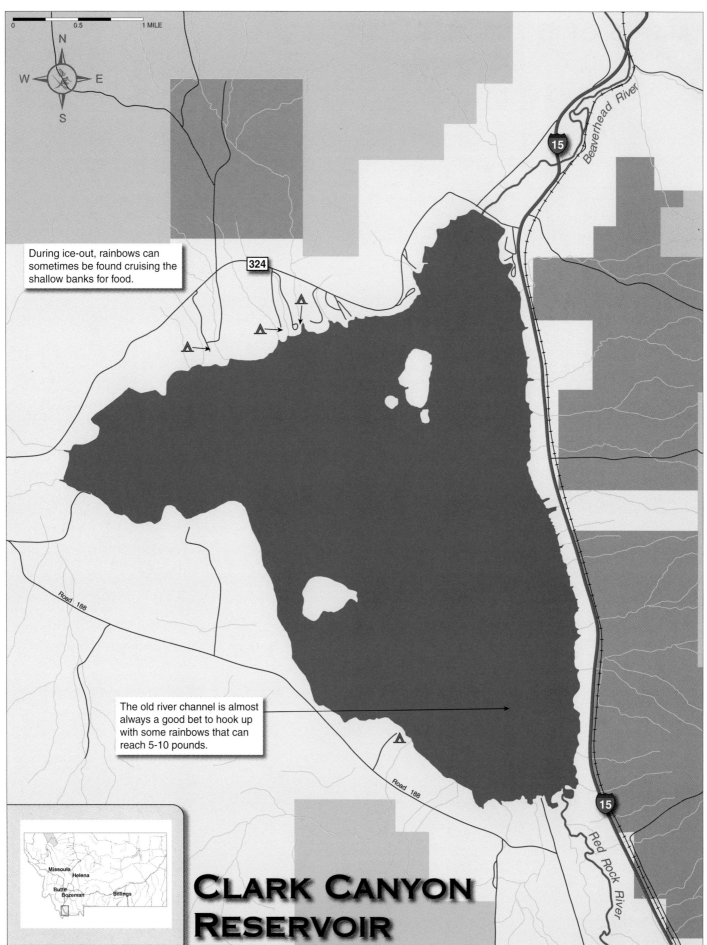

During ice-out, rainbows can sometimes be found cruising the shallow banks for food.

The old river channel is almost always a good bet to hook up with some rainbows that can reach 5-10 pounds.

CLARK CANYON
RESERVOIR

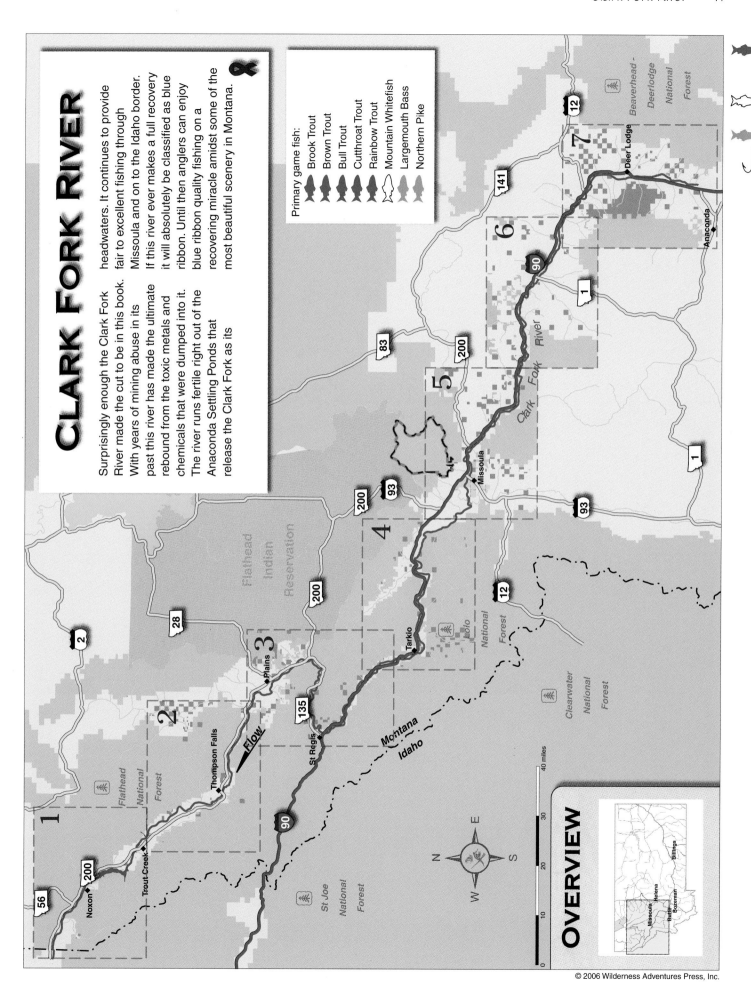

CLARK FORK RIVER

Surprisingly enough the Clark Fork River made the cut to be in this book. With years of mining abuse in its past this river has made the ultimate rebound from the toxic metals and chemicals that were dumped into it. The river runs fertile right out of the Anaconda Settling Ponds that release the Clark Fork as its

headwaters. It continues to provide fair to excellent fishing through Missoula and on to the Idaho border. If this river ever makes a full recovery it will absolutely be classified as blue ribbon. Until then anglers can enjoy a blue ribbon quality fishing on a recovering miracle amidst some of the most beautiful scenery in Montana.

Primary game fish:
Brook Trout
Brown Trout
Bull Trout
Cutthroat Trout
Rainbow Trout
Mountain Whitefish
Largemouth Bass
Northern Pike

OVERVIEW

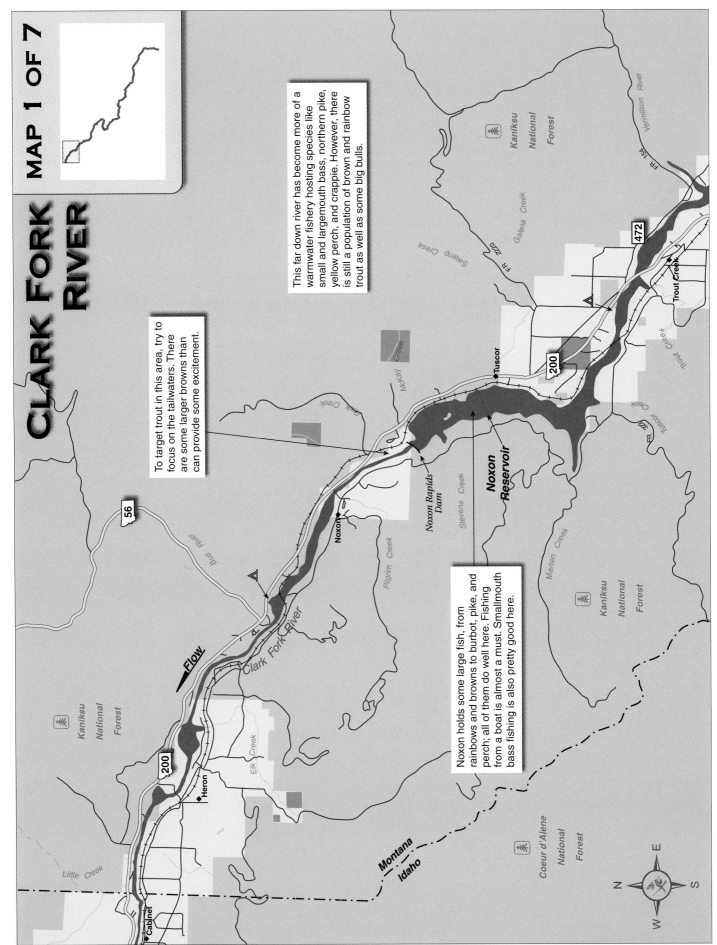

CLARK FORK RIVER

MAP 1 OF 7

This far down river has become more of a warmwater fishery hosting species like small and largemouth bass, northern pike, yellow perch, and crappie. However, there is still a population of brown and rainbow trout as well as some big bulls.

To target trout in this area, try to focus on the tailwaters. There are some larger browns than can provide some excitement.

Noxon holds some large fish, from rainbows and browns to burbot, pike, and perch; all of them do well here. Fishing from a boat is almost a must. Smallmouth bass fishing is also pretty good here.

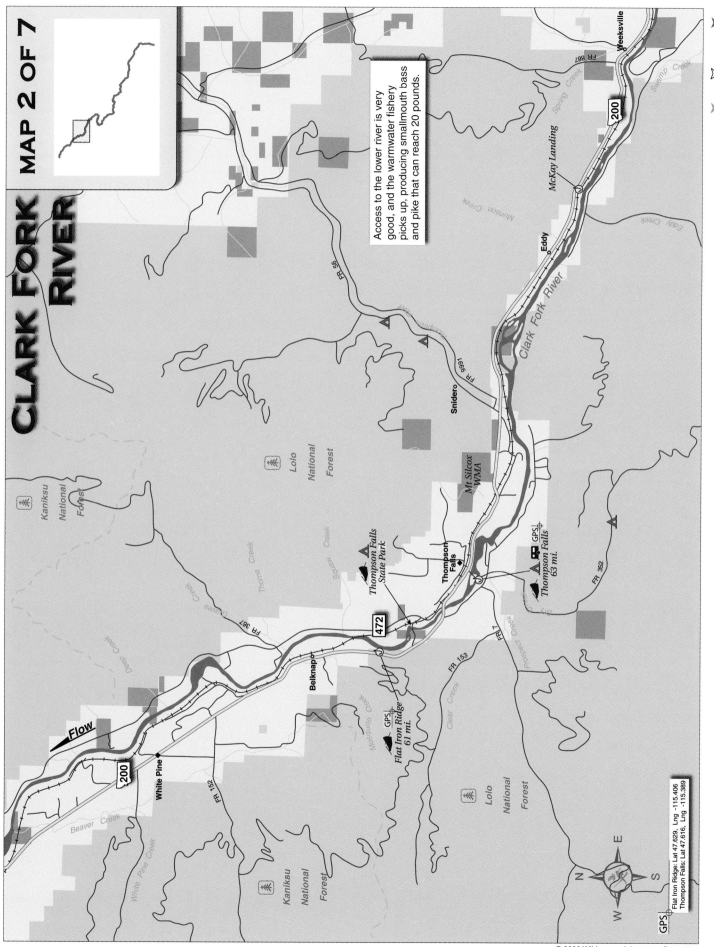

CLARK FORK RIVER

MAP 2 OF 7

Access to the lower river is very good, and the warmwater fishery picks up, producing smallmouth bass and pike that can reach 20 pounds.

Weeksville

FR 887

200

McKay Landing

Eddy

Spring Creek

Munson Creek

Swamp Creek

Eddy Creek

Clark Fork River

FR 56

Snidero

FR 9696

Mt Silcox WMA

Lolo National Forest

Kaniksu National Forest

Thorne Creek

Squaw Creek

Graves Creek

FR 367

Thompson Falls State Park

Thompson Falls

GPS

GPS Thompson Falls 63 mi.

FR 352

472

Belknap

Mosquito Creek

GPS Flat Iron Ridge 61 mi.

FR 153

Clear Creek

Prospect Creek

FR 7

Deep Creek

Flow

200

White Pine

FR 152

White Pine Creek

Beaver Creek

Lolo National Forest

Kaniksu National Forest

N
E
S
W

GPS Flat Iron Ridge: Lat 47.629, Lng -115.406
Thompson Falls: Lat 47.616, Lng -115.389

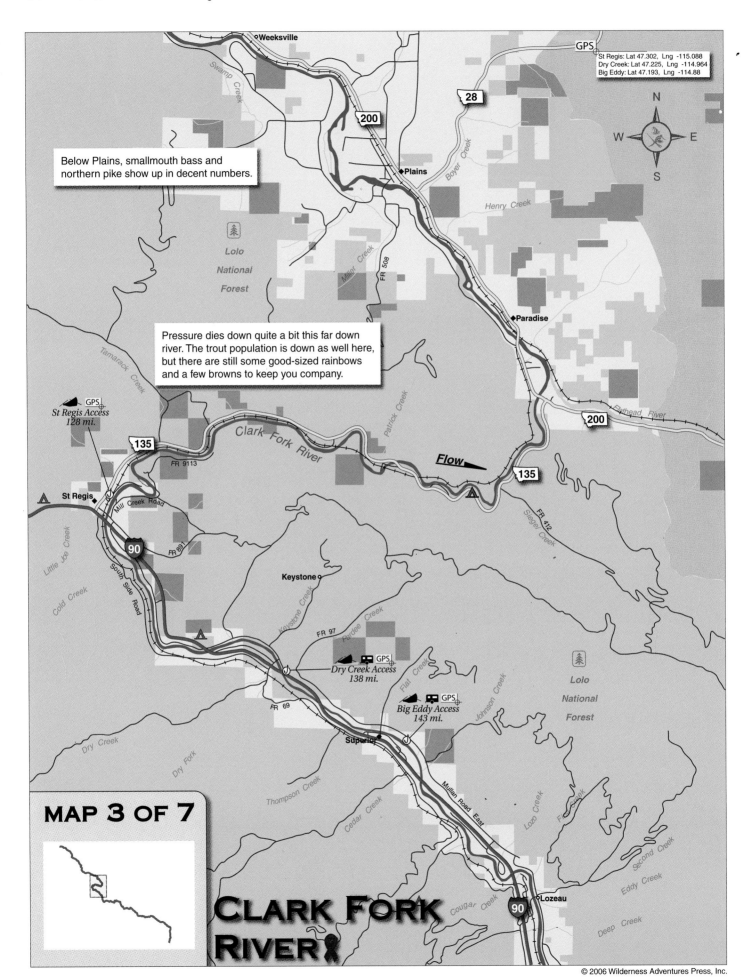

St Regis: Lat 47.302, Lng -115.088
Dry Creek: Lat 47.225, Lng -114.964
Big Eddy: Lat 47.193, Lng -114.88

Below Plains, smallmouth bass and
northern pike show up in decent numbers.

Pressure dies down quite a bit this far down
river. The trout population is down as well here,
but there are still some good-sized rainbows
and a few browns to keep you company.

St Regis Access
128 mi.

Dry Creek Access
138 mi.

Big Eddy Access
143 mi.

MAP 3 OF 7

CLARK FORK RIVER

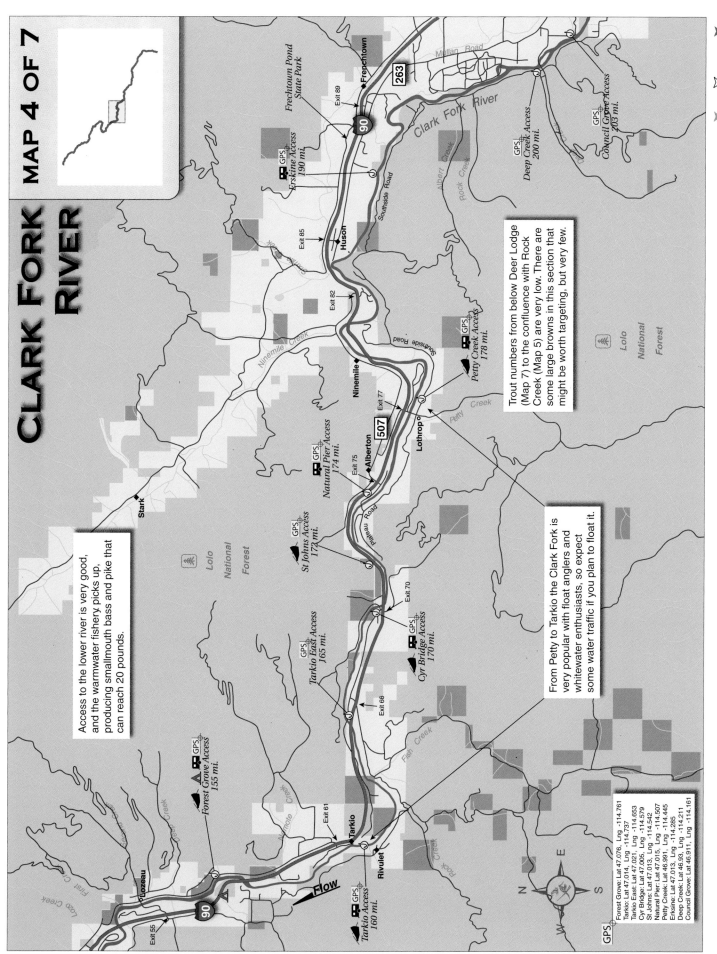

CLARK FORK RIVER

MAP 4 OF 7

Access to the lower river is very good, and the warmwater fishery picks up, producing smallmouth bass and pike that can reach 20 pounds.

Trout numbers from below Deer Lodge (Map 7) to the confluence with Rock Creek (Map 5) are very low. There are some large browns in this section that might be worth targeting, but very few.

From Petty to Tarkio the Clark Fork is very popular with float anglers and whitewater enthusiasts, so expect some water traffic if you plan to float it.

Frechtown Pond State Park

Erskine Access 190 mi.

Council Grove Access 203 mi.

Deep Creek Access 200 mi.

Clark Fork River

Huson

Petty Creek Access 178 mi.

Ninemile

Natural Pier Access 174 mi.

Alberton

Lothrop

St Johns Access 172 mi.

Tarkio East Access 165 mi.

Cyr Bridge Access 170 mi.

Forest Grove Access 155 mi.

Tarkio

Rivulet

Tarkio Access 160 mi.

Stark

Lolo National Forest

Lolo National Forest

Flow

Forest Grove: Lat 47.076, Lng -114.761
Tarkio: Lat 47.014, Lng -114.737
Tarkio East: Lat 47.021, Lng -114.653
Cyr Bridge: Lat 47.005, Lng -114.579
St Johns: Lat 47.013, Lng -114.542
Natural Pier: Lat 47.015, Lng -114.507
Petty Creek: Lat 46.991, Lng -114.445
Erksine: Lat 47.013, Lng -114.285
Deep Creek: Lat 46.93, Lng -114.211
Council Grove: Lat 46.911, Lng -114.161

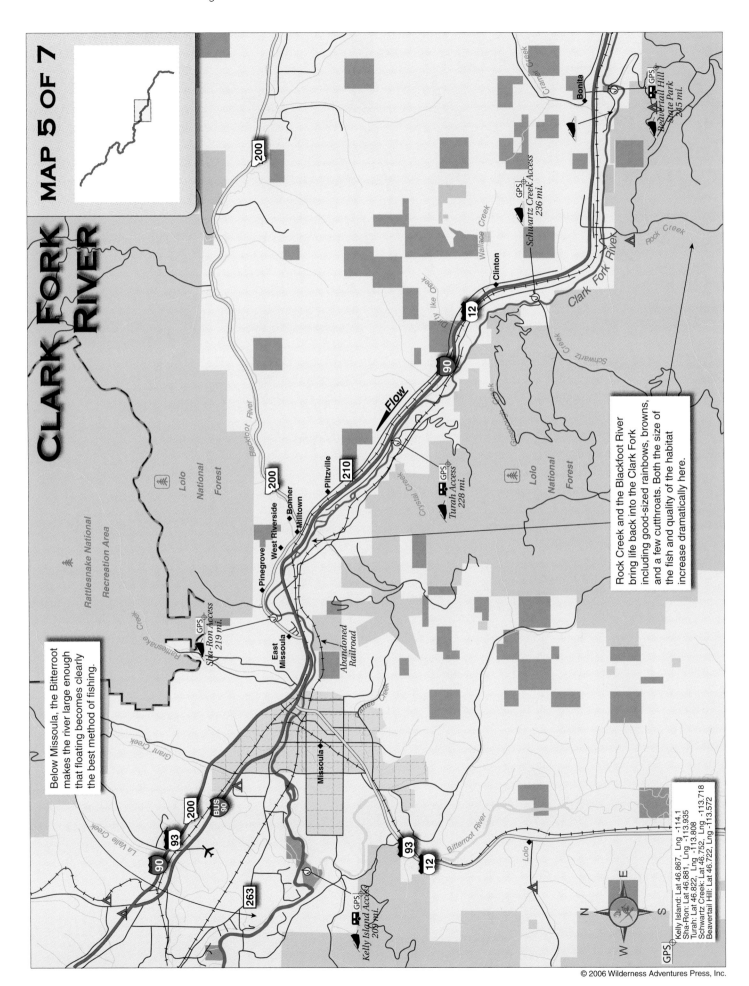

MAP 5 OF 7

CLARK FORK RIVER

Below Missoula, the Bitterroot makes the river large enough that floating becomes clearly the best method of fishing.

Rock Creek and the Blackfoot River bring life back into the Clark Fork including good-sized rainbows, browns, and a few cutthroats. Both the size of the fish and quality of the habitat increase dramatically here.

Flow

Sha-Ron Access 219 mi.

Turah Access 228 mi.

Schwartz Creek Access 236 mi.

Beavertail Hill State Park 245 mi.

Kelly Island Access 200 mi.

200
200
90
12
210
93
BUS 90
263

Missoula
East Missoula
Pinegrove
West Riverside
Bonner
Milltown
Piltzville
Clinton
Bonita

Lolo National Forest
Rattlesnake National Recreation Area

Abandoned Railroad

Blackfoot River
Bitterroot River
Rattlesnake Creek
Grant Creek
La Valle Creek
Rock Creek
Schwartz Creek
Wallace Creek
Cramer Creek
Dirty Ike Creek
Crystal Creek
Lolo

GPS
Kelly Island: Lat 46.867, Lng -114.1
Sha-Ron: Lat 46.881, Lng -113.935
Turah: Lat 46.822, Lng -113.808
Schwartz Creek: Lat 46.752, Lng -113.718
Beavertail Hill: Lat 46.722, Lng -113.572

N E W S

© 2006 Wilderness Adventures Press, Inc.

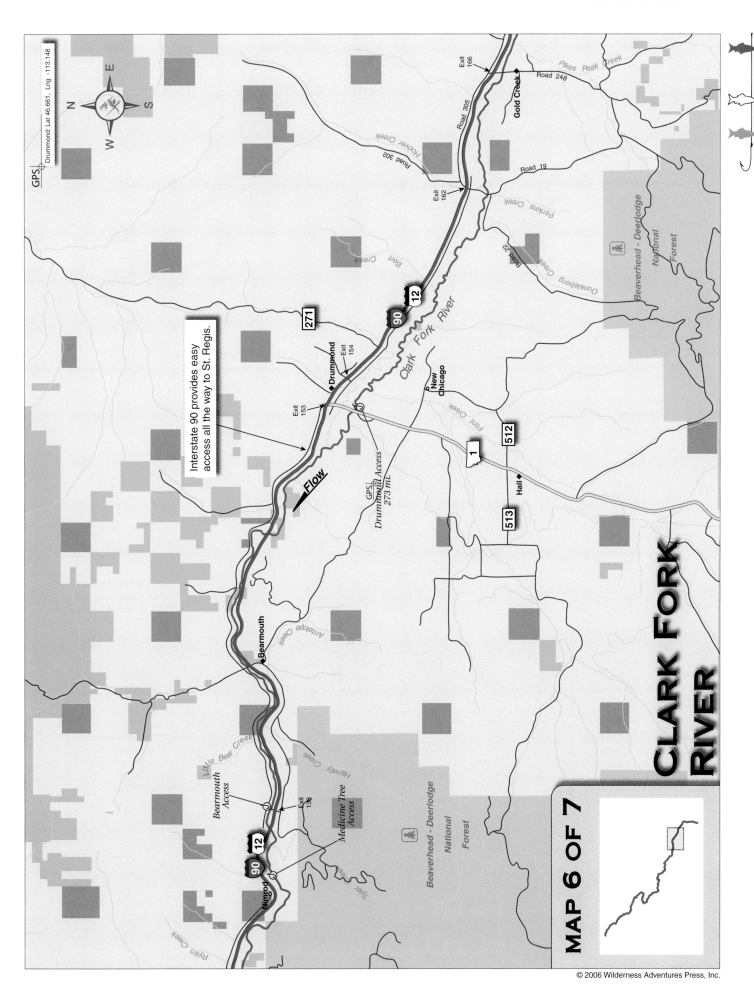

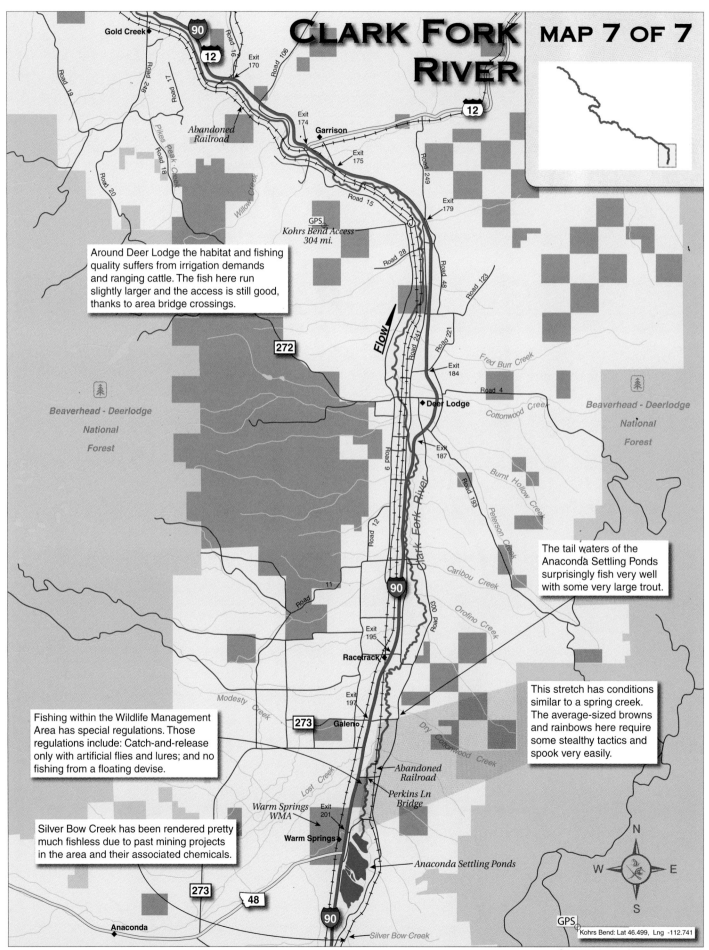

CLARK FORK RIVER

MAP 7 OF 7

Gold Creek

Road 19

Road 248

Road 17

Road 16

Exit 170

Road 106

Abandoned Railroad

Exit 174

Garrison

Exit 175

Road 249

Exit 179

Road 15

Pikes Peak Creek

Road 18

Road 20

Willow Creek

GPS Kohrs Bend Access 304 mi.

Around Deer Lodge the habitat and fishing quality suffers from irrigation demands and ranging cattle. The fish here run slightly larger and the access is still good, thanks to area bridge crossings.

Road 28

Road 48

Road 123

272

Flow

Road 241

Road 221

Exit 184

Fred Burr Creek

Road 4

Beaverhead - Deerlodge National Forest

Deer Lodge

Cottonwood Creek

Exit 187

Beaverhead - Deerlodge National Forest

Burnt Hollow Creek

Road 9

Road 193

Peterson Creek

The tail waters of the Anaconda Settling Ponds surprisingly fish very well with some very large trout.

Road 12

Clark Fork River

Caribou Creek

11

Road

90

Orofino Creek

Road 600

Exit 195

Racetrack

This stretch has conditions similar to a spring creek. The average-sized browns and rainbows here require some stealthy tactics and spook very easily.

Modesty Creek

Exit 197

273

Galeno

Dry Cottonwood Creek

Fishing within the Wildlife Management Area has special regulations. Those regulations include: Catch-and-release only with artificial flies and lures; and no fishing from a floating devise.

Lost Creek

Abandoned Railroad

Perkins Ln Bridge

Warm Springs WMA

Exit 201

Silver Bow Creek has been rendered pretty much fishless due to past mining projects in the area and their associated chemicals.

Warm Springs

Anaconda Settling Ponds

273

48

N
W E
S

GPS

Anaconda

90

Silver Bow Creek

Kohrs Bend: Lat 46.499, Lng -112.741

© 2006 Wilderness Adventures Press, Inc.

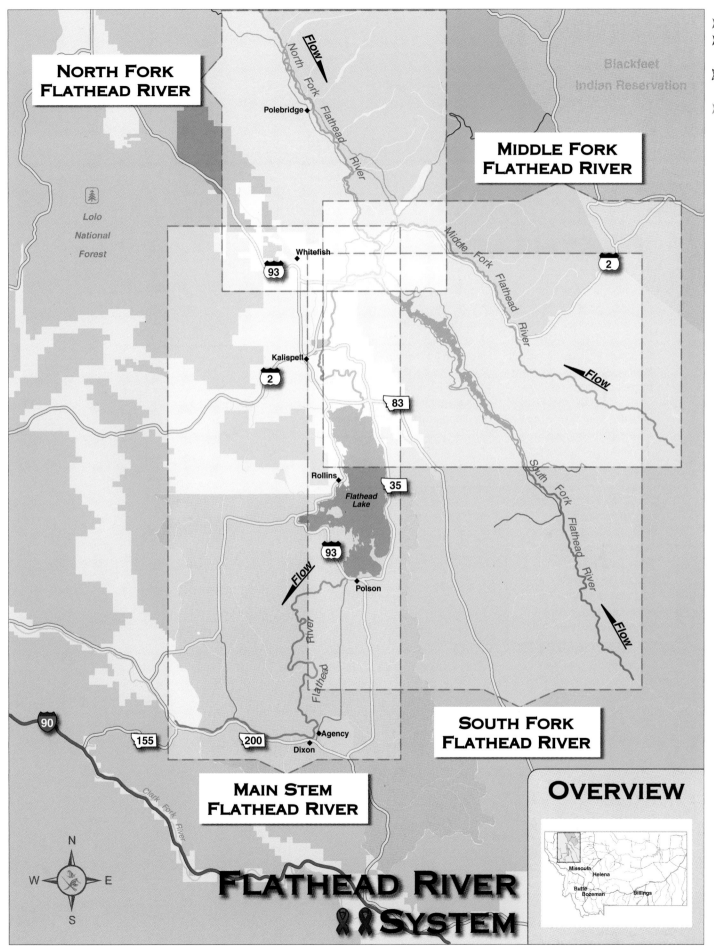

© 2006 Wilderness Adventures Press, Inc.

OVERVIEW

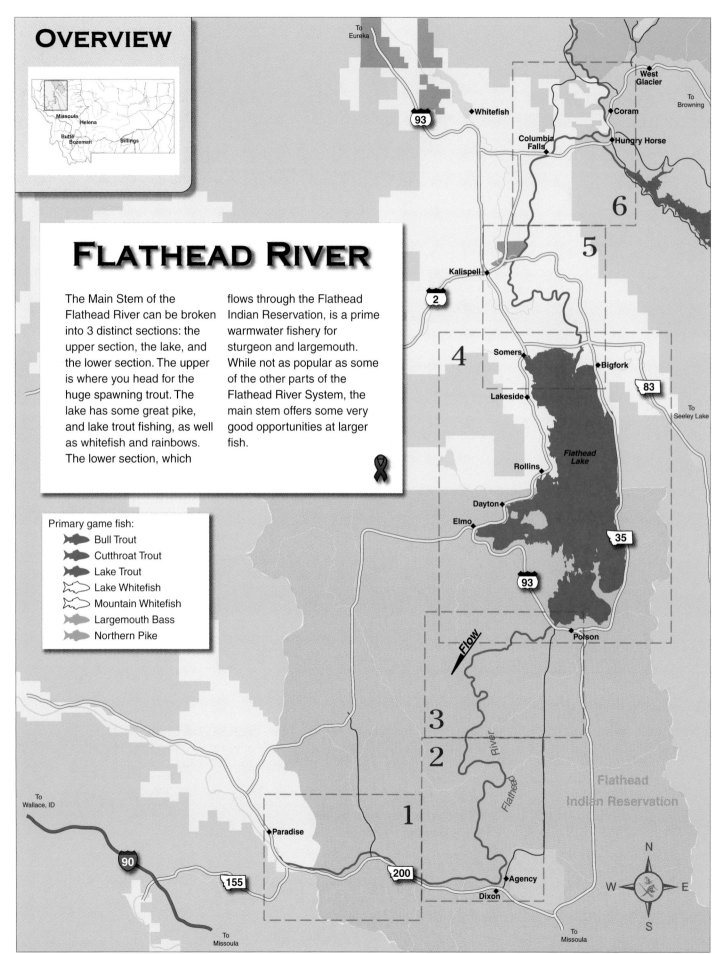

FLATHEAD RIVER

The Main Stem of the Flathead River can be broken into 3 distinct sections: the upper section, the lake, and the lower section. The upper is where you head for the huge spawning trout. The lake has some great pike, and lake trout fishing, as well as whitefish and rainbows. The lower section, which flows through the Flathead Indian Reservation, is a prime warmwater fishery for sturgeon and largemouth. While not as popular as some of the other parts of the Flathead River System, the main stem offers some very good opportunities at larger fish.

Primary game fish:
- Bull Trout
- Cutthroat Trout
- Lake Trout
- Lake Whitefish
- Mountain Whitefish
- Largemouth Bass
- Northern Pike

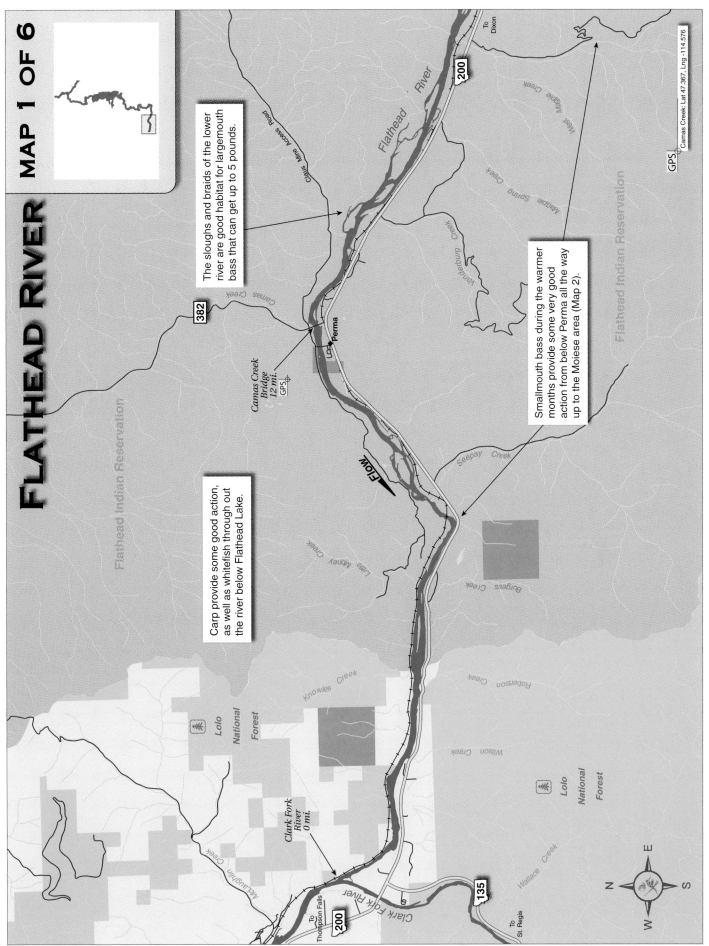

FLATHEAD RIVER MAP 1 OF 6

The sloughs and braids of the lower river are good habitat for largemouth bass that can get up to 5 pounds.

Smallmouth bass during the warmer months provide some very good action from below Perma all the way up to the Moiese area (Map 2).

Carp provide some good action, as well as whitefish through out the river below Flathead Lake.

Camas Creek Bridge 12 mi.

Clark Fork River 0 mi.

Perma

FLOW

382

200

135

200

Flathead Indian Reservation

Lolo National Forest

Lolo National Forest

Flathead River

Claus Mine Access Road

Camas Creek

Vandenburg Creek

Magpie Spring Creek

West Magpie Creek

Seepay Creek

Little Money Creek

Burgess Creek

Robertson Creek

Wilson Creek

Knowles Creek

McLaughlin Creek

Wallace Creek

Clark Fork River

To Dixon

To Thompson Falls

To St. Regis

GPS Camas Creek: Lat 47.367, Lng -114.576

© 2006 Wilderness Adventures Press, Inc.

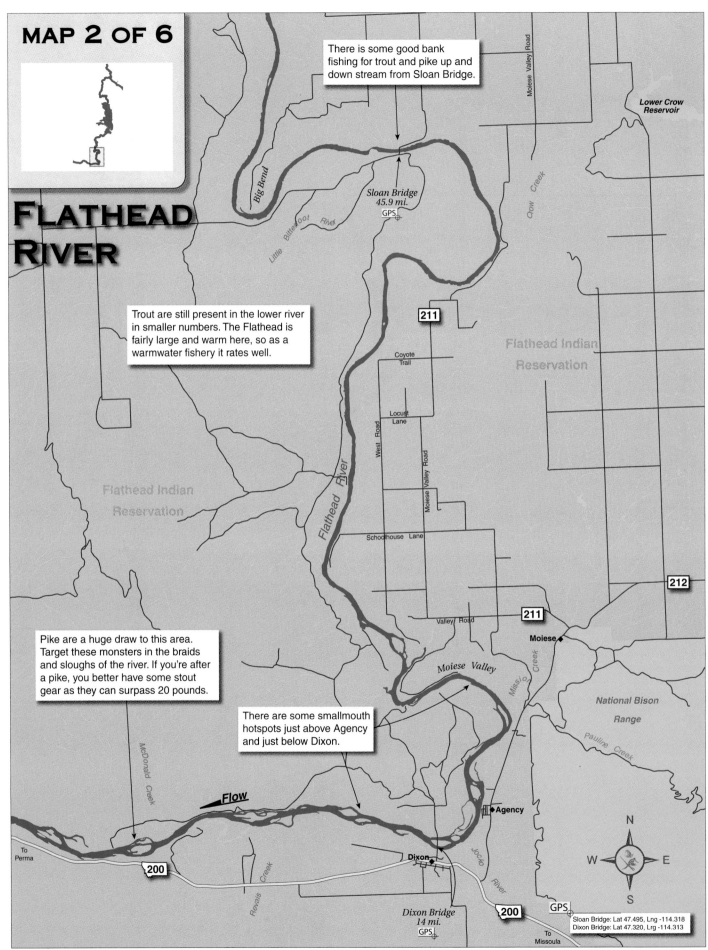

MAP 2 OF 6

FLATHEAD RIVER

There is some good bank fishing for trout and pike up and down stream from Sloan Bridge.

Sloan Bridge 45.9 mi.

Trout are still present in the lower river in smaller numbers. The Flathead is fairly large and warm here, so as a warmwater fishery it rates well.

Pike are a huge draw to this area. Target these monsters in the braids and sloughs of the river. If you're after a pike, you better have some stout gear as they can surpass 20 pounds.

There are some smallmouth hotspots just above Agency and just below Dixon.

Flow

Dixon Bridge 14 mi.

Sloan Bridge: Lat 47.495, Lng -114.318
Dixon Bridge: Lat 47.320, Lrg -114.313

© 2006 Wilderness Adventures Press, Inc.

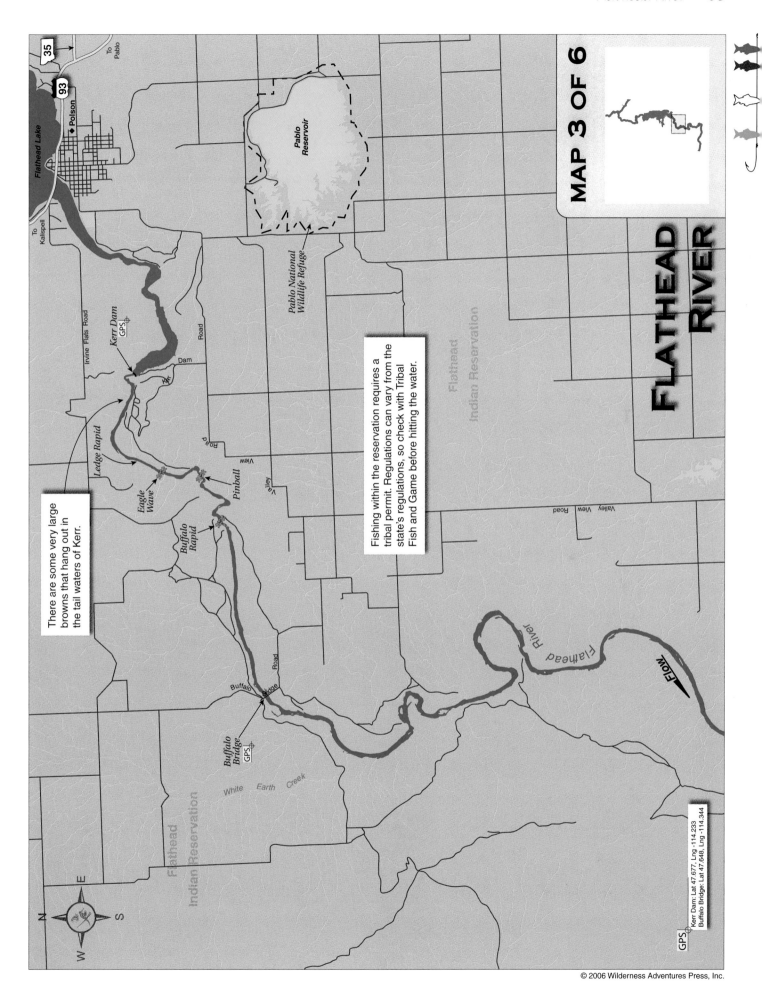

MAP 3 OF 6

FLATHEAD RIVER

There are some very large browns that hang out in the tail waters of Kerr.

Fishing within the reservation requires a tribal permit. Regulations can vary from the state's regulations, so check with Tribal Fish and Game before hitting the water.

Kerr Dam: Lat 47.677, Lng -114.233
Buffalo Bridge: Lat 47.648, Lng -114.344

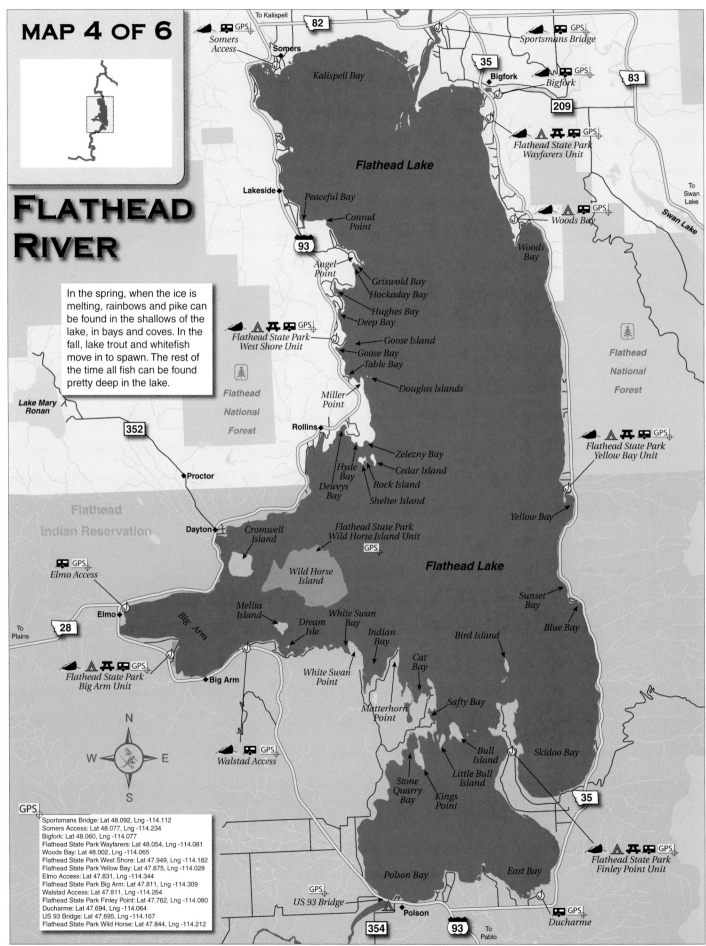

MAP 4 OF 6

FLATHEAD RIVER

In the spring, when the ice is melting, rainbows and pike can be found in the shallows of the lake, in bays and coves. In the fall, lake trout and whitefish move in to spawn. The rest of the time all fish can be found pretty deep in the lake.

To Kalispell

Somers Access
Somers

Kalispell Bay

Sportsmans Bridge

Bigfork
Bigfork

Flathead State Park
Wayfarers Unit

To Swan Lake

Flathead Lake

Swan Lake

Lakeside

Peaceful Bay

Conrad Point

Woods Bay

Woods Bay

Angel Point

Griswold Bay
Hockaday Bay

Hughes Bay
Deep Bay

Flathead State Park
West Shore Unit

Goose Island

Goose Bay
Table Bay

Flathead
National
Forest

Douglas Islands

Miller Point

Rollins

Zelezny Bay

Cedar Island

Hyde Bay

Rock Island

Deweys Bay

Shelter Island

Flathead State Park
Yellow Bay Unit

Yellow Bay

Lake Mary Ronan

Flathead
National
Forest

Proctor

Flathead
Indian Reservation

Dayton

Cromwell Island

Flathead State Park
Wild Horse Island Unit

Flathead Lake

Wild Horse Island

Sunset Bay

Elmo Access

Melita Island

White Swan Bay

Blue Bay

Elmo

Big Arm

Dream Isle

Indian Bay

Bird Island

To Plains

White Swan Point

Cat Bay

Flathead State Park
Big Arm Unit

Big Arm

Matterhorn Point

Safty Bay

Walstad Access

Bull Island

Skidoo Bay

Little Bull Island

Stone Quarry Bay

Kings Point

Flathead State Park
Finley Point Unit

Polson Bay

East Bay

US 93 Bridge

Polson

Ducharme

To Pablo

Sportsmans Bridge: Lat 48.092, Lng -114.112
Somers Access: Lat 48.077, Lng -114.234
Bigfork: Lat 48.060, Lng -114.077
Flathead State Park Wayfarers: Lat 48.054, Lng -114.081
Woods Bay: Lat 48.002, Lng -114.065
Flathead State Park West Shore: Lat 47.949, Lng -114.182
Flathead State Park Yellow Bay: Lat 47.875, Lng -114.028
Elmo Access: Lat 47.831, Lng -114.344
Flathead State Park Big Arm: Lat 47.811, Lng -114.309
Walstad Access: Lat 47.811, Lng -114.264
Flathead State Park Finley Point: Lat 47.762, Lng -114.080
Ducharme: Lat 47.694, Lng -114.064
US 93 Bridge: Lat 47.695, Lng -114.167
Flathead State Park Wild Horse: Lat 47.844, Lng -114.212

© 2006 Wilderness Adventures Press, Inc.

MAP 5 OF 6

FLATHEAD RIVER

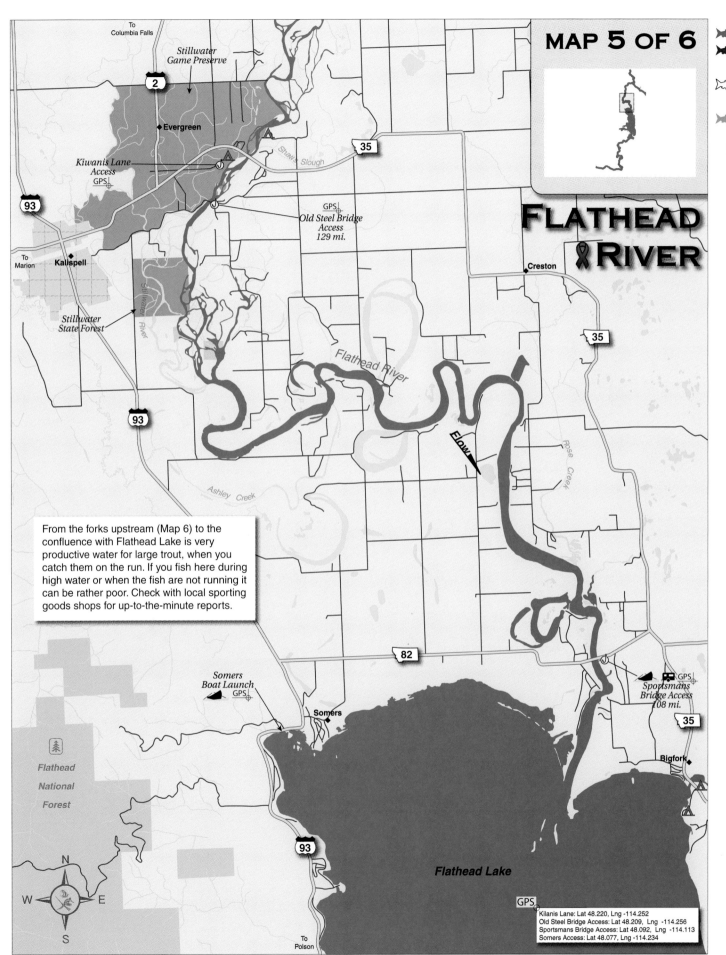

To
Columbia Falls

*Stillwater
Game Preserve*

US 2

◆ Evergreen

*Kiwanis Lane
Access*
GPS

93

Shaw's Slough

35

GPS
*Old Steel Bridge
Access
129 mi.*

To
Marion

◆ Kalispell

*Stillwater
State Forest*

Stillwater River

◆ Creston

35

Flathead River

35

Elow

93

Ashley Creek

Rose Creek

From the forks upstream (Map 6) to the confluence with Flathead Lake is very productive water for large trout, when you catch them on the run. If you fish here during high water or when the fish are not running it can be rather poor. Check with local sporting goods shops for up-to-the-minute reports.

82

*Somers
Boat Launch*
GPS

GPS
*Sportsmans
Bridge Access
108 mi.*

35

◆ Somers

◆ Bigfork

*Flathead
National
Forest*

N
W   E
S

Flathead Lake

To
Polson

GPS

Kilanis Lane: Lat 48.220, Lng -114.252
Old Steel Bridge Access: Lat 48.209, Lng -114.256
Sportsmans Bridge Access: Lat 48.092, Lng -114.113
Somers Access: Lat 48.077, Lng -114.234

© 2006 Wilderness Adventures Press, Inc.

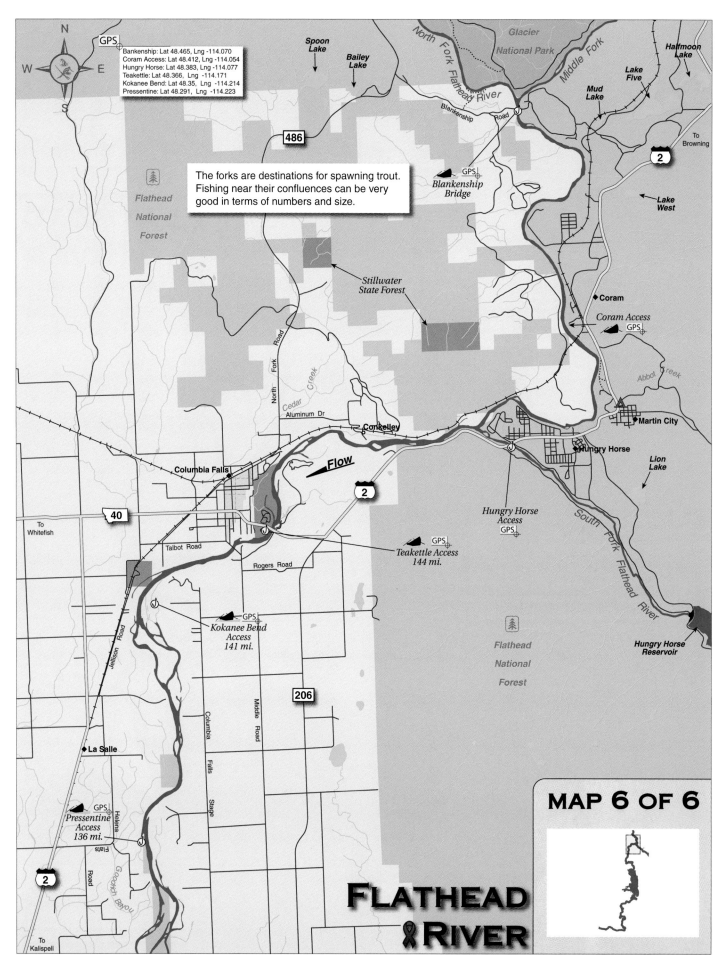

GPS

Bankenship: Lat 48.465, Lng -114.070
Coram Access: Lat 48.412, Lng -114.054
Hungry Horse: Lat 48.383, Lng -114.077
Teakettle: Lat 48.366, Lng -114.171
Kokanee Bend: Lat 48.35, Lng -114.214
Pressentine: Lat 48.291, Lng -114.223

North Fork Flathead River

Glacier National Park

Middle Fork

Spoon Lake

Bailey Lake

Halfmoon Lake

Lake Five

Mud Lake

To Browning

2

486

Blankenship Road

The forks are destinations for spawning trout. Fishing near their confluences can be very good in terms of numbers and size.

GPS
Blankenship Bridge

Lake West

Flathead National Forest

Stillwater State Forest

Coram

Coram Access
GPS

Abbot Creek

North Fork Road

Cedar Creek

Aluminum Dr

Conkelley

Martin City

Hungry Horse

Lion Lake

Columbia Falls

Flow

2

Hungry Horse Access
GPS

South Fork Flathead River

40

To Whitefish

Talbot Road

Teakettle Access
144 mi.

GPS

Rogers Road

Kokanee Bend Access
141 mi.

GPS

Flathead National Forest

206

Columbia Falls Stage

Middle Road

Jellison Road

Hungry Horse Reservoir

La Salle

Pressentine Access
136 mi.

GPS

Helena Flats Road

MAP 6 OF 6

2

To Kalispell

Goodrich Bayou

FLATHEAD RIVER

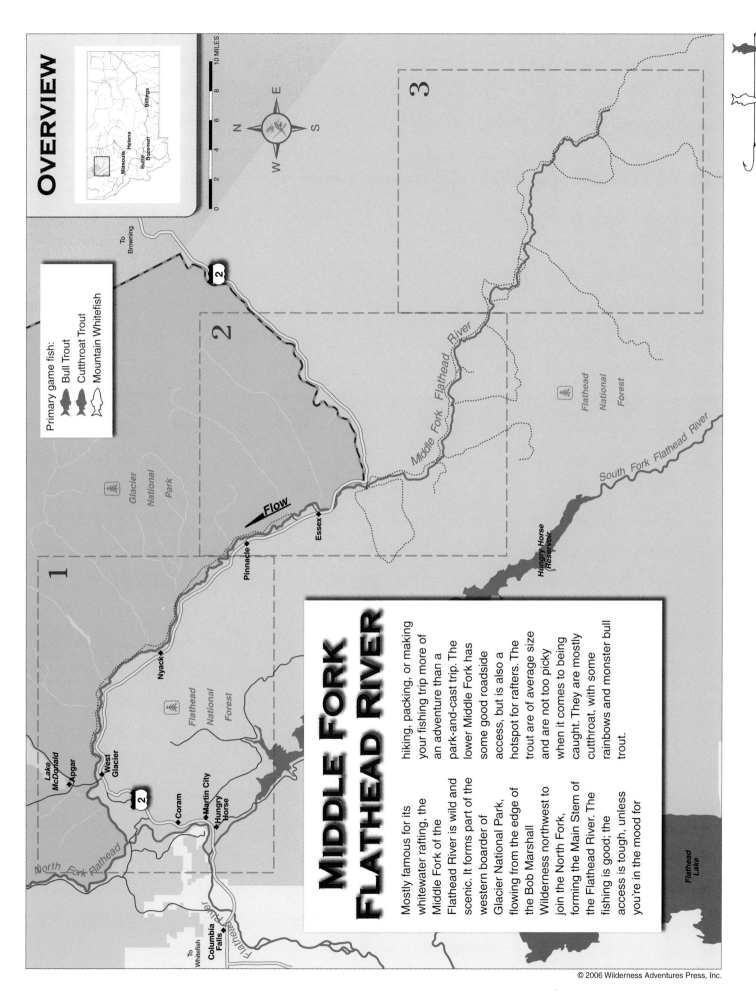

OVERVIEW

Primary game fish:
- Bull Trout
- Cutthroat Trout
- Mountain Whitefish

MIDDLE FORK FLATHEAD RIVER

Mostly famous for its whitewater rafting, the Middle Fork of the Flathead River is wild and scenic. It forms part of the western boarder of Glacier National Park, flowing from the edge of the Bob Marshall Wilderness northwest to join the North Fork, forming the Main Stem of the Flathead River. The fishing is good; the access is tough, unless you're in the mood for hiking, packing, or making your fishing trip more of an adventure than a park-and-cast trip. The lower Middle Fork has some good roadside access, but is also a hotspot for rafters. The trout are of average size and are not too picky when it comes to being caught. They are mostly cutthroat, with some rainbows and monster bull trout.

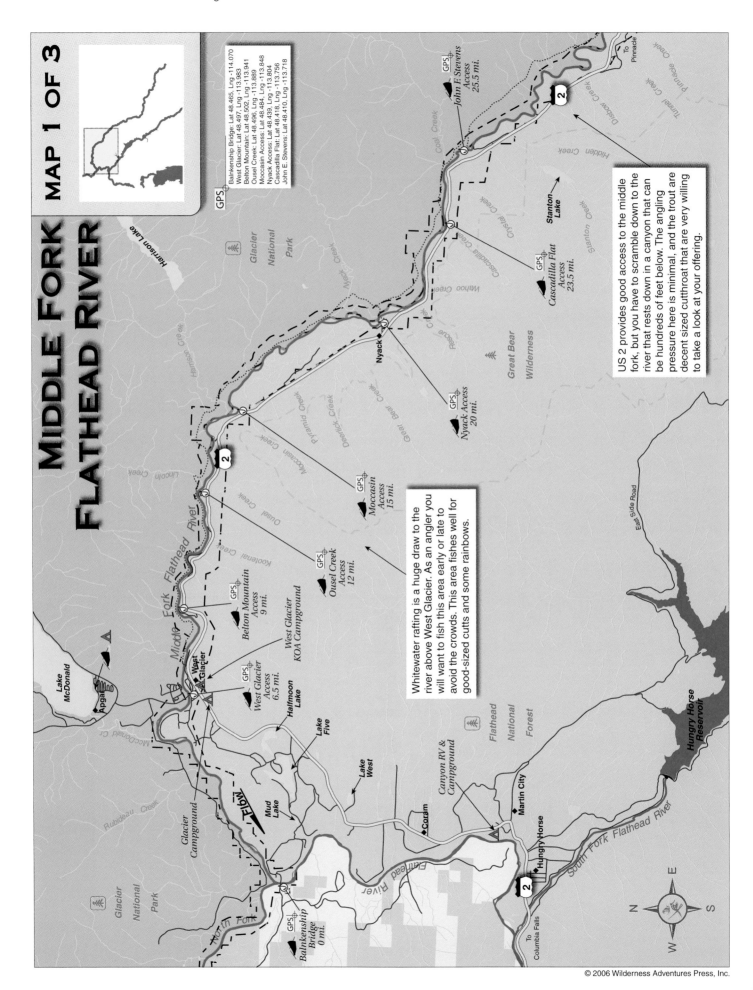

MIDDLE FORK FLATHEAD RIVER

MAP 1 OF 3

GPS

Balnkenship Bridge: Lat 48.465, Lng -114.070
West Glacier: Lat 48.497, Lng -113.983
Belton Mountain: Lat 48.502, Lng -113.941
Ousel Creek: Lat 48.496, Lng -113.889
Moccasin Access: Lat 48.484, Lng -113.848
Nyack Access: Lat 48.439, Lng -113.804
Cascadilla Flat: Lat 48.418, Lng -113.756
John E. Stevens: Lat 48.410, Lng -113.718

US 2 provides good access to the middle fork, but you have to scramble down to the river that rests down in a canyon that can be hundreds of feet below. The angling pressure here is minimal, and the trout are decent sized cutthroat that are very willing to take a look at your offering.

Whitewater rafting is a huge draw to the river above West Glacier. As an angler you will want to fish this area early or late to avoid the crowds. This area fishes well for good-sized cutts and some rainbows.

Glacier National Park

Harrison Lake

John F. Stevens Access 25.5 mi.

Coal Creek

Stanton Lake

Cascadilla Flat Access 23.5 mi.

Great Bear Wilderness

Nyack Access 20 mi.

Nyack

Moccasin Access 15 mi.

Ousel Creek Access 12 mi.

Belton Mountain Access 9 mi.

West Glacier KOA Campground

West Glacier Access 6.5 mi.

West Glacier

Halfmoon Lake

Lake Five

Lake West

Lake McDonald

Apgar

Middle Fork Flathead River

Flow

Mud Lake

Glacier Campground

Canyon RV & Campground

Flathead National Forest

Martin City

Coram

Hungry Horse

Hungry Horse Reservoir

South Fork Flathead River

Flathead River

North Fork

Balnkenship Bridge 0 mi.

To Columbia Falls

N E W S

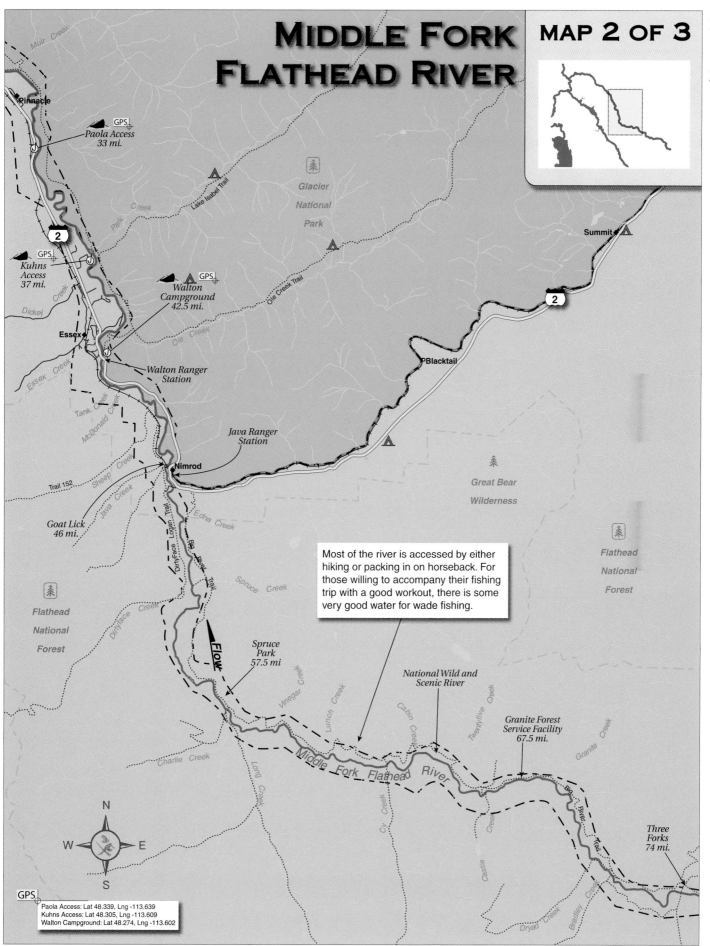

MIDDLE FORK FLATHEAD RIVER

MAP 2 OF 3

Pinnacle

Paola Access
33 mi. GPS

Kuhns
Access
37 mi. GPS

Lake Isabel Trail

Glacier

National

Park

Muir Creek

Creek

Park Creek

Ole Creek Trail

2

Summit

2

PBlacktail

Walton
Campground
42.5 mi. GPS

Essex

Walton Ranger
Station

Dickel Creek

Essex Creek

Tank Creek

McDonald Creek

Sheep Creek

Java Creek

Java Ranger
Station

Nimrod

Trail 152

Ole Creek

Great Bear

Wilderness

Goat Lick
46 mi.

DirtyFace Logan Trail

Edna Creek

Big River Trail

DirtyFace Creek

Spruce Creek

Flathead

National

Forest

Flathead

National

Forest

Flow

Spruce
Park
57.5 mi

Most of the river is accessed by either
hiking or packing in on horseback. For
those willing to accompany their fishing
trip with a good workout, there is some
very good water for wade fishing.

National Wild and
Scenic River

Granite Forest
Service Facility
67.5 mi.

Vinegar Creek

Lunch Creek

Cabin Creek

Twentyfive Creek

Granite Creek

Charlie Creek

Long Creek

Cr. Creek

Middle Fork Flathead River

Big River Trail

Three
Forks
74 mi.

Castle Creek

Bradley Creek

Dryad Creek

N
W   E
S

GPS
Paola Access: Lat 48.339, Lng -113.639
Kuhns Access: Lat 48.305, Lng -113.609
Walton Campground: Lat 48.274, Lng -113.602

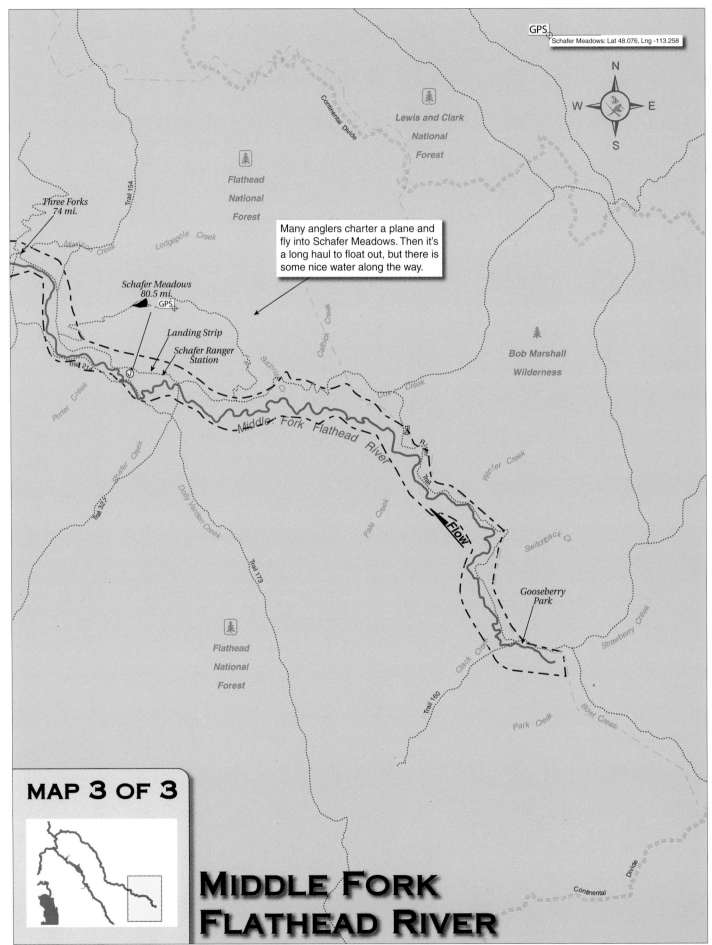

GPS
Schafer Meadows: Lat 48.076, Lng -113.258

N
W E
S

Lewis and Clark

National

Forest

Continental Divide

Flathead

National

Forest

Three Forks
74 mi.

Trail 154

Lodgepole Creek

Catlbck Creek

Many anglers charter a plane and
fly into Schafer Meadows. Then it's
a long haul to float out, but there is
some nice water along the way.

Schafer Meadows
80.5 mi.
GPS

Landing Strip

Schafer Ranger
Station

Surprise Cr.

Bob Marshall

Wilderness

Trail 27

Porter Creek

Middle Fork Flathead River

Cox Creek

River

Trail

Winter Creek

Morrison Creek

Schafer Creek

Trail 327

Dolly Varden Creek

Pale Creek

Flow

Switchback Cr.

Gooseberry
Park

Trail 173

Flathead

National

Forest

Clack Cr.

Strawberry Creek

Trail 160

Park Creek

Bowl Creek

Divide

Continental

MAP 3 OF 3

MIDDLE FORK
FLATHEAD RIVER

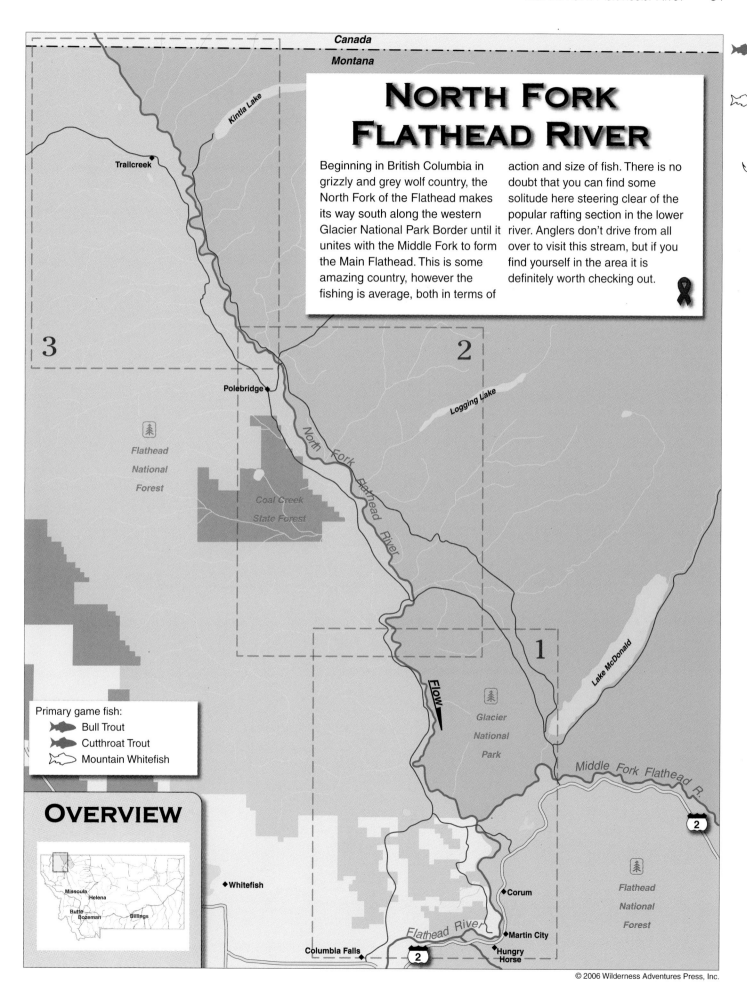

NORTH FORK FLATHEAD RIVER

Beginning in British Columbia in grizzly and grey wolf country, the North Fork of the Flathead makes its way south along the western Glacier National Park Border until it unites with the Middle Fork to form the Main Flathead. This is some amazing country, however the fishing is average, both in terms of action and size of fish. There is no doubt that you can find some solitude here steering clear of the popular rafting section in the lower river. Anglers don't drive from all over to visit this stream, but if you find yourself in the area it is definitely worth checking out.

Canada
Montana

Kintla Lake

Trailcreek

3

Polebridge

Flathead National Forest

Coal Creek State Forest

2

Logging Lake

North Fork Flathead River

1

Lake McDonald

Flow

Glacier National Park

Middle Fork Flathead R.

2

Flathead National Forest

Primary game fish:
Bull Trout
Cutthroat Trout
Mountain Whitefish

OVERVIEW

Missoula
Helena
Butte
Bozeman
Billings

Whitefish

Corum

Flathead River

Martin City

Columbia Falls

2

Hungry Horse

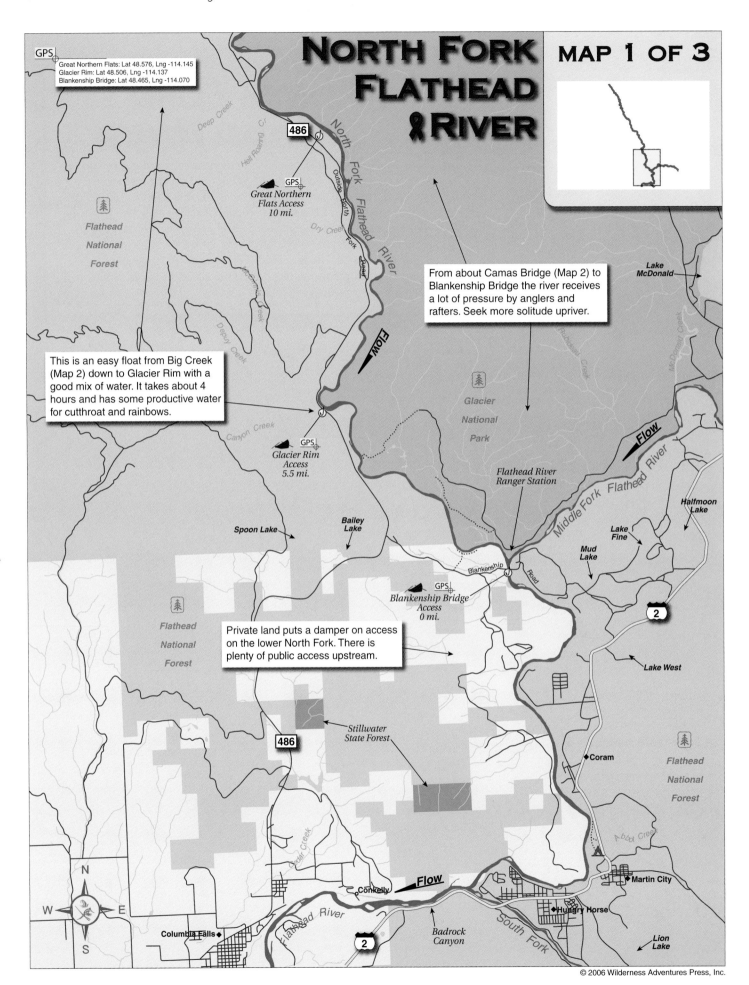

GPS
Great Northern Flats: Lat 48.576, Lng -114.145
Glacier Rim: Lat 48.506, Lng -114.137
Blankenship Bridge: Lat 48.465, Lng -114.070

486

GPS
Great Northern
Flats Access
10 mi.

Deep Creek

Hell Roaring C.

Outside — North Fork

Dry Creek

North Fork Flathead River

FLOW

Flathead
National
Forest

From about Camas Bridge (Map 2) to
Blankenship Bridge the river receives
a lot of pressure by anglers and
rafters. Seek more solitude upriver.

Lake
McDonald

McDonald Creek

This is an easy float from Big Creek
(Map 2) down to Glacier Rim with a
good mix of water. It takes about 4
hours and has some productive water
for cutthroat and rainbows.

Canyon Creek

GPS
Glacier Rim
Access
5.5 mi.

Glacier
National
Park

Flow

Middle Fork Flathead River

Flathead River
Ranger Station

Halfmoon
Lake

Spoon Lake

Bailey
Lake

Lake
Fine

Mud
Lake

Blankenship

Road

2

Flathead
National
Forest

486

Private land puts a damper on access
on the lower North Fork. There is
plenty of public access upstream.

GPS
Blankenship Bridge
Access
0 mi.

Lake West

Stillwater
State Forest

Coram

Flathead
National
Forest

Abbot Creek

N
W   E
S

Crook Creek

Flow

Conkelly

Flathead River

Columbia Falls

2

Flow

Badrock
Canyon

South Fork

Martin City

Hungry Horse

Lion
Lake

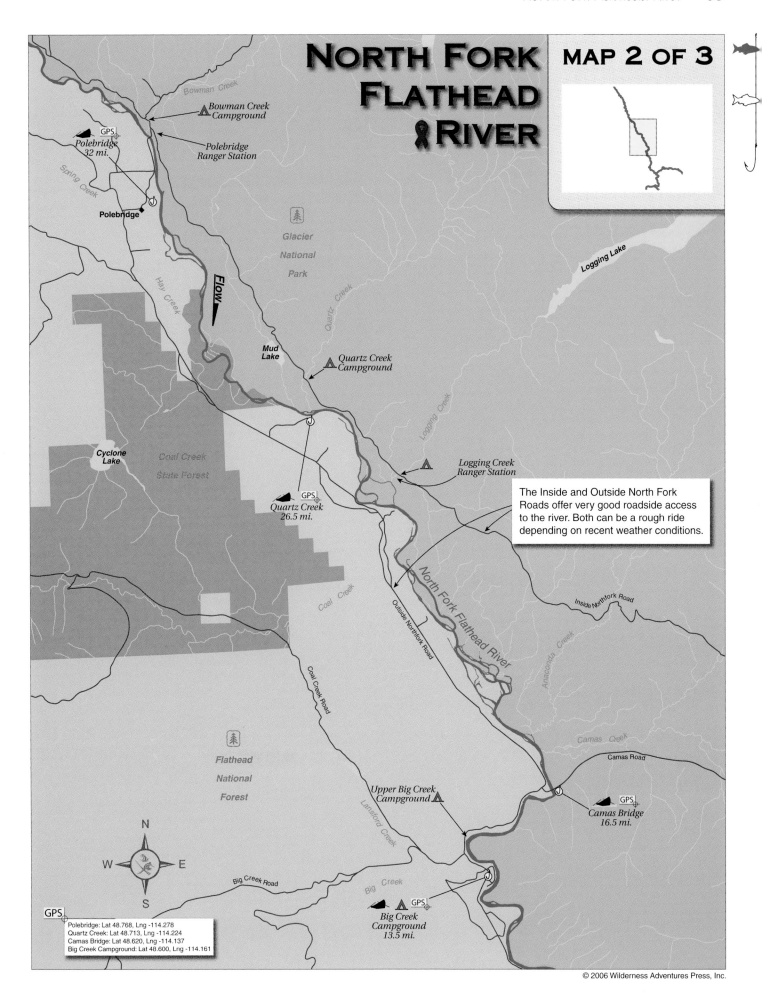

NORTH FORK FLATHEAD RIVER

MAP 2 OF 3

Bowman Creek

Bowman Creek Campground

GPS
Polebridge 32 mi.

Polebridge Ranger Station

Spring Creek

Polebridge

Glacier National Park

Quartz Creek

Logging Lake

Flow

Hay Creek

Mud Lake

Quartz Creek Campground

Logging Creek

Cyclone Lake

Coal Creek State Forest

Logging Creek Ranger Station

GPS
Quartz Creek 26.5 mi.

The Inside and Outside North Fork Roads offer very good roadside access to the river. Both can be a rough ride depending on recent weather conditions.

Coal Creek

North Fork Flathead River

Outside Northfork Road

Inside Northfork Road

Anaconda Creek

Coal Creek Road

Camas Creek

Camas Road

Flathead National Forest

Upper Big Creek Campground

Lansford Creek

GPS
Camas Bridge 16.5 mi.

N
W   E
S

Big Creek Road

Big Creek

GPS

GPS
Big Creek Campground 13.5 mi.

Polebridge: Lat 48.768, Lng -114.278
Quartz Creek: Lat 48.713, Lng -114.224
Camas Bridge: Lat 48.620, Lng -114.137
Big Creek Campground: Lat 48.600, Lng -114.161

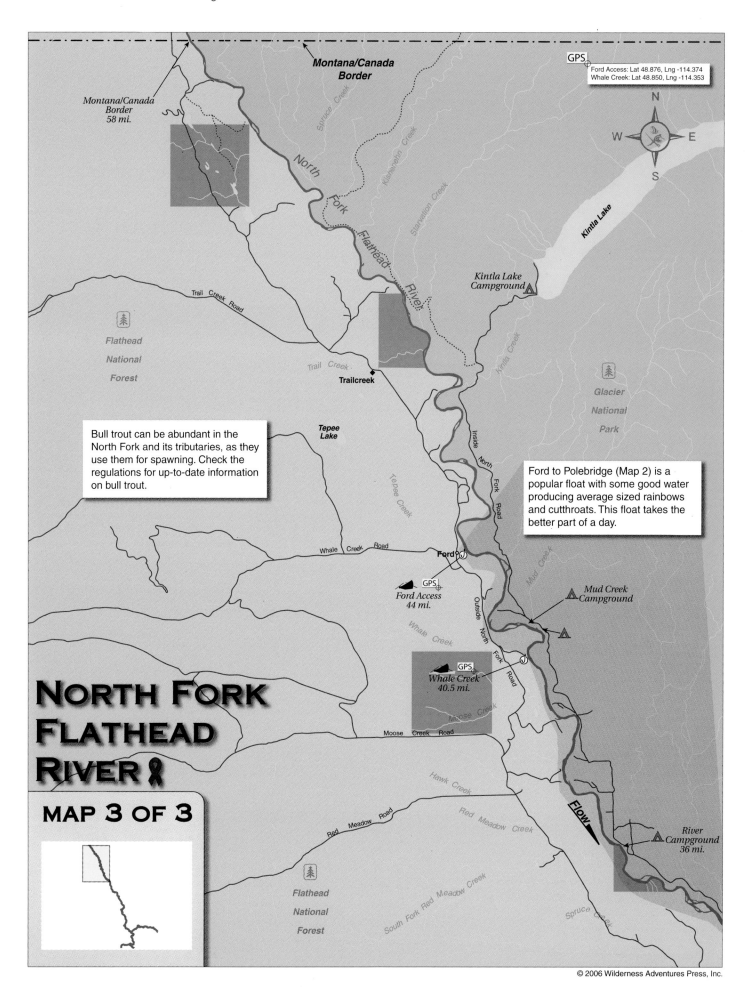

GPS
Ford Access: Lat 48.876, Lng -114.374
Whale Creek: Lat 48.850, Lng -114.353

Montana/Canada Border

Montana/Canada Border 58 mi.

Spruce Creek

North Fork

Kishenehn Creek

Starvation Creek

Flathead River

Kintla Lake

N
W   E
S

Kintla Lake Campground

Trail Creek Road

Flathead National Forest

Trail Creek

Trailcreek

Kintla Creek

Glacier National Park

Tepee Lake

Bull trout can be abundant in the North Fork and its tributaries, as they use them for spawning. Check the regulations for up-to-date information on bull trout.

Tepee Creek

Inside North Fork Road

Ford to Polebridge (Map 2) is a popular float with some good water producing average sized rainbows and cutthroats. This float takes the better part of a day.

Whale Creek Road

Ford

GPS
Ford Access 44 mi.

Whale Creek

Mud Creek

Mud Creek Campground

Outside North Fork Road

GPS
Whale Creek 40.5 mi.

NORTH FORK FLATHEAD RIVER

Moose Creek

Moose Creek Road

MAP 3 OF 3

Hawk Creek

Red Meadow Road

Red Meadow Creek

Flow

River Campground 36 mi.

Flathead National Forest

South Fork Red Meadow Creek

Spruce Creek

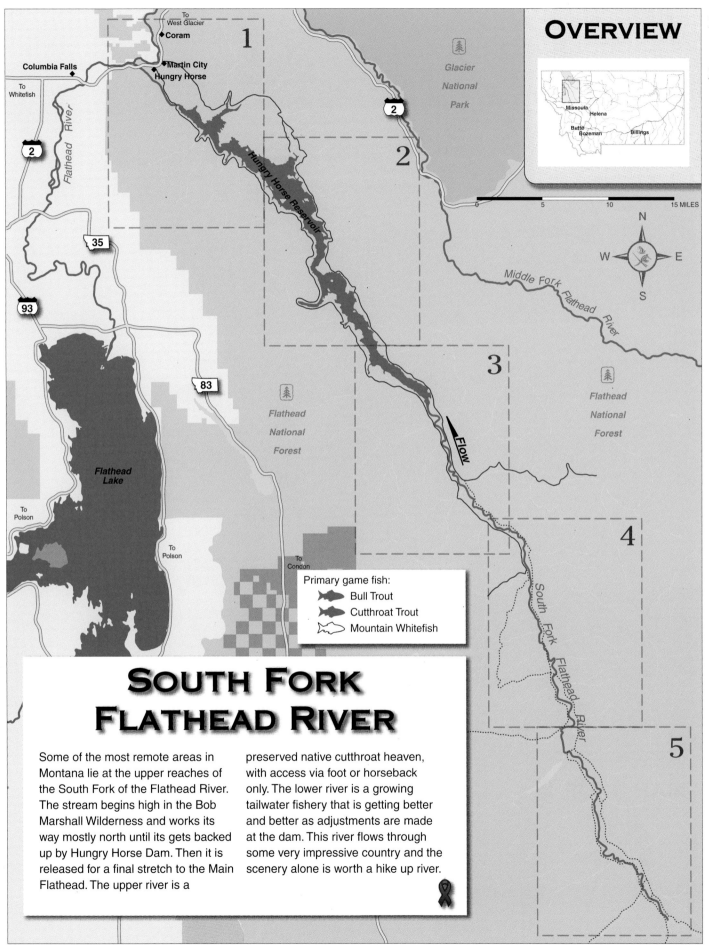

OVERVIEW

0 5 10 15 MILES

Primary game fish:
- Bull Trout
- Cutthroat Trout
- Mountain Whitefish

SOUTH FORK FLATHEAD RIVER

Some of the most remote areas in Montana lie at the upper reaches of the South Fork of the Flathead River. The stream begins high in the Bob Marshall Wilderness and works its way mostly north until its gets backed up by Hungry Horse Dam. Then it is released for a final stretch to the Main Flathead. The upper river is a preserved native cutthroat heaven, with access via foot or horseback only. The lower river is a growing tailwater fishery that is getting better and better as adjustments are made at the dam. This river flows through some very impressive country and the scenery alone is worth a hike up river.

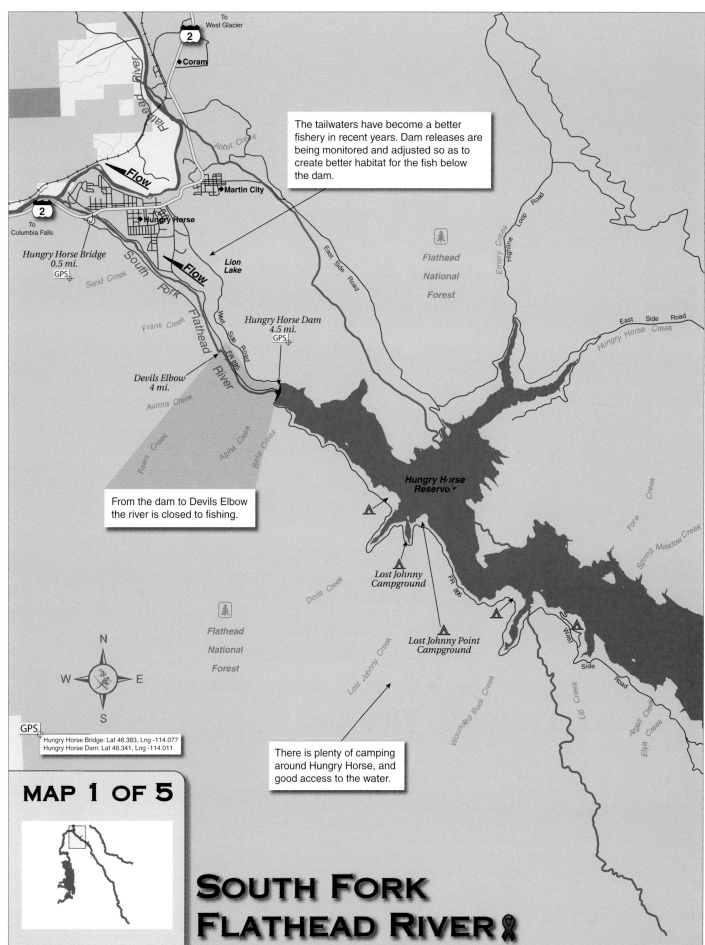

The tailwaters have become a better fishery in recent years. Dam releases are being monitored and adjusted so as to create better habitat for the fish below the dam.

From the dam to Devils Elbow the river is closed to fishing.

There is plenty of camping around Hungry Horse, and good access to the water.

Hungry Horse Bridge 0.5 mi.

Hungry Horse Dam 4.5 mi.

Devils Elbow 4 mi.

Hungry Horse Bridge: Lat 48.383, Lng -114.077
Hungry Horse Dam: Lat 48.341, Lng -114.011

MAP 1 OF 5

SOUTH FORK FLATHEAD RIVER

MAP 2 OF 5

SOUTH FORK FLATHEAD RIVER

Hungry Horse Reservoir has whitefish and cutthroat present, but the fishing is just so-so. You would have better luck fishing upstream from the reservoir or hitting the tailwaters.

Riverside Creek

Murray Creek

McInernie Creek

Deep Creek

Hungry Horse Reservoir

East Side Road

FR 38

Corinda Creek

Canyon Creek

Harris Creek

Flathead National Forest

Goldie Creek

Nairona Creek

FR 895

Parnora Creek

West Side Road

Lakeview Campground

Knieff Creek

Emma Cr.

Pearl Creek

Anna Creek

Flathead National Forest

Felix Creek

Trout Lake

Pain Creek

Ben Creek

Mazie Creek

Logan Creek

Handkerchief Lake

Graves Creek

Jones Creek

Baker Creek

South Fork Logan Creek

Hungry Horse Reservoir

East Side Road

Devils Corkscrew Creek

Devils Corkscrew Campground

West Side Road

Forest Creek

Margaret Lake

Hoke Creek

FR 895

Wheeler Creek

Baptiste Creek

N
W E
S

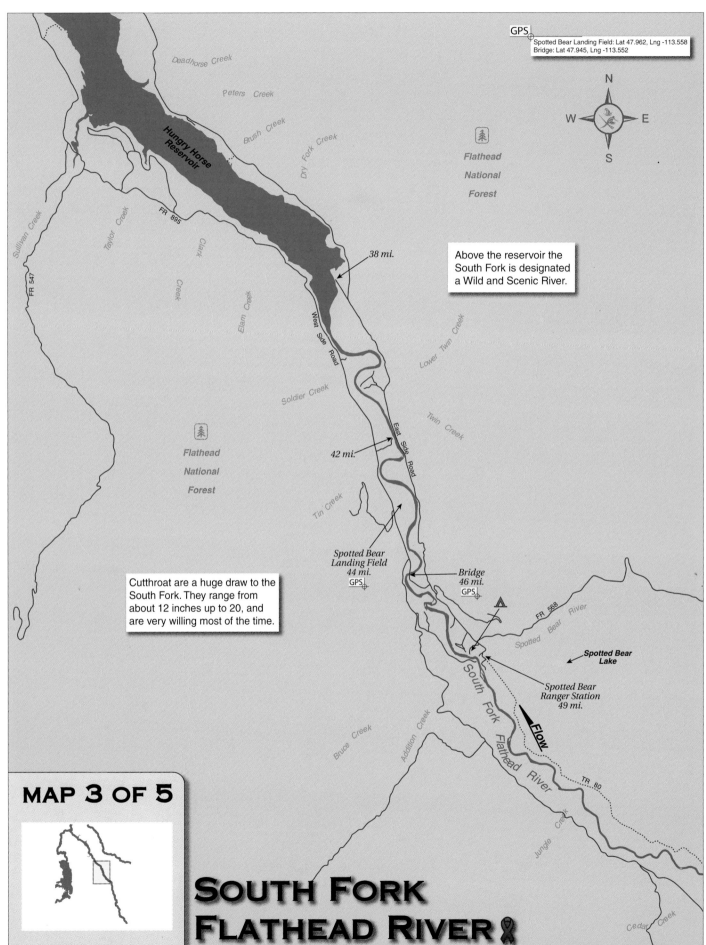

GPS

Spotted Bear Landing Field: Lat 47.962, Lng -113.558
Bridge: Lat 47.945, Lng -113.552

N
W E
S

Deadhorse Creek

Peters Creek

Brush Creek

Dry Fork Creek

Hungry Horse Reservoir

Flathead National Forest

FR 895

Sullivan Creek

FR 547

Taylor Creek

Clark Creek

Elam Creek

West Side Road

38 mi.

Above the reservoir the South Fork is designated a Wild and Scenic River.

Soldier Creek

Lower Twin Creek

East Side Road

Twin Creek

Flathead National Forest

42 mi.

Tin Creek

Cutthroat are a huge draw to the South Fork. They range from about 12 inches up to 20, and are very willing most of the time.

Spotted Bear Landing Field 44 mi.
GPS

Bridge 46 mi.
GPS

FR 568

Spotted Bear River

Spotted Bear Lake

Spotted Bear Ranger Station 49 mi.

Bruce Creek

Addition Creek

South Fork Flathead River

Flow

TR 80

Jungle Creek

Cedar Creek

MAP 3 OF 5

SOUTH FORK FLATHEAD RIVER

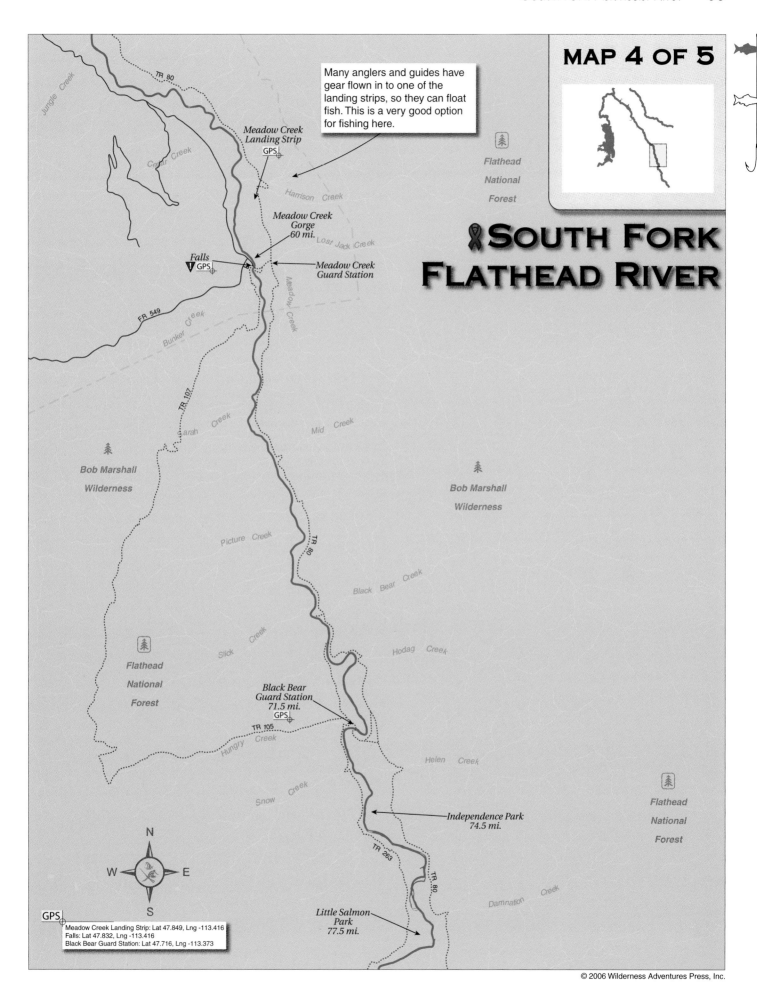

MAP **4** OF **5**

Many anglers and guides have gear flown in to one of the landing strips, so they can float fish. This is a very good option for fishing here.

Flathead National Forest

SOUTH FORK FLATHEAD RIVER

TR 80

Jungle Creek

Cedar Creek

Meadow Creek Landing Strip
GPS

Harrison Creek

Lost Jack Creek

Meadow Creek Gorge 60 mi.

Falls
GPS

Meadow Creek Guard Station

FR 549

Bunker Creek

Meadow Creek

TR 107

Sarah Creek

Mid Creek

Bob Marshall Wilderness

Bob Marshall Wilderness

Picture Creek

TR 80

Black Bear Creek

Slick Creek

Hodag Creek

Flathead National Forest

Black Bear Guard Station 71.5 mi.
GPS

TR 105

Hungry Creek

Helen Creek

Snow Creek

Flathead National Forest

N
W E
S

TR 263

Independence Park 74.5 mi.

TR 80

Damnation Creek

GPS

Little Salmon Park 77.5 mi.

Meadow Creek Landing Strip: Lat 47.849, Lng -113.416
Falls: Lat 47.832, Lng -113.416
Black Bear Guard Station: Lat 47.716, Lng -113.373

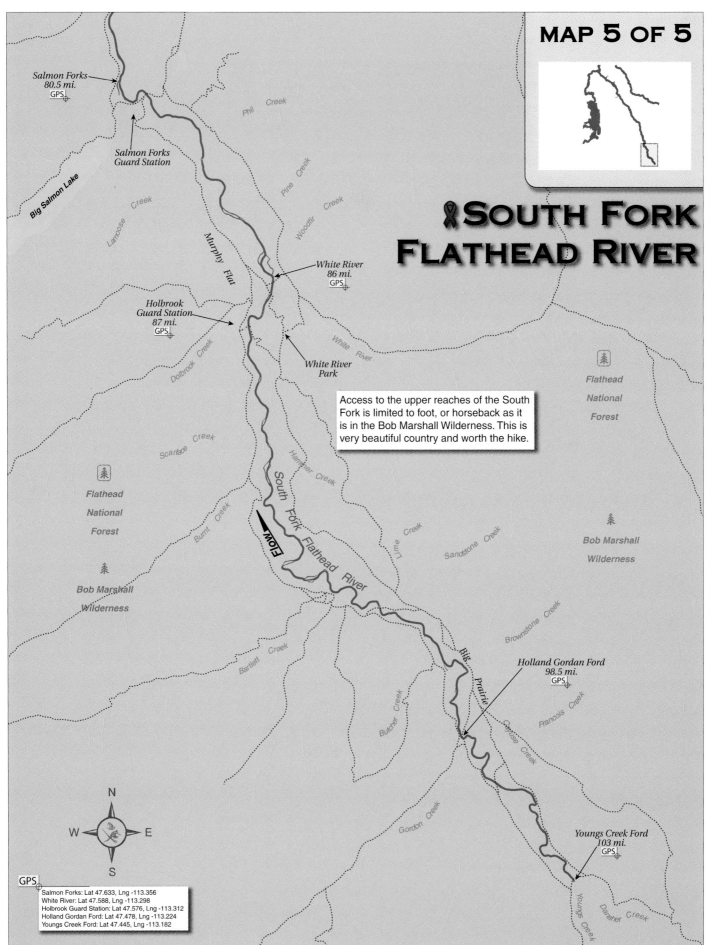

MAP 5 OF 5

SOUTH FORK FLATHEAD RIVER

Salmon Forks
80.5 mi.
GPS

Salmon Forks
Guard Station

Big Salmon Lake

Phil Creek

Lamoose Creek

Pine Creek

Woodfir Creek

Murphy Flat

White River
86 mi.
GPS

Holbrook
Guard Station
87 mi.
GPS

White River

White River
Park

Dolbrook Creek

Flathead
National
Forest

Scarface Creek

Flathead
National
Forest

Bob Marshall
Wilderness

Burnt Creek

FLOW

South Fork Flathead River

Hammer Creek

Lime Creek

Sandstone Creek

Bob Marshall
Wilderness

Access to the upper reaches of the South
Fork is limited to foot, or horseback as it
is in the Bob Marshall Wilderness. This is
very beautiful country and worth the hike.

Bartlett Creek

Butcher Creek

Big Prairie

Brownstone Creek

Holland Gordan Ford
98.5 mi.
GPS

Francois Creek

Cayuse Creek

Gordon Creek

Youngs Creek Ford
103 mi.
GPS

Youngs Creek

Danaher Creek

N
W   E
S

GPS

Salmon Forks: Lat 47.633, Lng -113.356
White River: Lat 47.588, Lng -113.298
Holbrook Guard Station: Lat 47.576, Lng -113.312
Holland Gordan Ford: Lat 47.478, Lng -113.224
Youngs Creek Ford: Lat 47.445, Lng -113.182

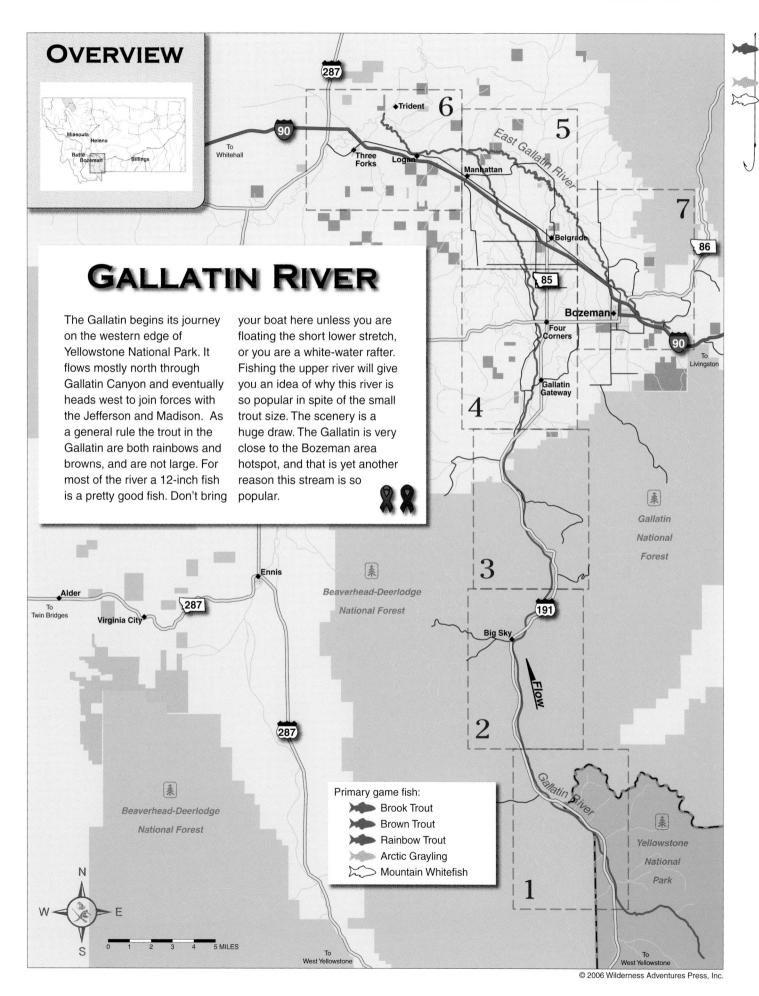

OVERVIEW

GALLATIN RIVER

The Gallatin begins its journey on the western edge of Yellowstone National Park. It flows mostly north through Gallatin Canyon and eventually heads west to join forces with the Jefferson and Madison. As a general rule the trout in the Gallatin are both rainbows and browns, and are not large. For most of the river a 12-inch fish is a pretty good fish. Don't bring your boat here unless you are floating the short lower stretch, or you are a white-water rafter. Fishing the upper river will give you an idea of why this river is so popular in spite of the small trout size. The scenery is a huge draw. The Gallatin is very close to the Bozeman area hotspot, and that is yet another reason this stream is so popular.

Primary game fish:
Brook Trout
Brown Trout
Rainbow Trout
Arctic Grayling
Mountain Whitefish

0 1 2 3 4 5 MILES

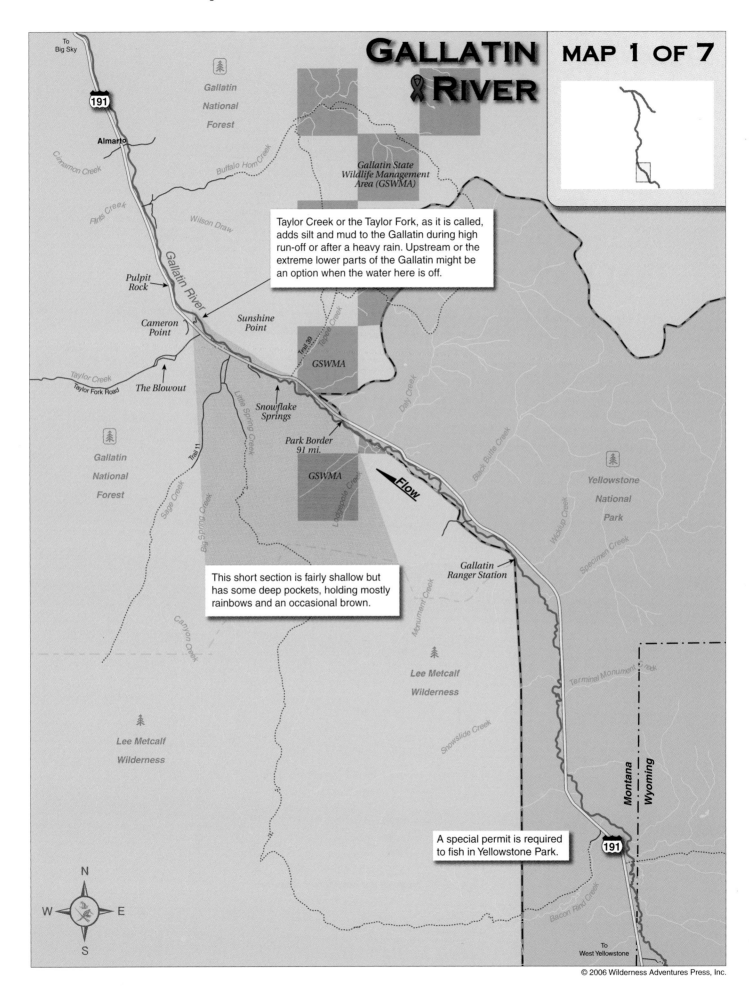

To Big Sky

191

Gallatin National Forest

Almarto

Cinnamon Creek

Buffalo Horn Creek

Flints Creek

Wilson Draw

Gallatin River

Pulpit Rock

Cameron Point

Sunshine Point

Taylor Creek

Taylor Fork Road

The Blowout

Little Spring Creek

Snowflake Springs

Trail 39

Tepee Creek

Gallatin State Wildlife Management Area (GSWMA)

GSWMA

Taylor Creek or the Taylor Fork, as it is called, adds silt and mud to the Gallatin during high run-off or after a heavy rain. Upstream or the extreme lower parts of the Gallatin might be an option when the water here is off.

Daly Creek

Gallatin National Forest

Trail 11

Sage Creek

Big Spring Creek

GSWMA

Lodgepole Creek

Park Border 91 mi.

Flow

Black Butte Creek

Yellowstone National Park

Wickup Creek

Specimen Creek

Gallatin Ranger Station

This short section is fairly shallow but has some deep pockets, holding mostly rainbows and an occasional brown.

Canyon Creek

Monument Creek

Lee Metcalf Wilderness

Lee Metcalf Wilderness

Snowslide Creek

Terminal Monument Creek

Montana

Wyoming

A special permit is required to fish in Yellowstone Park.

191

Bacon Rind Creek

N
W   E
S

To West Yellowstone

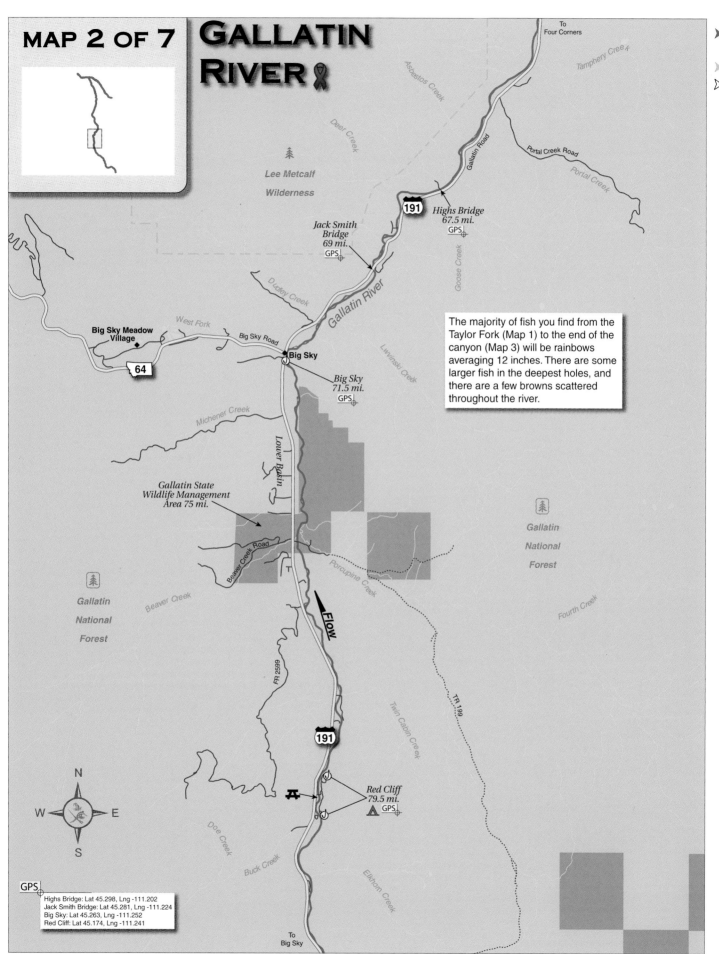

MAP 2 OF 7 GALLATIN RIVER

To Four Corners

Tamphery Creek

Asbestos Creek

Deer Creek

Lee Metcalf Wilderness

Gallatin Road

Portal Creek Road

Portal Creek

191

Highs Bridge
67.5 mi.
GPS

Jack Smith Bridge
69 mi.
GPS

Goose Creek

Dudley Creek

West Fork

Gallatin River

Big Sky Meadow Village

Big Sky Road

Big Sky

Lwinski Creek

64

Big Sky
71.5 mi.
GPS

The majority of fish you find from the Taylor Fork (Map 1) to the end of the canyon (Map 3) will be rainbows averaging 12 inches. There are some larger fish in the deepest holes, and there are a few browns scattered throughout the river.

Michener Creek

Lower Basin

Gallatin State Wildlife Management Area 75 mi.

Gallatin National Forest

Beaver Creek Road

Porcupine Creek

Fourth Creek

Gallatin National Forest

Beaver Creek

Flow

FR 2599

TR 199

Twin Cabin Creek

191

Red Cliff
79.5 mi.
GPS

N
W E
S

Doe Creek

Buck Creek

Elkhorn Creek

GPS

Highs Bridge: Lat 45.298, Lng -111.202
Jack Smith Bridge: Lat 45.281, Lng -111.224
Big Sky: Lat 45.263, Lng -111.252
Red Cliff: Lat 45.174, Lng -111.241

To Big Sky

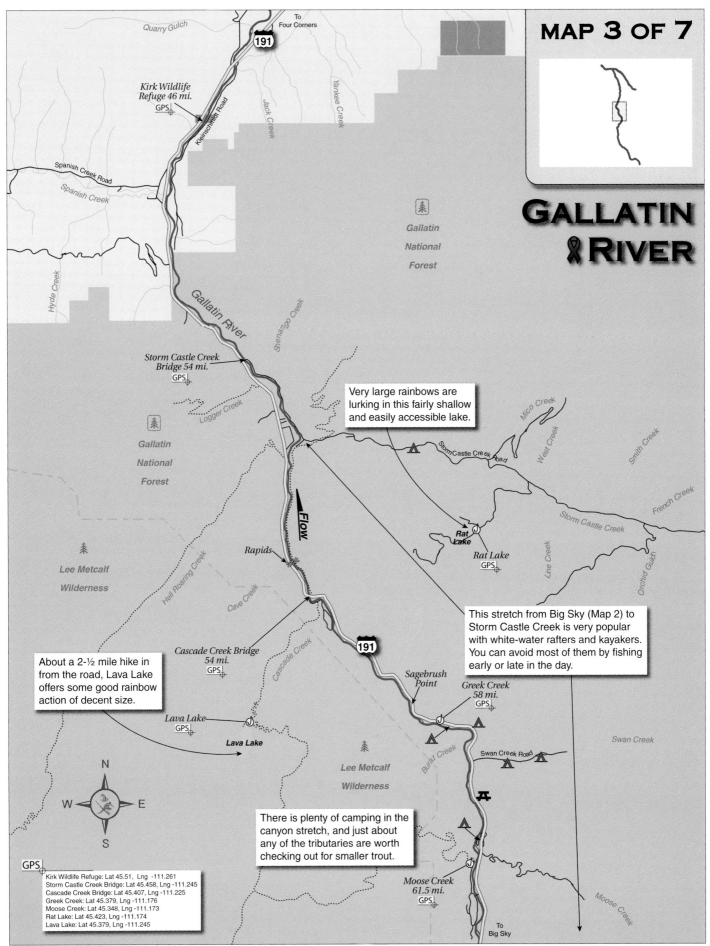

MAP 3 OF 7

GALLATIN ❧RIVER

Quarry Gulch

To Four Corners

191

Kirk Wildlife Refuge 46 mi.
GPS

Kleinschmidt Road

Jack Creek

Yankee Creek

Gallatin National Forest

Spanish Creek Road

Spanish Creek

Hyde Creek

Gallatin River

Shenango Creek

Storm Castle Creek Bridge 54 mi.
GPS

Logger Creek

Gallatin National Forest

Storm Castle Creek Road

Mico Creek

West Creek

Smith Creek

French Creek

Very large rainbows are lurking in this fairly shallow and easily accessible lake.

Rat Lake

Rat Lake
GPS

Line Creek

Storm Castle Creek

Orchid Gulch

Flow

Rapids

Lee Metcalf Wilderness

Hell Roaring Creek

Cave Creek

This stretch from Big Sky (Map 2) to Storm Castle Creek is very popular with white-water rafters and kayakers. You can avoid most of them by fishing early or late in the day.

About a 2-½ mile hike in from the road, Lava Lake offers some good rainbow action of decent size.

Cascade Creek Bridge 54 mi.
GPS

Cascade Creek

191

Sagebrush Point

Greek Creek 58 mi.
GPS

Swan Creek

Swan Creek Road

Lava Lake
GPS

Lava Lake

Lee Metcalf Wilderness

Bufal Creek

N
W   E
S

There is plenty of camping in the canyon stretch, and just about any of the tributaries are worth checking out for smaller trout.

Moose Creek 61.5 mi.
GPS

Moose Creek

To Big Sky

GPS
Kirk Wildlife Refuge: Lat 45.51, Lng -111.261
Storm Castle Creek Bridge: Lat 45.458, Lng -111.245
Cascade Creek Bridge: Lat 45.407, Lng -111.225
Greek Creek: Lat 45.379, Lng -111.176
Moose Creek: Lat 45.348, Lng -111.173
Rat Lake: Lat 45.423, Lng -111.174
Lava Lake: Lat 45.379, Lng -111.245

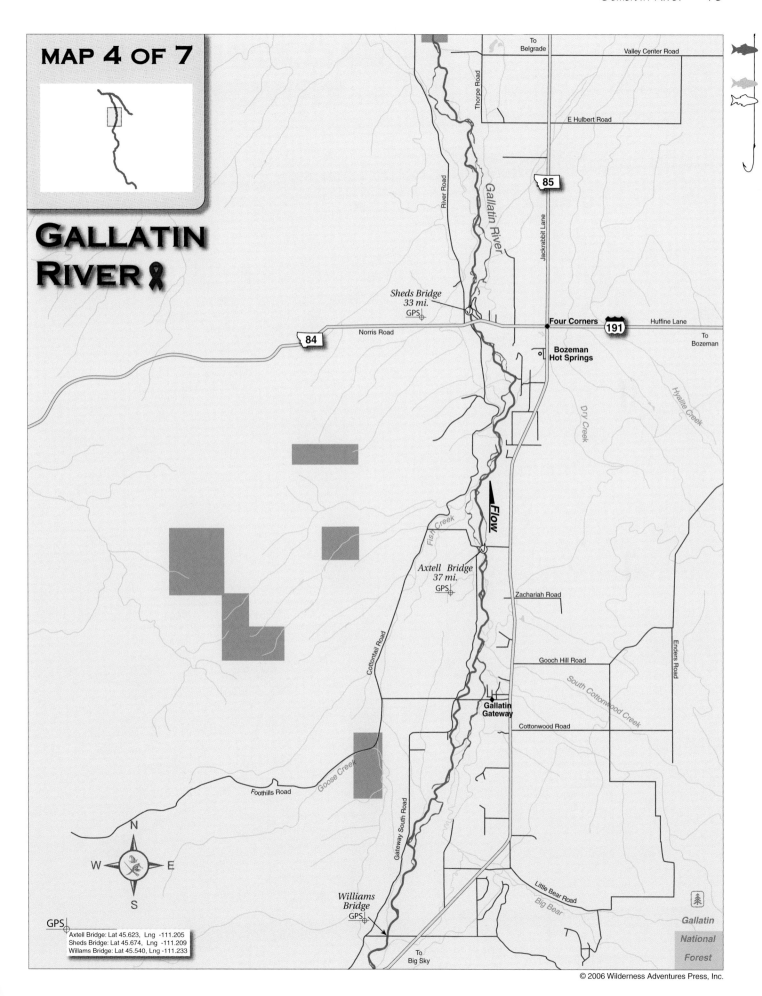

MAP **4** OF **7**

GALLATIN
RIVER

To Belgrade

Valley Center Road

Thorpe Road

E Hulbert Road

River Road

Gallatin River

Jackrabbit Lane

85

Sheds Bridge
33 mi.
GPS

Norris Road

84

Four Corners

191

Huffine Lane

To Bozeman

Bozeman
Hot Springs

Dry Creek

Hyalite Creek

Fish Creek

Flow

Axtell Bridge
37 mi.
GPS

Zachariah Road

Cottontail Road

Gooch Hill Road

Enders Road

South Cottonwood Creek

Gallatin
Gateway

Cottonwood Road

Goose Creek

Foothills Road

Gateway South Road

Little Bear Road

Big Bear

Gallatin

N
W   E
S

Williams
Bridge
GPS

National

Forest

To
Big Sky

GPS

Axtell Bridge: Lat 45.623, Lng -111.205
Sheds Bridge: Lat 45.674, Lng -111.209
Willams Bridge: Lat 45.540, Lng -111.233

© 2006 Wilderness Adventures Press, Inc.

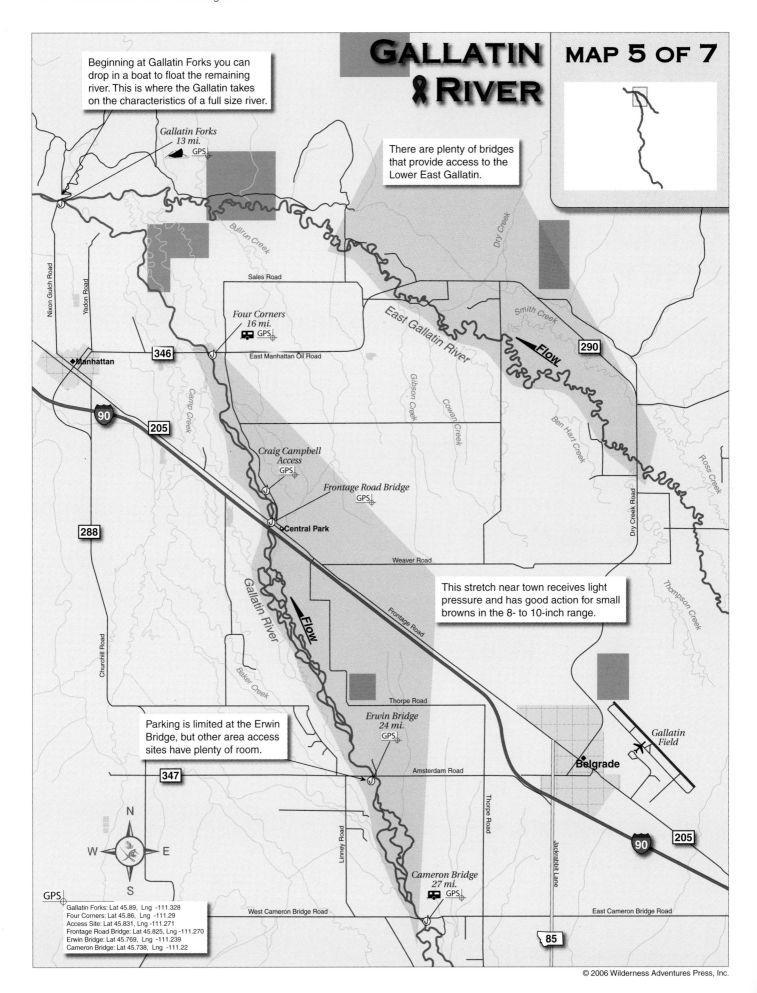

Beginning at Gallatin Forks you can drop in a boat to float the remaining river. This is where the Gallatin takes on the characteristics of a full size river.

GALLATIN RIVER

MAP 5 OF 7

Gallatin Forks
13 mi.
GPS

There are plenty of bridges that provide access to the Lower East Gallatin.

Bullrun Creek

Dry Creek

Sales Road

Four Corners
16 mi.
GPS

East Gallatin River

Smith Creek

East Manhattan Oil Road

346

◆Manhattan

290

Flow

Camp Creek

Gibson Creek

Cowan Creek

Ben Hart Creek

Ross Creek

90

205

Craig Campbell
Access
GPS

Frontage Road Bridge
GPS

Dry Creek Road

288

Central Park

Weaver Road

This stretch near town receives light pressure and has good action for small browns in the 8- to 10-inch range.

Thompson Creek

Gallatin River

Flow

Frontage Road

Baker Creek

Thorpe Road

Parking is limited at the Erwin Bridge, but other area access sites have plenty of room.

Erwin Bridge
24 mi.
GPS

Gallatin Field

✈

Belgrade

347

Amsterdam Road

Thorpe Road

Linney Road

N
W · E
S

Jackrabbit Lane

205

90

Cameron Bridge
27 mi.
GPS

GPS

West Cameron Bridge Road

East Cameron Bridge Road

85

Gallatin Forks: Lat 45.89, Lng -111.328
Four Corners: Lat 45.86, Lng -111.29
Access Site: Lat 45.831, Lng -111.271
Frontage Road Bridge: Lat 45.825, Lng -111.270
Erwin Bridge: Lat 45.769, Lng -111.239
Cameron Bridge: Lat 45.738, Lng -111.22

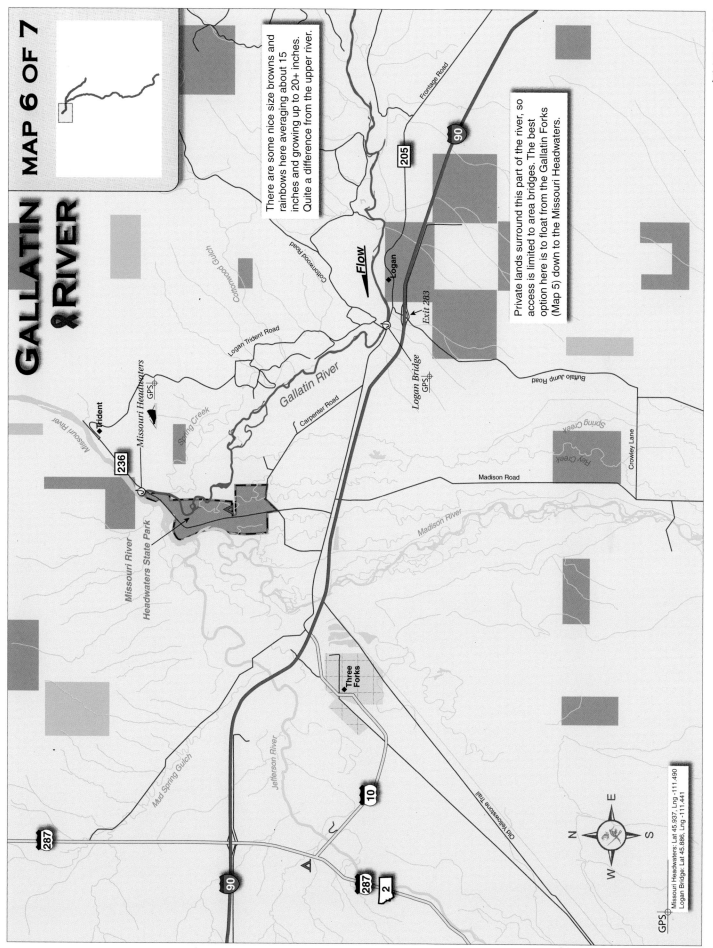

GALLATIN RIVER

MAP 6 OF 7

There are some nice size browns and rainbows here averaging about 15 inches and growing up to 20+ inches. Quite a difference from the upper river.

Private lands surround this part of the river, so access is limited to area bridges. The best option here is to float from the Gallatin Forks (Map 5) down to the Missouri Headwaters.

Frontage Road

90

205

Flow

Logan

Exit 283

Cottonwood Road

Logan Trident Road

Gallatin River

Carpenter Road

Logan Bridge
GPS

Buffalo Jump Road

Cottonwood Gulch

Missouri Headwaters
GPS

Trident

Missouri River

Missouri River
Headwaters State Park

236

Spring Creek

Madison Road

Rev Creek

Spring Creek

Crowley Lane

Madison River

Three Forks

Mud Spring Gulch

Jefferson River

Old Yellowstone Trail

10

287

2

287

90

N
W   E
S

GPS
Missouri Headwaters: Lat 45.937, Lng -111.490
Logan Bridge: Lat 45.886, Lng -111.441

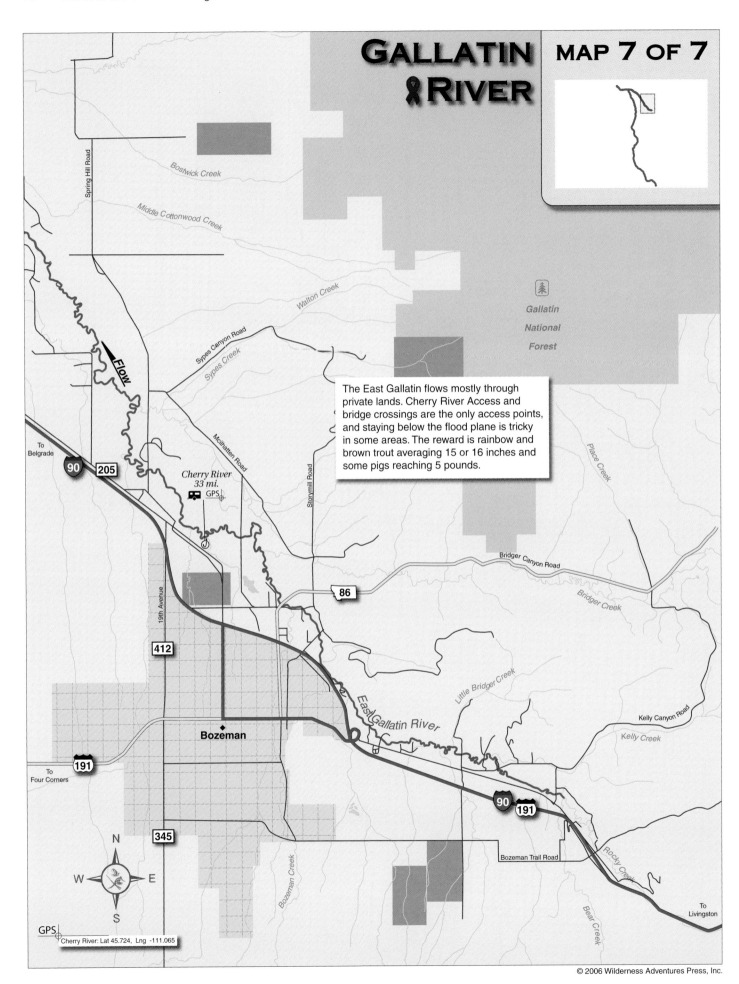

GALLATIN RIVER

MAP 7 OF 7

Bostwick Creek

Spring Hill Road

Middle Cottonwood Creek

Walton Creek

Gallatin

National

Forest

Flow

Sypes Canyon Road

Sypes Creek

McIlhatten Road

To
Belgrade

90

205

Cherry River
33 mi.

GPS

Storymill Road

Place Creek

Bridger Canyon Road

Bridger Creek

The East Gallatin flows mostly through
private lands. Cherry River Access and
bridge crossings are the only access points,
and staying below the flood plane is tricky
in some areas. The reward is rainbow and
brown trout averaging 15 or 16 inches and
some pigs reaching 5 pounds.

19th Avenue

412

86

Little Bridger Creek

Kelly Canyon Road

Kelly Creek

Bozeman

To
Four Corners

191

East Gallatin River

90

191

345

N

W E

S

GPS

Cherry River: Lat 45.724, Lng -111.065

Bozeman Creek

Bozeman Trail Road

Rocky Creek

Bear Creek

To
Livingston

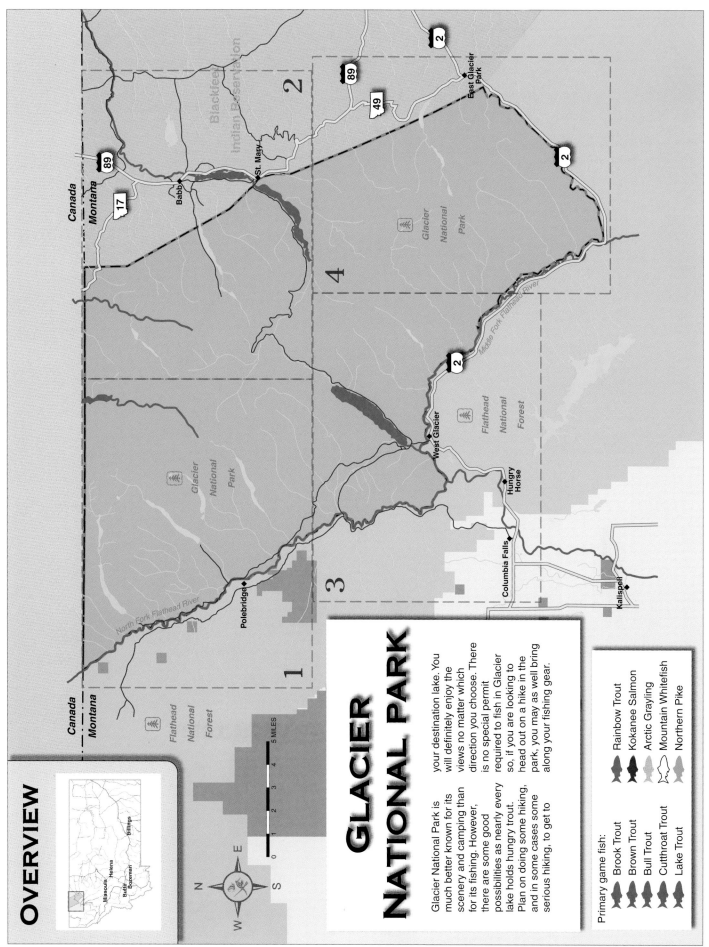

OVERVIEW

GLACIER NATIONAL PARK

Glacier National Park is much better known for its scenery and camping than for its fishing. However, there are some good possibilities as nearly every lake holds hungry trout. Plan on doing some hiking, and in some cases some serious hiking, to get to your destination lake. You will definitely enjoy the views no matter which direction you choose. There is no special permit required to fish in Glacier so, if you are looking to head out on a hike in the park, you may as well bring along your fishing gear.

Primary game fish:

Brook Trout
Brown Trout
Bull Trout
Cutthroat Trout
Lake Trout

Rainbow Trout
Kokanee Salmon
Arctic Grayling
Mountain Whitefish
Northern Pike

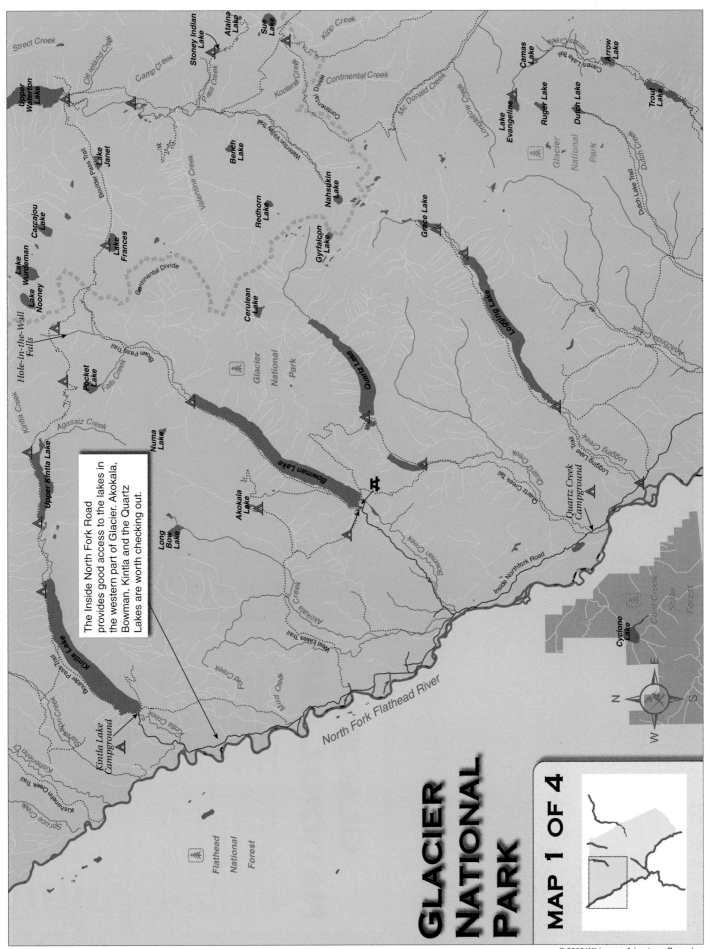

The Inside North Fork Road provides good access to the lakes in the western part of Glacier. Akokala, Bowman, Kintla and the Quartz Lakes are worth checking out.

Street Creek

Cleveland Creek

Camp Creek

Upper Waterton Lake

Stoney Indian Lake

Pass Creek

Ataina Lake

Sue Lake

Kipp Creek

Kootenai Creek

Continental Creek

Continental Divide

Mc Donald Creek

Longfellow Creek

Camas Creek

Camas Lake

Arrow Lake

Camas Lake Trail

Lake Evangeline

Ruger Lake

Dutch Lake

Trout Lake

Glacier National Park

Dutch Lake Trail

Dutch Creek

Boulder Pass Trail

Lake Janet

Bench Lake

Valentine Creek

Nahsukin Lake

Cacajou Lake

Lake Wurdeman

Lake Nooney

Lake Frances

Redhorn Lake

Gyrfalcon Lake

Grace Lake

Continental Divide

Cerulean Lake

Logging Lake

Anaconda Creek

Hole-in-the-Wall Falls

Bown Pass Trail

Falls Creek

Kintla Creek

Pocket Lake

Agassiz Creek

Quartz Lake

Glacier National Park

Quartz Creek

Quartz Creek Trail

Logging Creek

Logging Lake Trail

Numa Lake

Upper Kintla Lake

Bowman Lake

Quartz Creek Campground

Akokala Lake

Long Bow Lake

Kintla Lake

Boulder Pass Trail

Akokala Creek

West Lakes Trail

Ford Creek

Mud Creek

Bowman Creek

Inside Northfork Road

Coal Creek

State Forest

Cyclone Lake

Kintla Lake Campground

Starvation Creek

Kishenehn Creek Trail

Kishenehn Cr.

Spruce Creek

Kintla Creek

North Fork Flathead River

Flathead National Forest

N
E
W
S

GLACIER NATIONAL PARK

MAP 1 OF 4

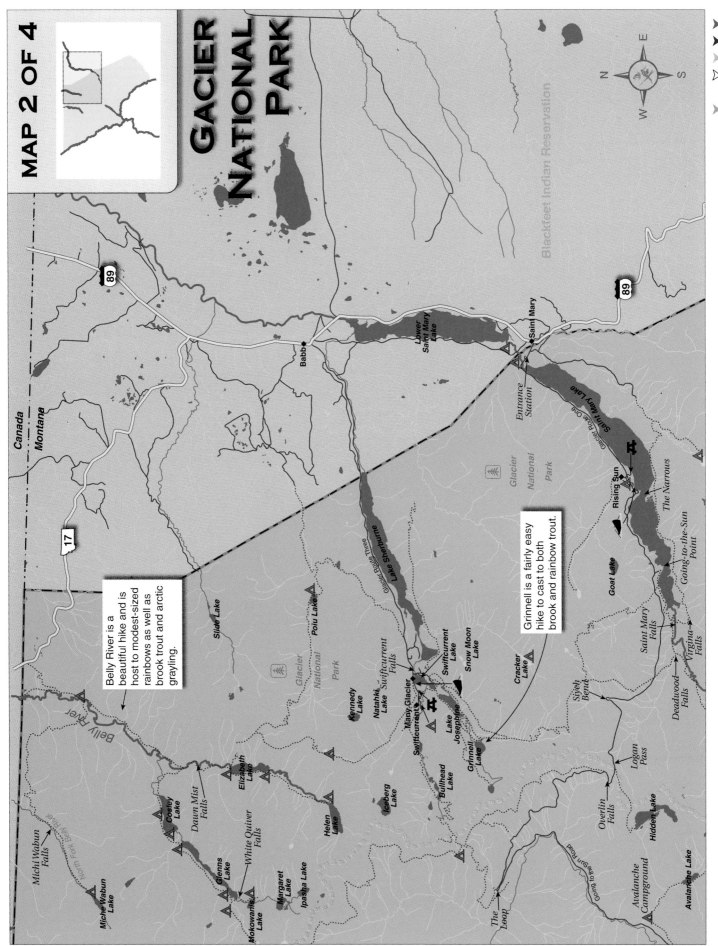

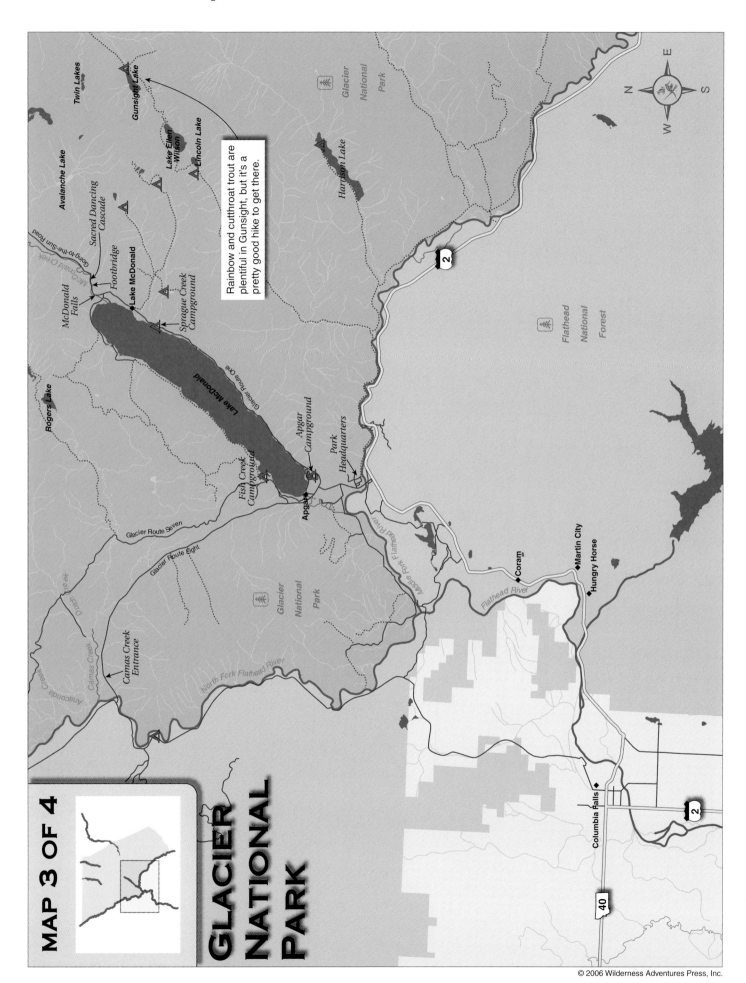

Rainbow and cutthroat trout are plentiful in Gunsight, but it's a pretty good hike to get there.

MAP 3 OF 4

GLACIER NATIONAL PARK

Twin Lakes

Gunsight Lake

Lake Ellen Wilson

Lincoln Lake

Avalanche Lake

Harrison Lake

Sacred Dancing Cascade

Glacier National Park

Going-to-the-Sun Road

McDonald Creek

Footbridge

Lake McDonald

McDonald Falls

Sprague Creek Campground

Rogers Lake

Lake McDonald

Glacier Route One

Apgar Campground

Park Headquarters

Flathead National Forest

Fish Creek Campground

Apgar

Middle Fork Flathead River

Martin City

Coram

Hungry Horse

Flathead River

Glacier Route Seven

Glacier Route Eight

Dutch Creek

Camas Creek

Anaconda Creek

Camas Creek Entrance

Glacier National Park

North Fork Flathead River

Columbia Falls

2

2

40

© 2006 Wilderness Adventures Press, Inc.

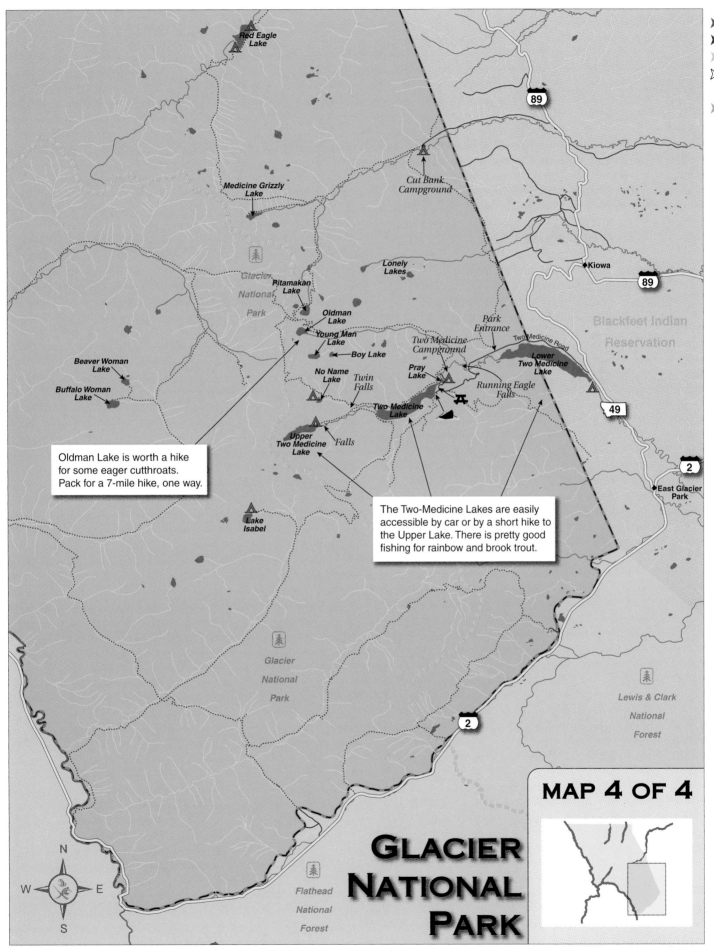

Oldman Lake is worth a hike for some eager cutthroats. Pack for a 7-mile hike, one way.

The Two-Medicine Lakes are easily accessible by car or by a short hike to the Upper Lake. There is pretty good fishing for rainbow and brook trout.

MAP 4 OF 4

GLACIER NATIONAL PARK

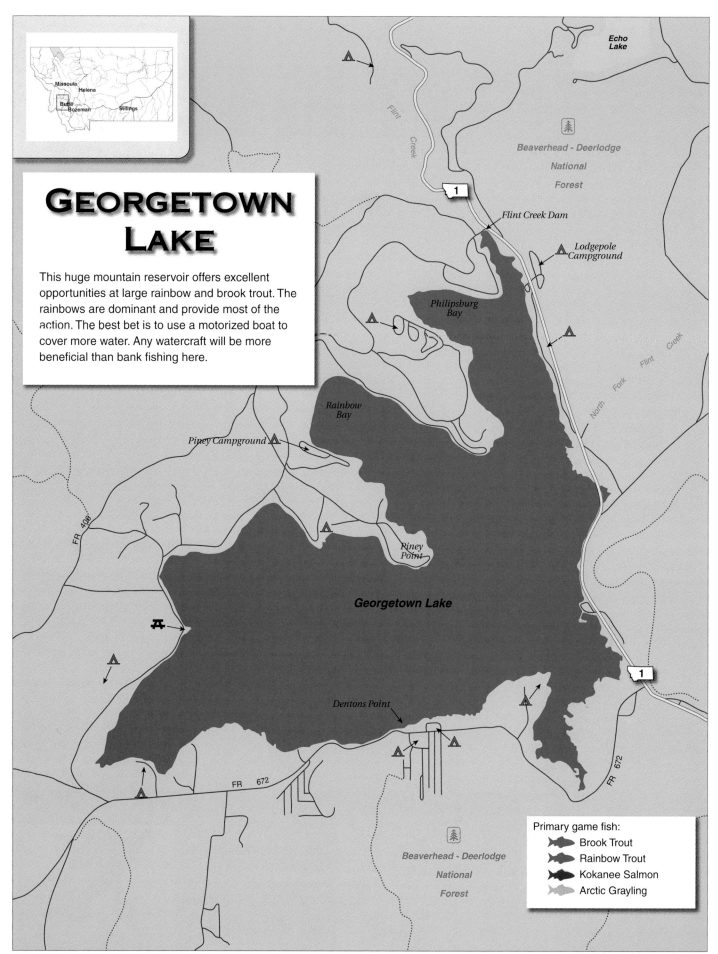

GEORGETOWN LAKE

This huge mountain reservoir offers excellent opportunities at large rainbow and brook trout. The rainbows are dominant and provide most of the action. The best bet is to use a motorized boat to cover more water. Any watercraft will be more beneficial than bank fishing here.

Echo Lake

Flint Creek

Beaverhead - Deerlodge National Forest

Flint Creek Dam

Lodgepole Campground

Philipsburg Bay

North Fork Flint Creek

Rainbow Bay

Piney Campground

Riney Point

Georgetown Lake

Dentons Point

FR 406

FR 672

FR 672

Beaverhead - Deerlodge National Forest

Primary game fish:
- Brook Trout
- Rainbow Trout
- Kokanee Salmon
- Arctic Grayling

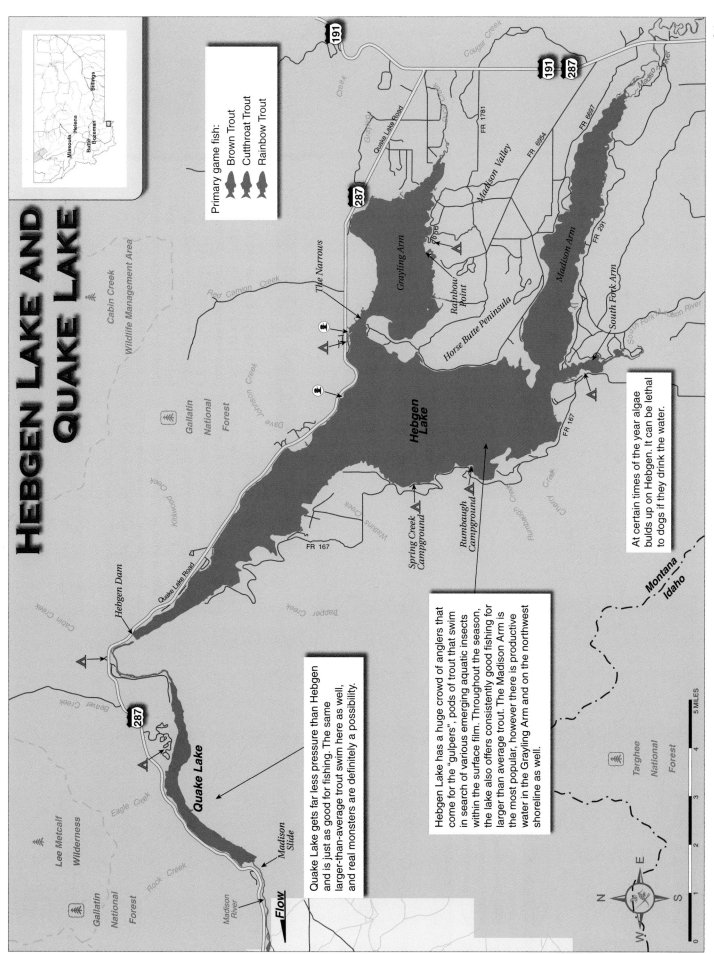

HEBGEN LAKE AND QUAKE LAKE

Primary game fish:
Brown Trout
Cutthroat Trout
Rainbow Trout

At certain times of the year algae builds up on Hebgen. It can be lethal to dogs if they drink the water.

Hebgen Lake has a huge crowd of anglers that come for the "gulpers", pods of trout that swim in search of various emerging aquatic insects within the surface film. Throughout the season, the lake also offers consistently good fishing for larger than average trout. The Madison Arm is the most popular, however there is productive water in the Grayling Arm and on the northwest shoreline as well.

Quake Lake gets far less pressure than Hebgen and is just as good for fishing. The same larger-than-average trout swim here as well, and real monsters are definitely a possibility.

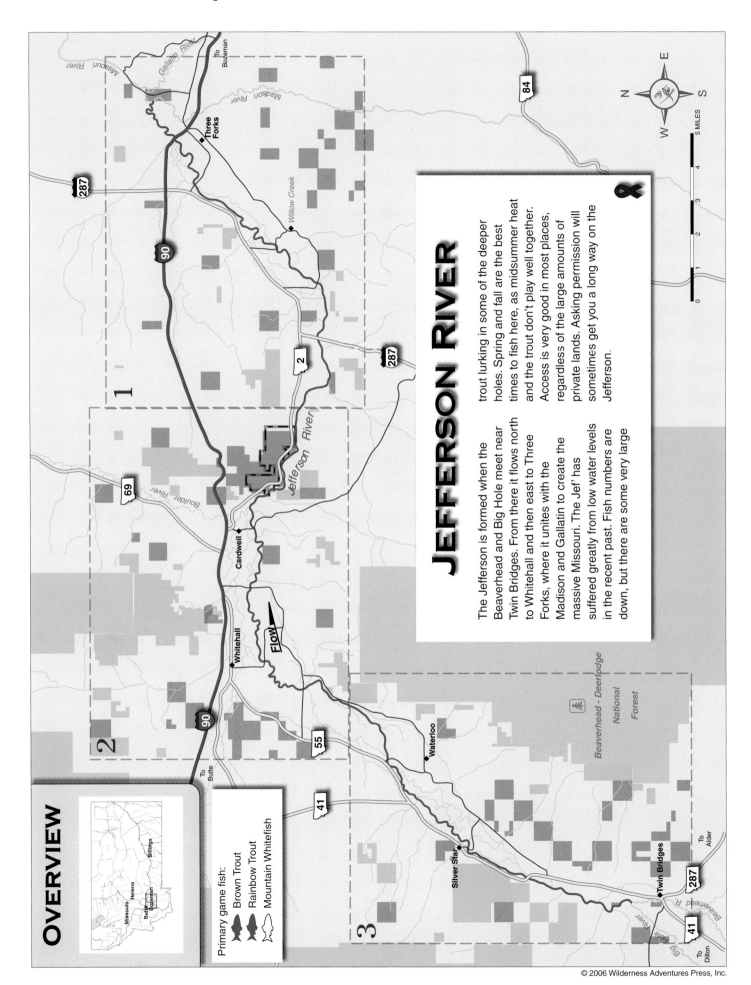

JEFFERSON RIVER

The Jefferson is formed when the Beaverhead and Big Hole meet near Twin Bridges. From there it flows north to Whitehall and then east to Three Forks, where it unites with the Madison and Gallatin to create the massive Missouri. The Jef' has suffered greatly from low water levels in the recent past. Fish numbers are down, but there are some very large trout lurking in some of the deeper holes. Spring and fall are the best times to fish here, as midsummer heat and the trout don't play well together. Access is very good in most places, regardless of the large amounts of private lands. Asking permission will sometimes get you a long way on the Jefferson.

OVERVIEW

Primary game fish:
- Brown Trout
- Rainbow Trout
- Mountain Whitefish

5 MILES

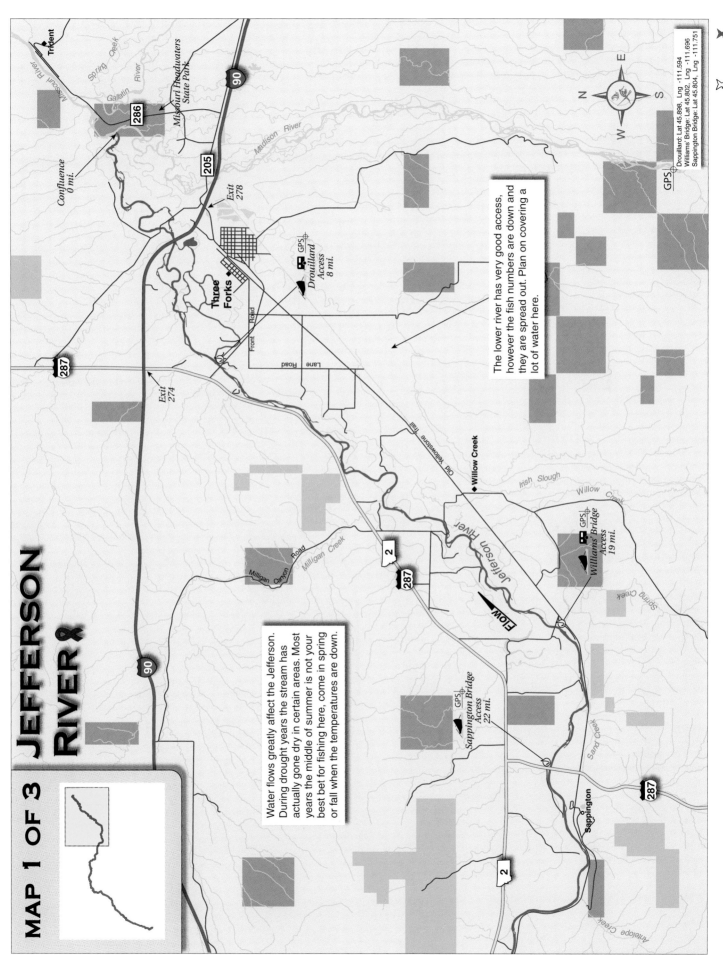

MAP 1 OF 3
JEFFERSON RIVER

Water flows greatly affect the Jefferson. During drought years the stream has actually gone dry in certain areas. Most years the middle of summer is not your best bet for fishing here, come in spring or fall when the temperatures are down.

The lower river has very good access, however the fish numbers are down and they are spread out. Plan on covering a lot of water here.

Droullard: Lat 45.896, Lng -111.594
Williams' Bridge: Lat 45.802, Lng -111.696
Sappington Bridge: Lat 45.804, Lng -111.751

Trident

Missouri Headwaters State Park

Confluence 0 mi.

Three Forks

Exit 278

Exit 274

Droullard Access 8 mi.

Front Road

Lane Road

Old Yellowstone Trail

Willow Creek

Irish Slough

Willow Creek

Jefferson River

Flow

Williams' Bridge Access 19 mi.

Spring Creek

Milligan Canyon Road

Milligan Creek

Sappington Bridge Access 22 mi.

Sappington

Sand Creek

Antelope Creek

Madison River

Spring Creek

Gallatin River

Missouri River

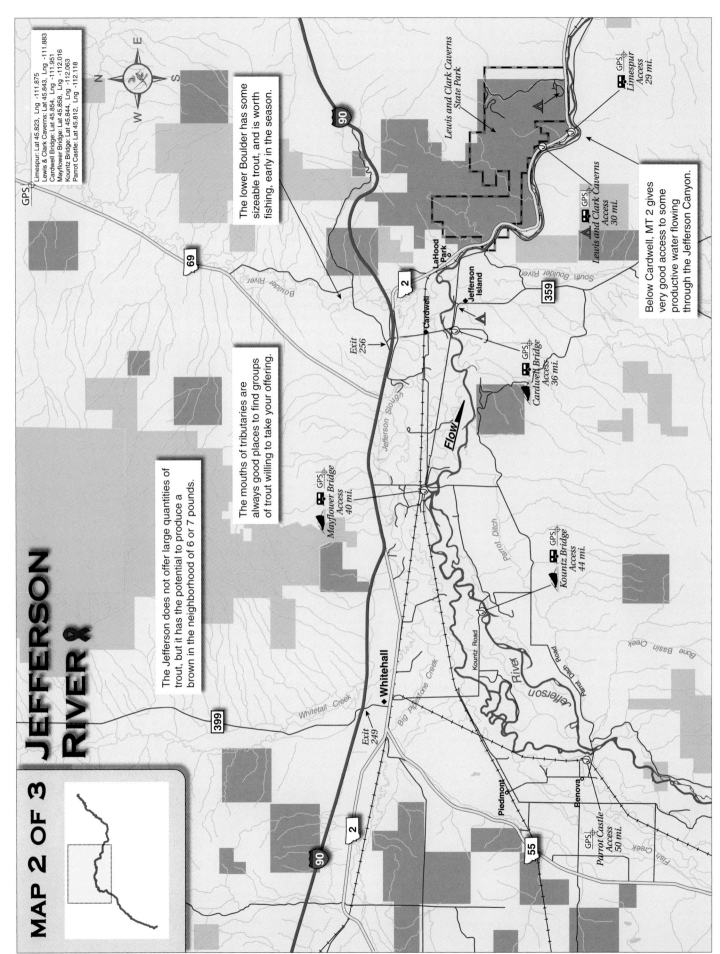

JEFFERSON RIVER

MAP 2 OF 3

Limespur: Lat 45.823, Lng -111.875
Lewis & Clark Caverns: Lat 45.843, Lng -111.883
Cardwell Bridge: Lat 45.854, Lng -111.951
Mayflower Bridge: Lat 45.858, Lng -112.016
Kountz Bridge: Lat 45.844, Lng -112.063
Parrot Castle: Lat 45.812, Lng -112.118

The lower Boulder has some sizeable trout, and is worth fishing, early in the season.

The mouths of tributaries are always good places to find groups of trout willing to take your offering.

The Jefferson does not offer large quantities of trout, but it has the potential to produce a brown in the neighborhood of 6 or 7 pounds.

Below Cardwell, MT 2 gives very good access to some productive water flowing through the Jefferson Canyon.

Lewis and Clark Caverns State Park

GPS Limespur Access 29 mi.

GPS Lewis and Clark Caverns Access 30 mi.

GPS Cardwell Bridge Access 36 mi.

LaHood Park

Cardwell

Jefferson Island

Exit 256

Flow

South Boulder River

359

Boulder River

69

90

2

Jefferson Slough

GPS Mayflower Bridge Access 40 mi.

GPS Kountz Bridge Access 44 mi.

Parrot Ditch

Kountz Road

Jefferson River

Whitehall

Exit 249

Big Pipestone Creek

Whitetall Creek

399

Piedmont

Benova

Parrot Ditch Road

Bone Basin Creek

GPS Parrot Castle Access 50 mi.

Fish Creek

55

2

90

© 2006 Wilderness Adventures Press, Inc.

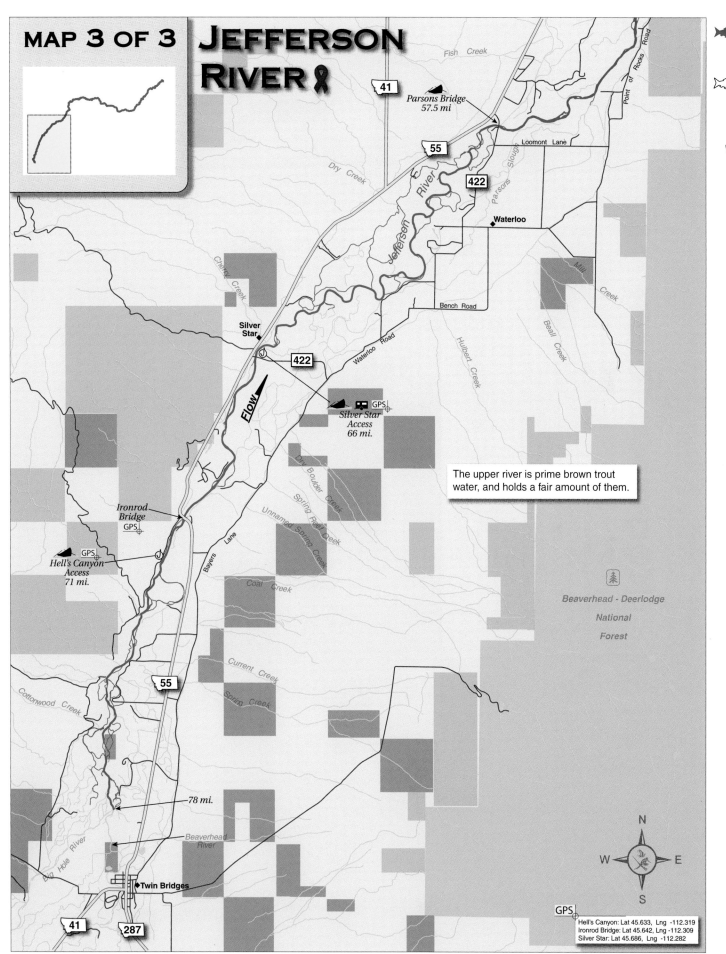

MAP 3 OF 3

JEFFERSON RIVER

Fish Creek

41

Parsons Bridge
57.5 mi

55

422

Loomont Lane

Jefferson River

Dry Creek

Parsons Slough

Waterloo

Cherry Creek

Bench Road

Mill Creek

Silver
Star

422

Waterloo Road

Beall Creek

Hulbert Creek

Flow

GPS
Silver Star
Access
66 mi.

The upper river is prime brown trout
water, and holds a fair amount of them.

Dry Boulder Creek

Spring Reef Creek

Ironrod
Bridge
GPS

Unnamed Spring Creek

Bayers Lane

GPS
Hell's Canyon
Access
71 mi.

Coal Creek

Beaverhead - Deerlodge

National

Forest

Current Creek

Spring Creek

55

Cottonwood Creek

78 mi.

Big Hole River

Beaverhead
River

N

W   E

S

Twin Bridges

GPS

41

287

Hell's Canyon: Lat 45.633, Lng -112.319
Ironrod Bridge: Lat 45.642, Lng -112.309
Silver Star: Lat 45.686, Lng -112.282

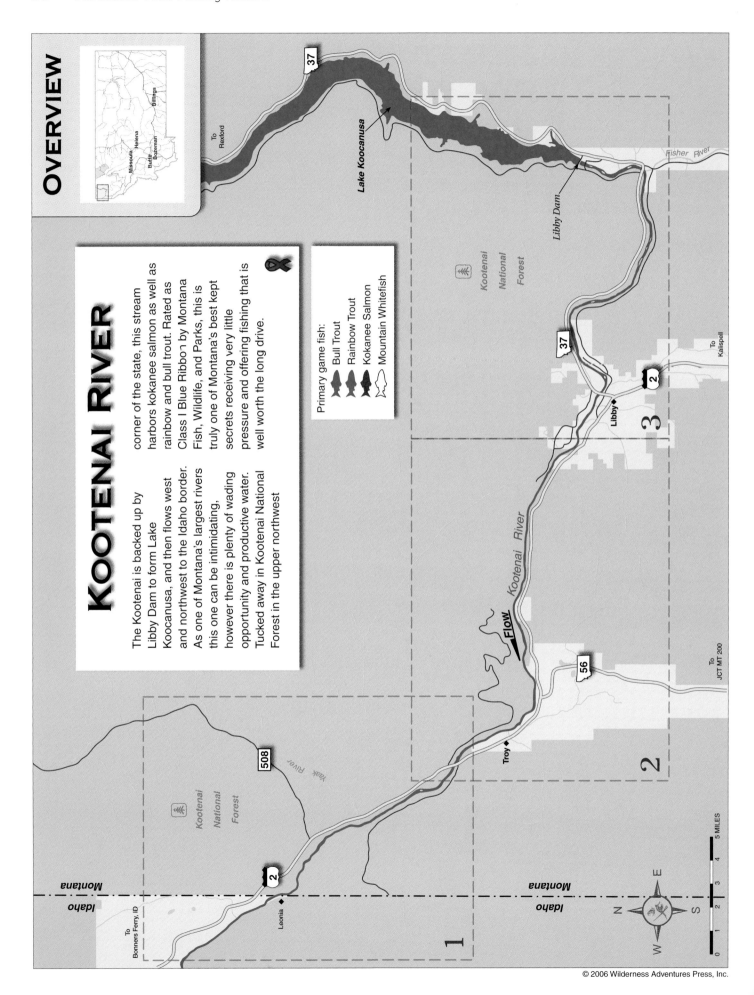

OVERVIEW

KOOTENAI RIVER

The Kootenai is backed up by Libby Dam to form Lake Koocanusa, and then flows west and northwest to the Idaho border. As one of Montana's largest rivers this one can be intimidating, however there is plenty of wading opportunity and productive water. Tucked away in Kootenai National Forest in the upper northwest corner of the state, this stream harbors kokanee salmon as well as rainbow and bull trout. Rated as Class I Blue Ribbon by Montana Fish, Wildlife, and Parks, this is truly one of Montana's best kept secrets receiving very little pressure and offering fishing that is well worth the long drive.

Primary game fish:
Bull Trout
Rainbow Trout
Kokanee Salmon
Mountain Whitefish

Missoula Helena Billings
Butte Bozeman

To Rexford

Lake Koocanusa

Fisher River

Libby Dam

Kootenai National Forest

To Kalispell

Libby

37

2

3

Kootenai River

Flow

56

To JCT MT 200

Troy

2

Kootenai National Forest

Yaak River

508

Montana
Idaho

To Bonners Ferry, ID

Leonia

2

1

Montana
Idaho

N E S W

0 1 2 3 4 5 MILES

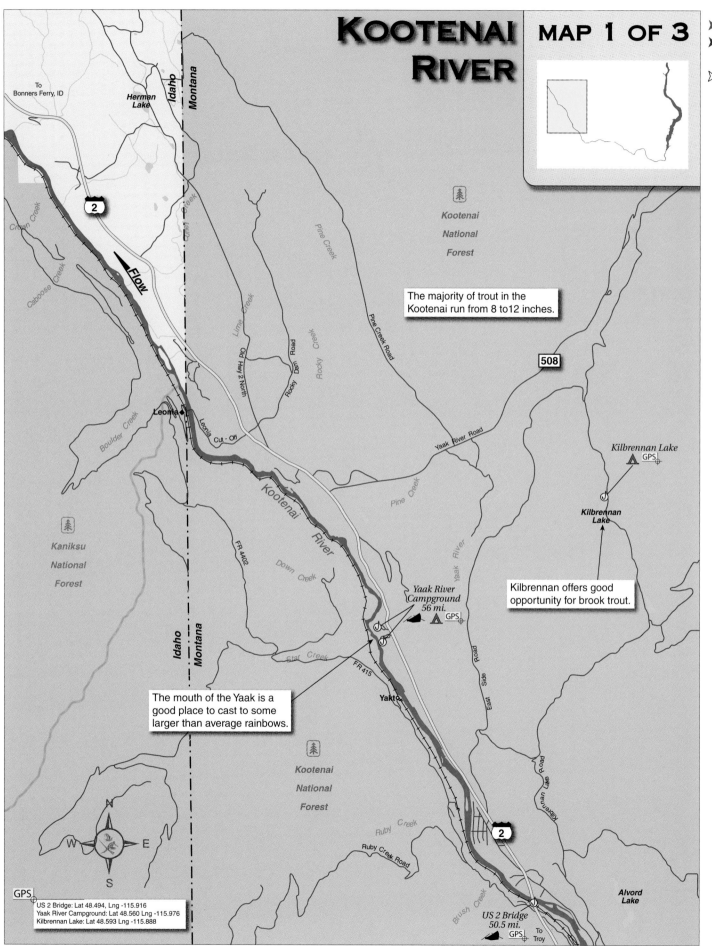

KOOTENAI RIVER

MAP 1 OF 3

To Bonners Ferry, ID

Herman Lake

Idaho

Montana

Crown Creek

Flow

Caboose Creek

Kootenai National Forest

The majority of trout in the Kootenai run from 8 to12 inches.

508

Pine Creek

Lime Creek

Old Hwy 2 North

Rocky Dam Road

Rocky Creek

Pine Creek Road

Yaak River Road

Leonia

Leonia Cut - Off

Boulder Creek

Kaniksu National Forest

Kootenai River

Down Creek

FR 4402

Pine Creek

Yaak River

Kilbrennan Lake
GPS

Kilbrennan Lake

Kilbrennan offers good opportunity for brook trout.

Yaak River Campground 56 mi.
GPS

The mouth of the Yaak is a good place to cast to some larger than average rainbows.

Star Creek

FR 415

Yakt

East Side Road

Idaho
Montana

Kootenai National Forest

Ruby Creek

Ruby Creek Road

Kilbrennan Lake Road

2

Brush Creek

US 2 Bridge 50.5 mi.
GPS
To Troy

Alvord Lake

N
W   E
S

GPS

US 2 Bridge: Lat 48.494, Lng -115.916
Yaak River Campground: Lat 48.560 Lng -115.976
Kilbrennan Lake: Lat 48.593 Lng -115.888

© 2006 Wilderness Adventures Press, Inc.

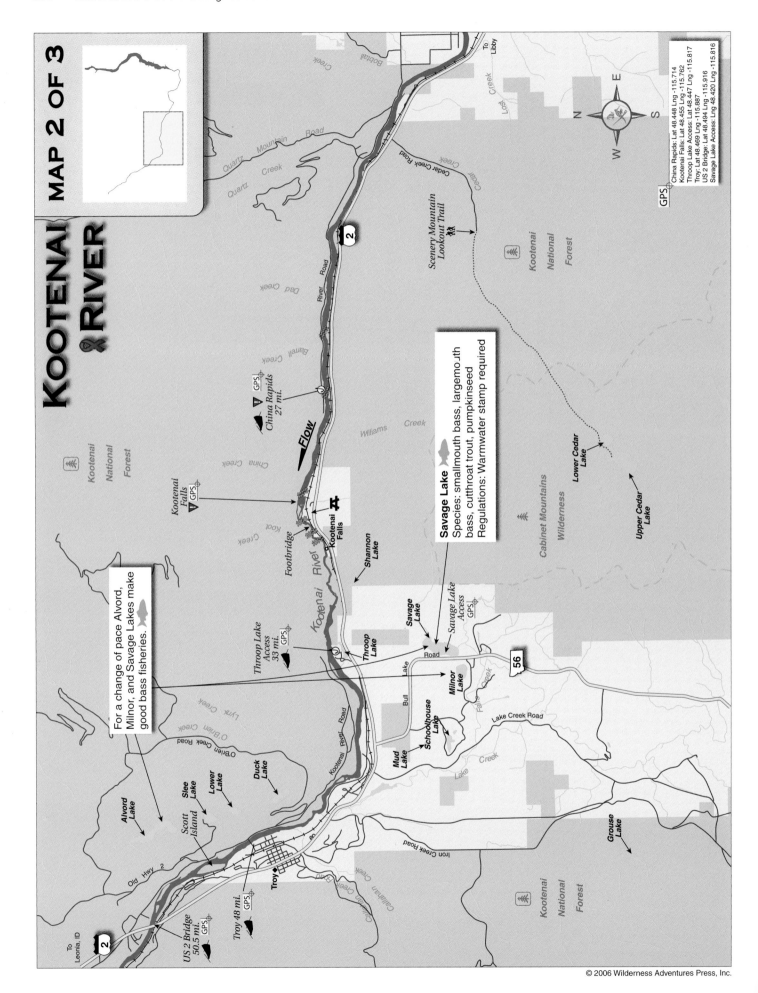

MAP 2 OF 3

KOOTENAI RIVER

For a change of pace Alvord, Milnor, and Savage Lakes make good bass fisheries.

Savage Lake
Species: smallmouth bass, largemouth bass, cutthroat trout, pumpkinseed
Regulations: Warmwater stamp required

China Rapids: Lat 48.448 Lng -115.714
Kootenai Falls: Lat 48.455 Lng -115.762
Throop Lake Access: Lat 48.447 Lng -115.817
Troy: Lat 48.469 Lng -115.887
US 2 Bridge: Lat 48.494 Lng -115.916
Savage Lake Access: Lng 48.420 Lng -115.816

To Libby

Lost Creek

Cedar Creek Road

Cedar Creek

Scenery Mountain Lookout Trail

Kootenai National Forest

Quartz Mountain Road

Quartz Creek

Creek

Bobtail Creek

2

River Road

Dad Creek

Barrell Creek

Williams Creek

China Creek

China Rapids 27 mi.
GPS

Flow

Kootenai Falls
GPS

Kootenai Falls

Footbridge

Kood Creek

Shannon Lake

Kootenai River

Throop Lake Access 33 mi.
GPS

Throop Lake

Milnor Lake

Savage Lake

Savage Lake Access
GPS

Road

Bull Lake

Lower Cedar Lake

Upper Cedar Lake

Cabinet Mountains Wilderness

Kootenai National Forest

56

Schoolhouse Lake

Falls Creek

Lake Creek Road

Mud Lake

Creek

Lake

Iron Creek Road

Grouse Lake

Kootenai National Forest

O'Brien Creek Road

O'Brien Creek

Lynx Creek

Kootenai River Road

Alvord Lake

Slee Lake

Lower Lake

Scott Island

Duck Lake

Old Hwy 2

Troy

Callahan Creek

Callahan Creek Road

To Leonia, ID

2

US 2 Bridge 50.5 mi.
GPS

Troy 48 mi.
GPS

N E S W

GPS

© 2006 Wilderness Adventures Press, Inc.

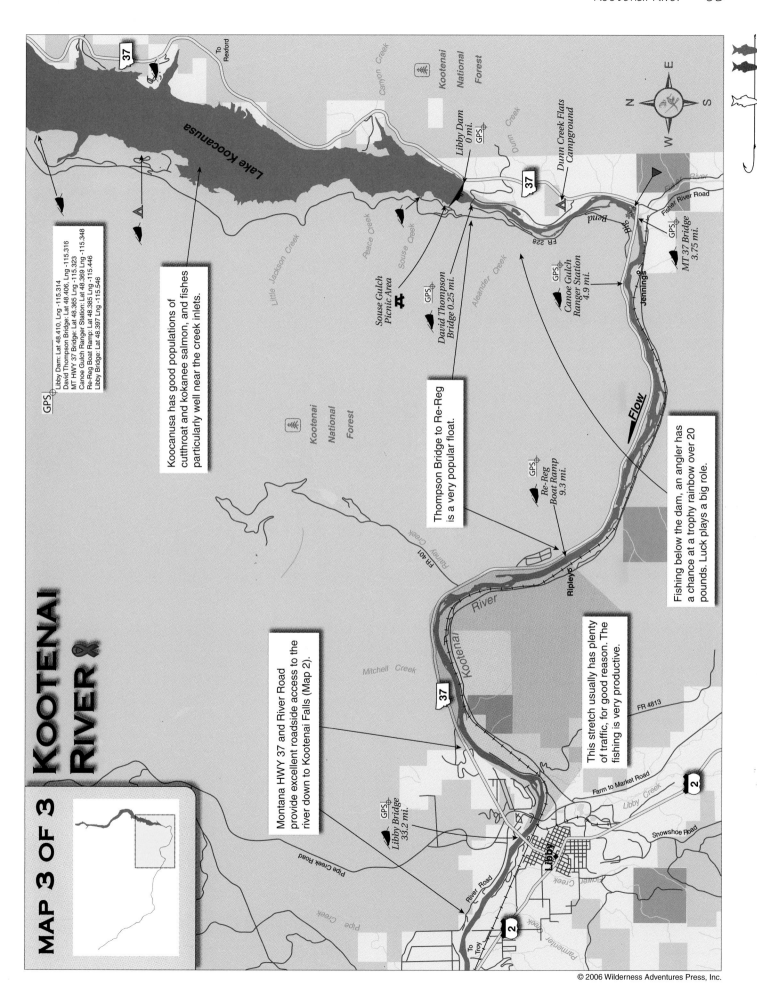

MAP 3 OF 3

KOOTENAI
RIVER

(Map 2)

GPS
Libby Dam: Lat 48.410, Lng -115.314
David Thompson Bridge: Lat 48.406, Lng -115.316
MT HWY 37 Bridge: Lat 48.365 Lng -115.323
Canoe Gulch Ranger Station: Lat 48.369 Lng -115.348
Re-Reg Boat Ramp: Lat 48.385 Lng -115.446
Libby Bridge: Lat 48.397 Lng -115.546

Koocanusa has good populations of cutthroat and kokanee salmon, and fishes particularly well near the creek inlets.

Thompson Bridge to Re-Reg is a very popular float.

Montana HWY 37 and River Road provide excellent roadside access to the river down to Kootenai Falls (Map 2).

Fishing below the dam, an angler has a chance at a trophy rainbow over 20 pounds. Luck plays a big role.

This stretch usually has plenty of traffic, for good reason. The fishing is very productive.

Lake Koocanusa

To Rexford

Canyon Creek

Kootenai National Forest

Libby Dam
0 mi.
GPS

Dunn Creek Flats Campground

Dunn Creek

37

Fisher River

Fisher River Road

GPS
MT 37 Bridge
3.75 mi.

Big Bend

FR 228

Jennings

GPS
Canoe Gulch Ranger Station
4.9 mi.

Aleander Creek

Souse Creek

Peace Creek

Little Jackson Creek

Souse Gulch Picnic Area

GPS
David Thompson Bridge 0.25 mi.

Kootenai National Forest

GPS
Re-Reg Boat Ramp
9.3 mi.

Ripley

Flow

FR 401

Rainey Creek

Kootenai River

Mitchell Creek

37

FR 4813

Farm to Market Road

Libby Creek

2

Snowshoe Road

GPS
Libby Bridge
33.2 mi.

Pipe Creek Road

River Road

Libby

Flower Creek

Pipe Creek

2

To Troy

Parmenter Creek

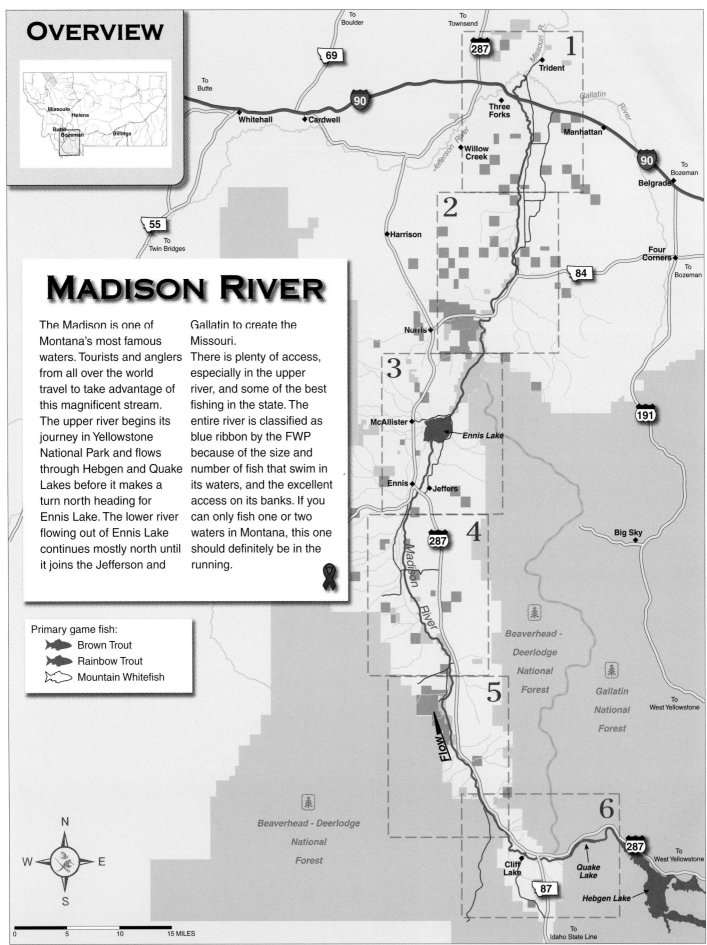

OVERVIEW

MADISON RIVER

The Madison is one of Montana's most famous waters. Tourists and anglers from all over the world travel to take advantage of this magnificent stream. The upper river begins its journey in Yellowstone National Park and flows through Hebgen and Quake Lakes before it makes a turn north heading for Ennis Lake. The lower river flowing out of Ennis Lake continues mostly north until it joins the Jefferson and Gallatin to create the Missouri.

There is plenty of access, especially in the upper river, and some of the best fishing in the state. The entire river is classified as blue ribbon by the FWP because of the size and number of fish that swim in its waters, and the excellent access on its banks. If you can only fish one or two waters in Montana, this one should definitely be in the running.

Primary game fish:
- Brown Trout
- Rainbow Trout
- Mountain Whitefish

0   5   10   15 MILES

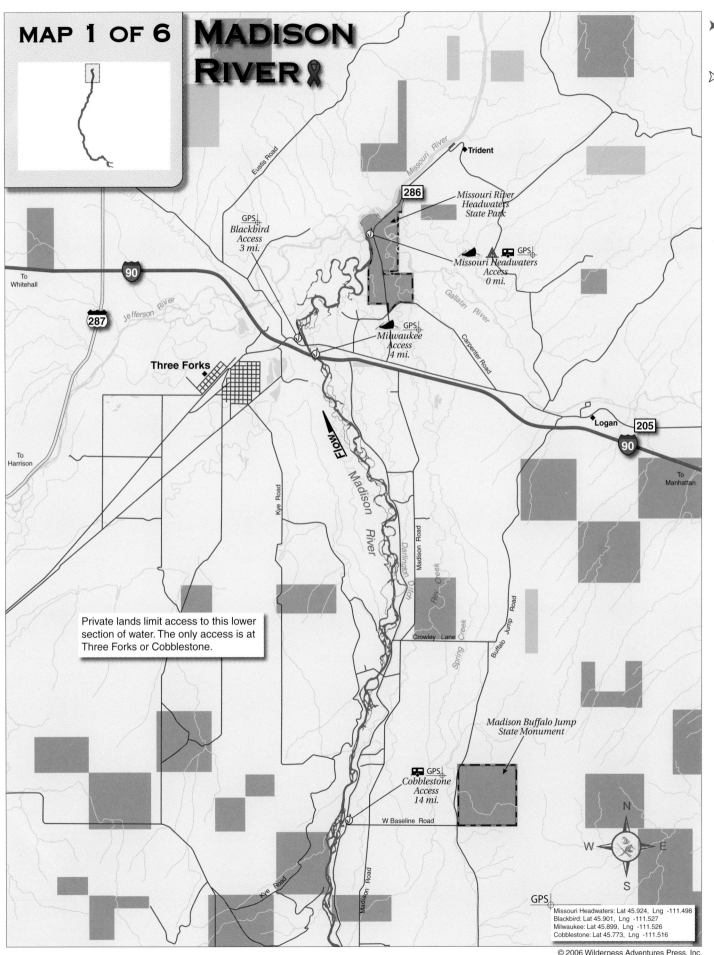

MAP 1 OF 6 | MADISON RIVER

Private lands limit access to this lower section of water. The only access is at Three Forks or Cobblestone.

Trident

286

Missouri River Headwaters State Park

GPS
Blackbird Access 3 mi.

GPS
Missouri Headwaters Access 0 mi.

Eustis Road

90

To Whitehall

287

Jefferson River

Gallatin River

Carpenter Road

GPS
Milwaukee Access 4 mi.

Three Forks

Logan

205

90

To Manhattan

FLOW

To Harrison

Kye Road

Madison River

Madison Road

Darlington Ditch

Rev Creek

Spring Creek

Buffalo Jump Road

Crowley Lane

Madison Buffalo Jump State Monument

GPS
Cobblestone Access 14 mi.

W Baseline Road

Kye Road

Madison Road

N
W · E
S

GPS
Missouri Headwaters: Lat 45.924, Lng -111.498
Blackbird: Lat 45.901, Lng -111.527
Milwaukee: Lat 45.899, Lng -111.526
Cobblestone: Lat 45.773, Lng -111.516

© 2006 Wilderness Adventures Press, Inc.

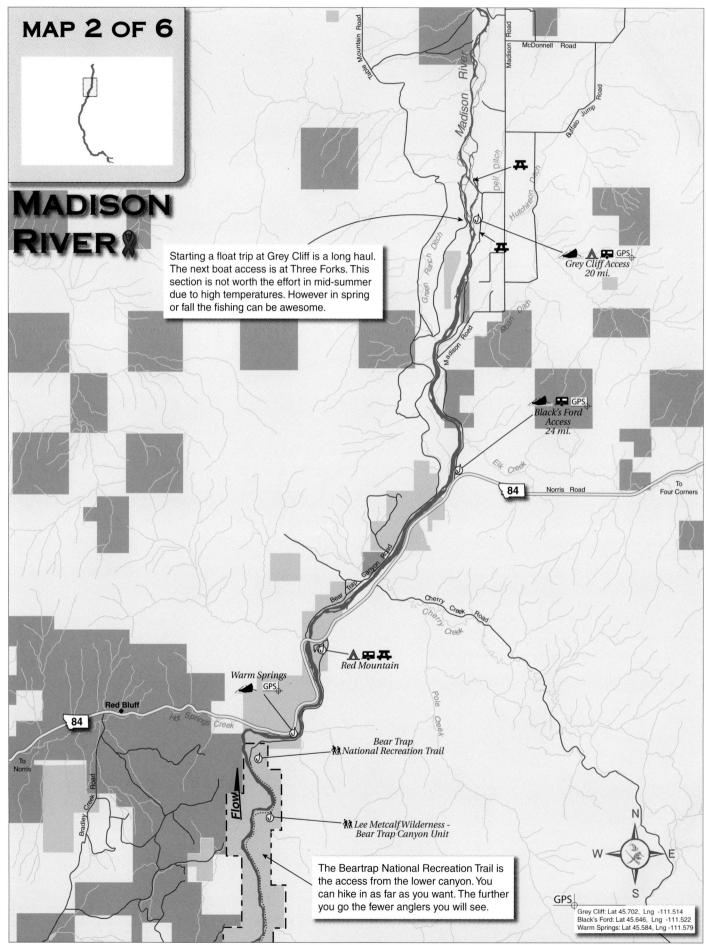

MAP 2 OF 6

MADISON RIVER

Table Mountain Road

Madison River

McDonnell Road

Madison Road

Buffalo Jump Road

Dell Ditch

Hutchinson Ditch

Green Ranch Ditch

Grey Cliff Access
20 mi.

GPS

Starting a float trip at Grey Cliff is a long haul. The next boat access is at Three Forks. This section is not worth the effort in mid-summer due to high temperatures. However in spring or fall the fishing can be awesome.

Shan Ditch

Madison Road

Black's Ford
Access
24 mi.

GPS

Elk Creek

84 Norris Road

To
Four Corners

Bear Trap Canyon Road

Cherry Creek Road

Cherry Creek

Red Mountain

Pole Creek

Warm Springs
GPS

Red Bluff

84

Hot Springs Creek

Bradley Creek Road

To
Norris

Flow

Bear Trap
National Recreation Trail

Lee Metcalf Wilderness -
Bear Trap Canyon Unit

The Beartrap National Recreation Trail is the access from the lower canyon. You can hike in as far as you want. The further you go the fewer anglers you will see.

N

W   E

S

GPS

Grey Cliff: Lat 45.702, Lng -111.514
Black's Ford: Lat 45.646, Lng -111.522
Warm Springs: Lat 45.584, Lng -111.579

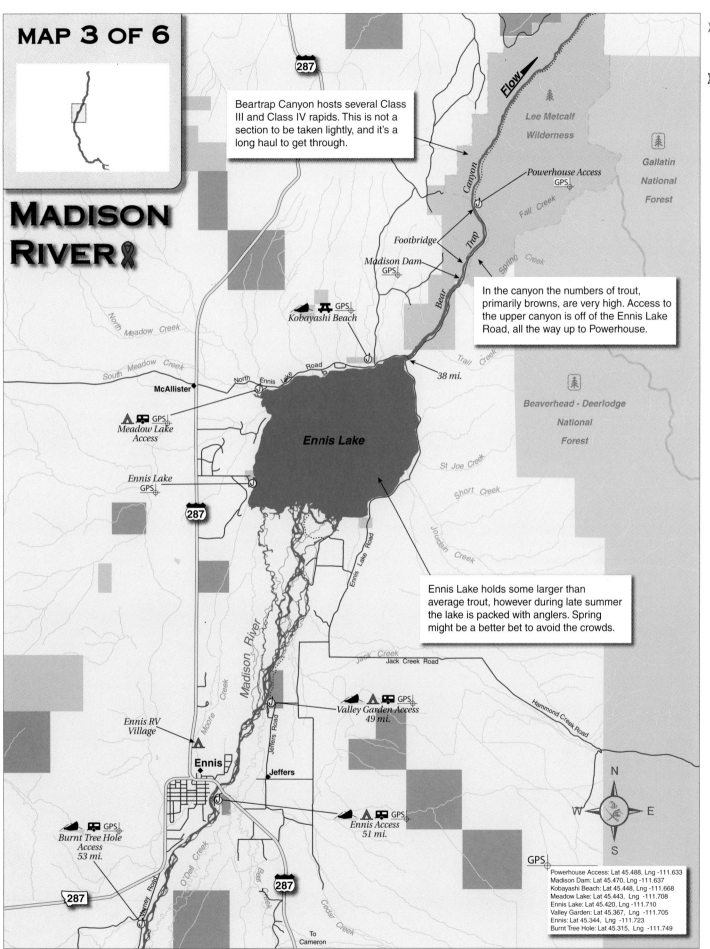

MAP 3 OF 6

MADISON RIVER

Beartrap Canyon hosts several Class III and Class IV rapids. This is not a section to be taken lightly, and it's a long haul to get through.

Flow

Lee Metcalf Wilderness

Powerhouse Access GPS

Gallatin National Forest

Footbridge

Madison Dam GPS

In the canyon the numbers of trout, primarily browns, are very high. Access to the upper canyon is off of the Ennis Lake Road, all the way up to Powerhouse.

GPS
Kobayashi Beach

38 mi.

Beaverhead - Deerlodge National Forest

North Meadow Creek

South Meadow Creek

North Ennis Lake Road

McAllister

GPS
Meadow Lake Access

Ennis Lake

Ennis Lake GPS

St Joe Creek

Short Creek

287

Jourdain Creek

Ennis Lake holds some larger than average trout, however during late summer the lake is packed with anglers. Spring might be a better bet to avoid the crowds.

Madison River

Moore Creek

Jack Creek
Jack Creek Road

Hammond Creek Road

GPS
Valley Garden Access
49 mi.

Jeffers Road

Ennis RV Village

Ennis

Jeffers

N
W — E
S

GPS
Burnt Tree Hole Access
53 mi.

Varney Road

O'Dell Creek

Bear Creek

GPS
Ennis Access
51 mi.

Cedar Creek

287

To Cameron

GPS
Powerhouse Access: Lat 45.488, Lng -111.633
Madison Dam: Lat 45.470, Lng -111.637
Kobayashi Beach: Lat 45.448, Lng -111.668
Meadow Lake: Lat 45.443, Lng -111.708
Ennis Lake: Lat 45.420, Lng -111.710
Valley Garden: Lat 45.367, Lng -111.705
Ennis: Lat 45.344, Lng -111.723
Burnt Tree Hole: Lat 45.315, Lng -111.749

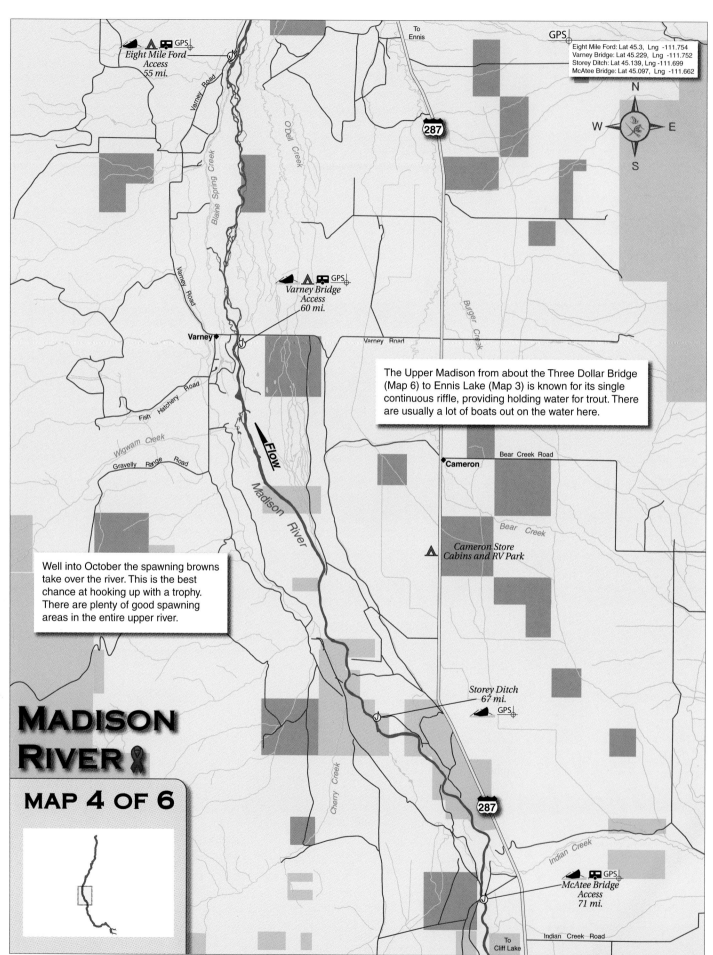

Eight Mile Ford
Access
55 mi.

GPS

Eight Mile Ford: Lat 45.3, Lng -111.754
Varney Bridge: Lat 45.229, Lng -111.752
Storey Ditch: Lat 45.139, Lng -111.699
McAtee Bridge: Lat 45.097, Lng -111.662

N
W — E
S

To
Ennis

GPS

287

Varney Road

O'Dell Creek

Blaine Spring Creek

Varney Bridge
Access
60 mi.

GPS

Varney

Varney Road

Burger Creek

Fish Hatchery Road

Wigwam Creek

Gravelly Range Road

Flow

Madison River

The Upper Madison from about the Three Dollar Bridge
(Map 6) to Ennis Lake (Map 3) is known for its single
continuous riffle, providing holding water for trout. There
are usually a lot of boats out on the water here.

Bear Creek Road

Cameron

Bear Creek

Cameron Store
Cabins and RV Park

Well into October the spawning browns
take over the river. This is the best
chance at hooking up with a trophy.
There are plenty of good spawning
areas in the entire upper river.

Storey Ditch
67 mi.

GPS

**MADISON
RIVER**

MAP 4 OF 6

Cherry Creek

287

Indian Creek

GPS

McAtee Bridge
Access
71 mi.

To
Cliff Lake

Indian Creek Road

© 2006 Wilderness Adventures Press, Inc.

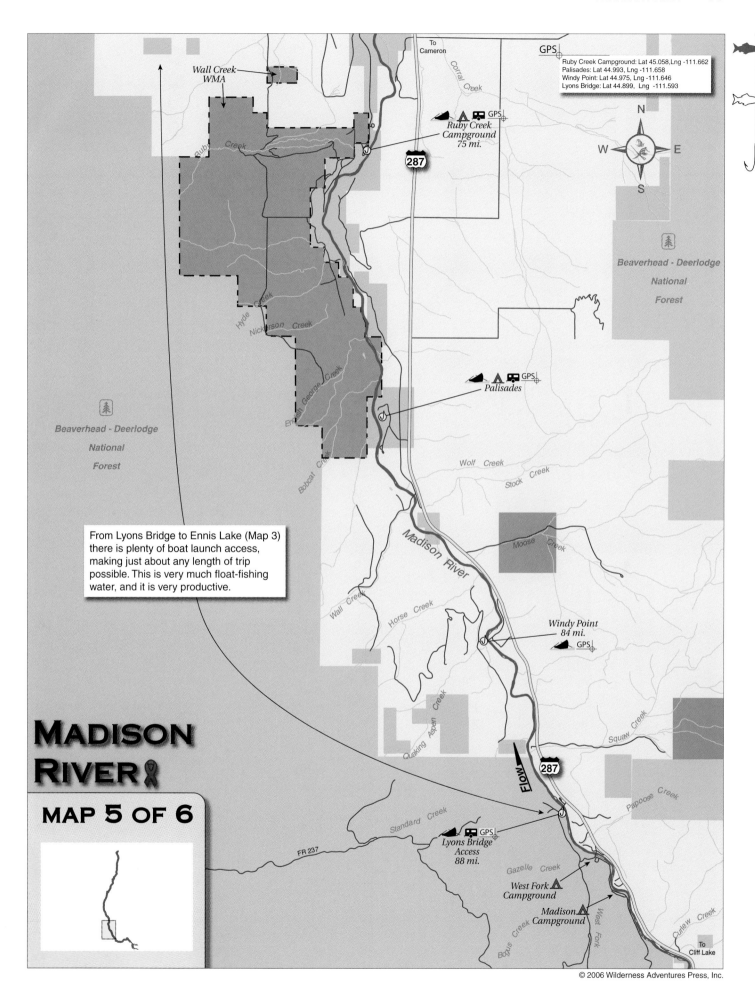

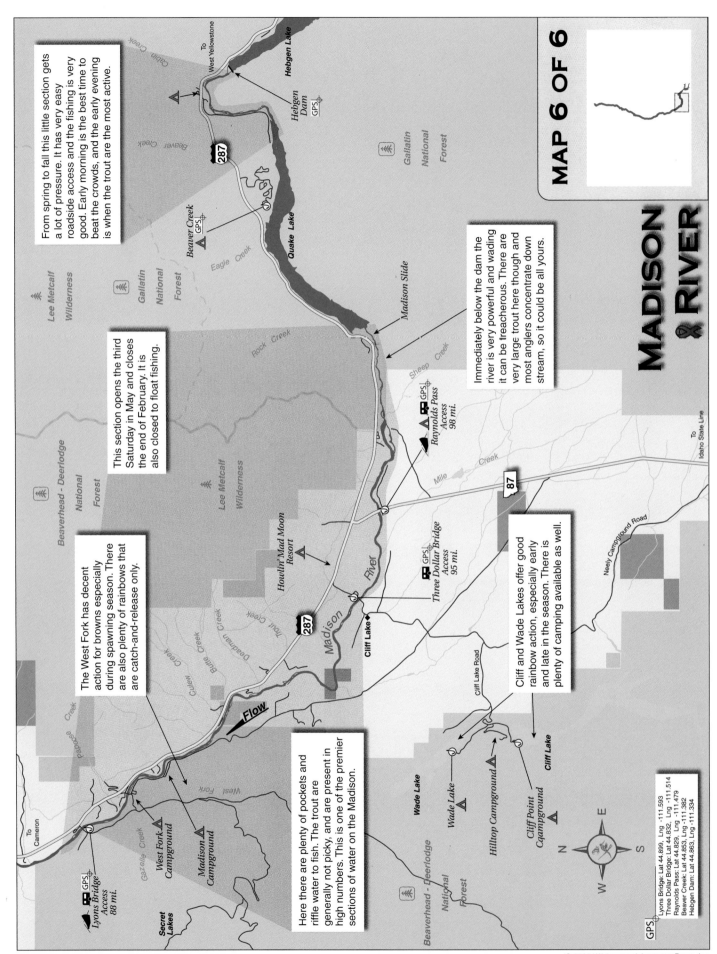

MAP 6 OF 6

MADISON RIVER

From spring to fall this little section gets a lot of pressure. It has very easy roadside access and the fishing is very good. Early morning is the best time to beat the crowds, and the early evening is when the trout are the most active.

This section opens the third Saturday in May and closes the end of February. It is also closed to float fishing.

Immediately below the dam the river is very powerful and wading it can be treacherous. There are very large trout here though and most anglers concentrate down stream, so it could be all yours.

The West Fork has decent action for browns especially during spawning season. There are also plenty of rainbows that are catch-and-release only.

Cliff and Wade Lakes offer good rainbow action, especially early and late in the season. There is plenty of camping available as well.

Here there are plenty of pockets and riffle water to fish. The trout are generally not picky, and are present in high numbers. This is one of the premier sections of water on the Madison.

Flow

Hebgen Lake

To West Yellowstone

Hebgen Dam
GPS

Cabin Creek

Beaver Creek

287

Beaver Creek
GPS

Quake Lake

Eagle Creek

Madison Slide

Gallatin National Forest

Lee Metcalf Wilderness

Gallatin National Forest

Rock Creek

Sheep Creek

Raynolds Pass Access 98 mi.
GPS

Mile Creek

87

To Idaho State Line

Beaverhead - Deerlodge National Forest

Lee Metcalf Wilderness

Howlin' Mad Moon Resort

Madison River

Three Dollar Bridge Access 95 mi.
GPS

Cliff Lake

Cliff Lake Road

Neely Campground Road

287

Deadman Creek

Trout Creek

Butte Creek

Cullen Creek

Gazelle Creek

Papoose Creek

To Cameron

Lyons Bridge Access 88 mi.
GPS

West Fork Campground

Madison Campground

Secret Lakes

West Fork

Wade Lake

Wade Lake

Hilltop Campground

Cliff Point Campground

Cliff Lake

Beaverhead - Deerlodge National Forest

N
E
S
W

GPS   Lyons Bridge: Lat 44.899, Lng -111.593
Three Dollar Bridge: Lat 44.832, Lng -111.514
Raynolds Pass: Lat 44.829, Lng -111.479
Beaver Creek: Lat 44.853, Lng -111.382
Hebgen Dam: Lat 44.863, Lng -111.334

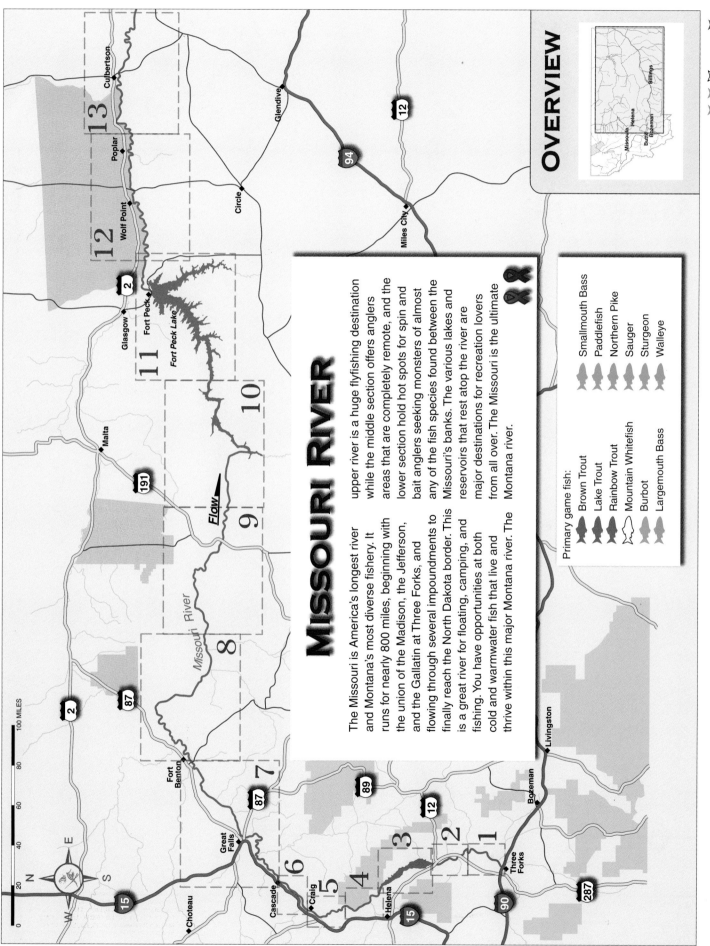

MISSOURI RIVER

The Missouri is America's longest river and Montana's most diverse fishery. It runs for nearly 800 miles, beginning with the union of the Madison, the Jefferson, and the Gallatin at Three Forks, and flowing through several impoundments to finally reach the North Dakota border. This is a great river for floating, camping, and fishing. You have opportunities at both cold and warmwater fish that live and thrive within this major Montana river. The upper river is a huge flyfishing destination while the middle section offers anglers areas that are completely remote, and the lower section hold hot spots for spin and bait anglers seeking monsters of almost any of the fish species found between the Missouri's banks. The various lakes and reservoirs that rest atop the river are major destinations for recreation lovers from all over. The Missouri is the ultimate Montana river.

OVERVIEW

Primary game fish:

Brown Trout
Lake Trout
Rainbow Trout
Mountain Whitefish
Burbot
Largemouth Bass

Smallmouth Bass
Paddlefish
Northern Pike
Sauger
Sturgeon
Walleye

Flow

100 MILES

MAP 1 OF 13

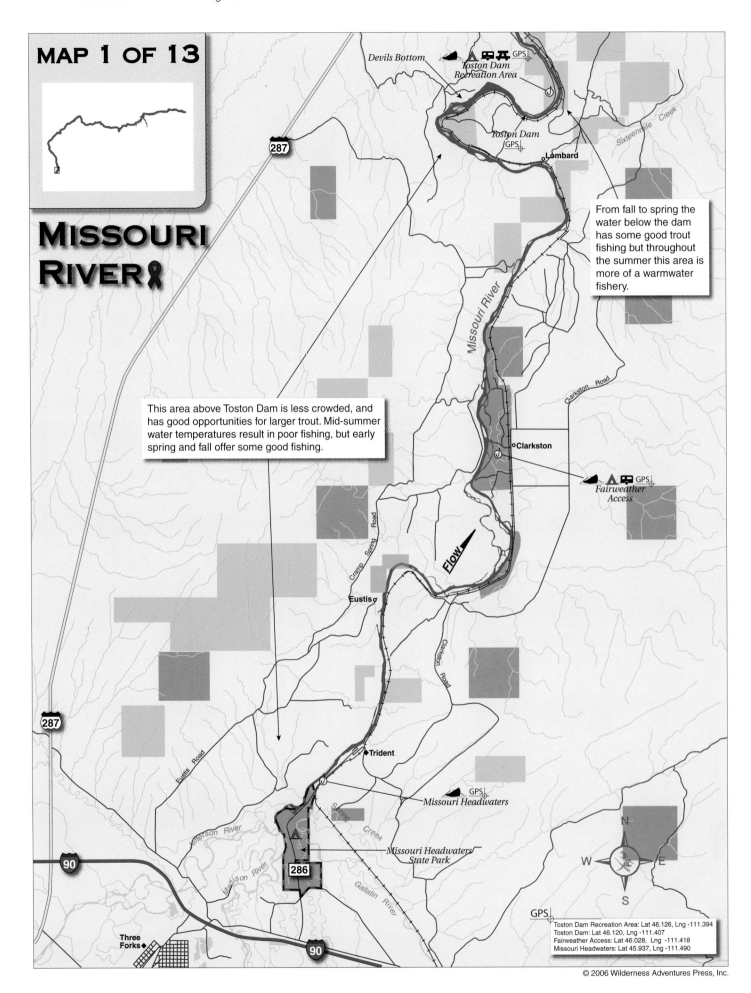

MISSOURI RIVER

Devils Bottom

Toston Dam Recreation Area GPS

Toston Dam GPS

Lombard

Sixteenmile Creek

From fall to spring the water below the dam has some good trout fishing but throughout the summer this area is more of a warmwater fishery.

Missouri River

Clarkston Road

This area above Toston Dam is less crowded, and has good opportunities for larger trout. Mid-summer water temperatures result in poor fishing, but early spring and fall offer some good fishing.

○**Clarkston**

Fairweather Access GPS

Cramp Spring Road

FLOW

Eustis○

Clarkston Road

Trident

GPS
Missouri Headwaters

Jefferson River

Spring Creek

△

286

Missouri Headwaters State Park

Madison River

Gallatin River

N
W · E
S

90

Three Forks◆

90

GPS

Toston Dam Recreation Area: Lat 46.126, Lng -111.394
Toston Dam: Lat 46.120, Lng -111.407
Fairweather Access: Lat 46.028, Lng -111.418
Missouri Headwaters: Lat 45.937, Lng -111.490

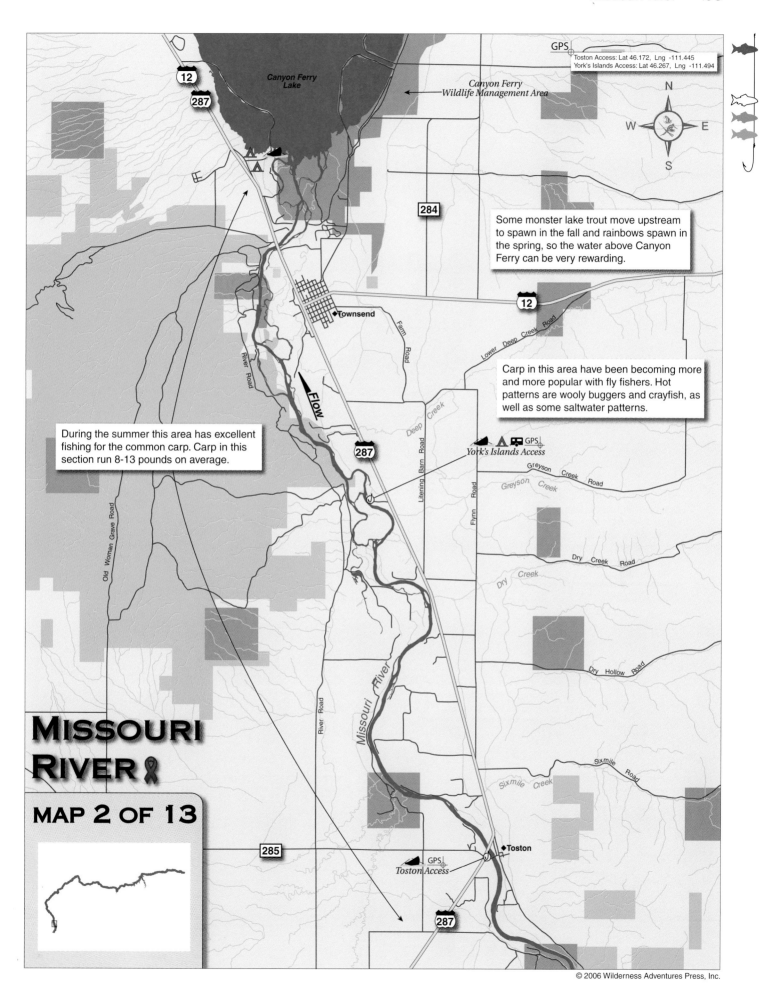

GPS

Canyon Ferry
Lake

Canyon Ferry
Wildlife Management Area

N
W   E
S

284

Some monster lake trout move upstream
to spawn in the fall and rainbows spawn in
the spring, so the water above Canyon
Ferry can be very rewarding.

12

◆Townsend

Farm Road

Lower Deep Creek Road

Carp in this area have been becoming more
and more popular with fly fishers. Hot
patterns are wooly buggers and crayfish, as
well as some saltwater patterns.

River Road

Flow

Deep Creek

Litening Barn Road

287

GPS
York's Islands Access

Greyson Creek Road

Greyson Creek

During the summer this area has excellent
fishing for the common carp. Carp in this
section run 8-13 pounds on average.

Flynn Road

Dry Creek Road

Old Woman Grave Road

Dry Creek

Dry Hollow Road

MISSOURI
RIVER

MAP 2 OF 13

Missouri River

River Road

Sixmile Road

Sixmile Creek

285

GPS
Toston Access

◆Toston

287

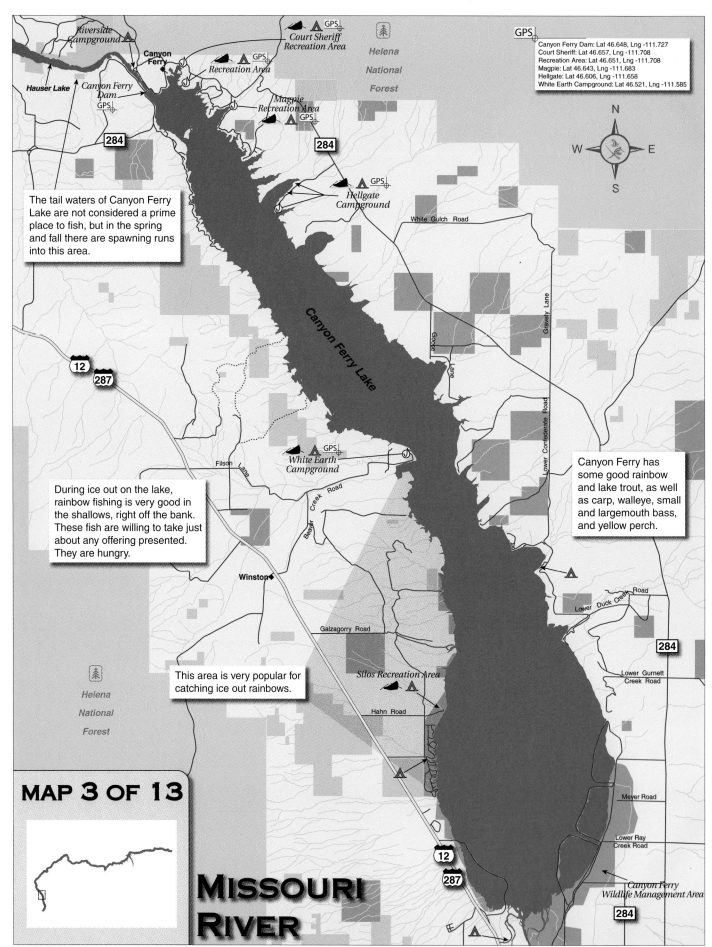

Riverside Campground

Canyon Ferry

Hauser Lake

Canyon Ferry Dam
GPS

284

Court Sheriff Recreation Area
GPS

Recreation Area
GPS

Magpie Recreation Area
GPS

Helena National Forest

284

Hellgate Campground
GPS

White Gulch Road

GPS
Canyon Ferry Dam: Lat 46.648, Lng -111.727
Court Sheriff: Lat 46.657, Lng -111.708
Recreation Area: Lat 46.651, Lng -111.708
Magpie: Lat 46.643, Lng -111.683
Hellgate: Lat 46.606, Lng -111.658
White Earth Campground: Lat 46.521, Lng -111.585

N
W   E
S

The tail waters of Canyon Ferry Lake are not considered a prime place to fish, but in the spring and fall there are spawning runs into this area.

Canyon Ferry Lake

12
287

Goose Lane

Gravely Lane

White Earth Campground
GPS

Filson Lane

Lower Confederate Road

Canyon Ferry has some good rainbow and lake trout, as well as carp, walleye, small and largemouth bass, and yellow perch.

During ice out on the lake, rainbow fishing is very good in the shallows, right off the bank. These fish are willing to take just about any offering presented. They are hungry.

Beaver Creek Road

Winston

Lower Duck Creek Road

Galzagorry Road

This area is very popular for catching ice out rainbows.

Silos Recreation Area

Hahn Road

Helena National Forest

284

Lower Gurnett Creek Road

Meyer Road

MAP 3 OF 13

Lower Ray Creek Road

12
287

MISSOURI RIVER

Canyon Ferry Wildlife Management Area

284

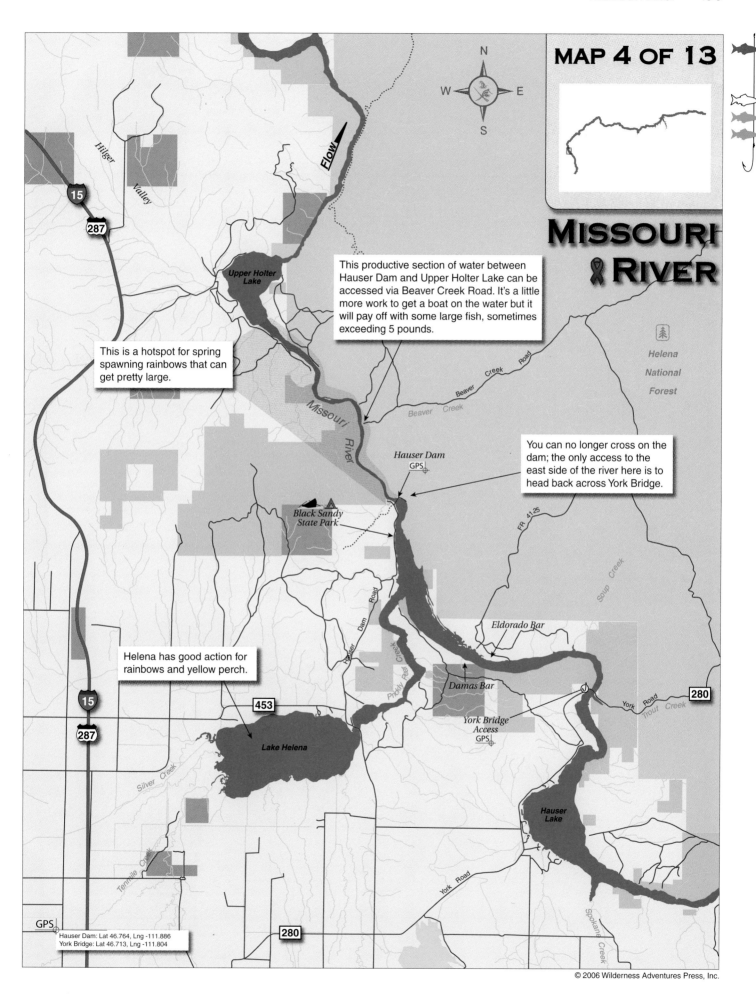

MAP 4 OF 13

MISSOURI
RIVER

This productive section of water between Hauser Dam and Upper Holter Lake can be accessed via Beaver Creek Road. It's a little more work to get a boat on the water but it will pay off with some large fish, sometimes exceeding 5 pounds.

This is a hotspot for spring spawning rainbows that can get pretty large.

Helena
National
Forest

You can no longer cross on the dam; the only access to the east side of the river here is to head back across York Bridge.

Hauser Dam
GPS

Black Sandy State Park

Helena has good action for rainbows and yellow perch.

Eldorado Bar

Damas Bar

York Bridge Access
GPS

Lake Helena

Hauser Lake

Hauser Dam: Lat 46.764, Lng -111.886
York Bridge: Lat 46.713, Lng -111.804

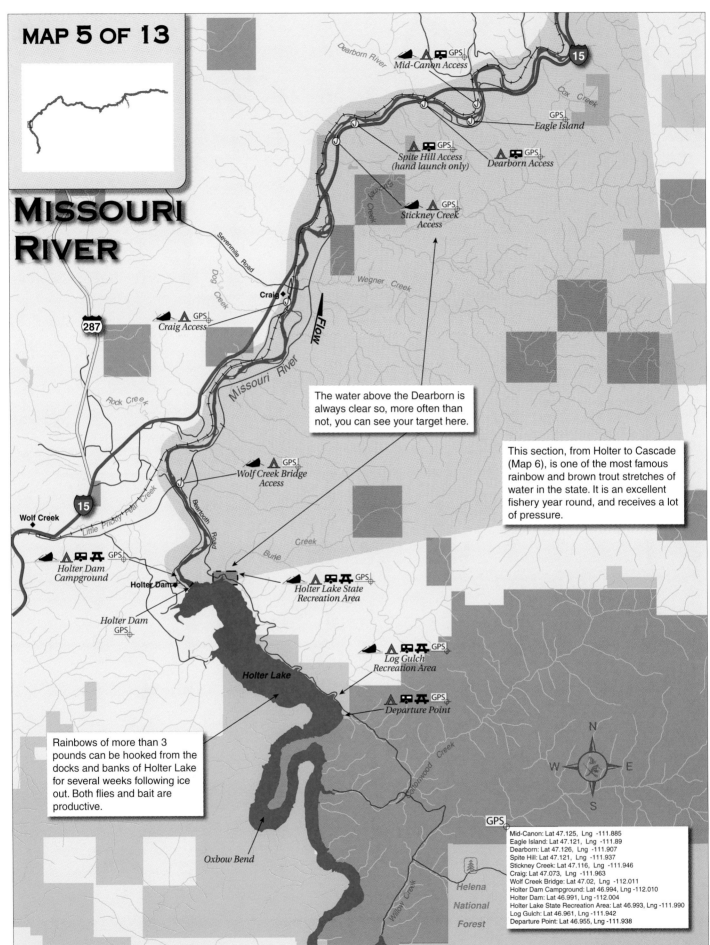

MAP 5 OF 13

MISSOURI RIVER

Mid-Canon Access

Eagle Island

Spite Hill Access
(hand launch only)

Dearborn Access

Stickney Creek
Access

Dearborn River

Cox Creek

Wegner Creek

The water above the Dearborn is always clear so, more often than not, you can see your target here.

This section, from Holter to Cascade (Map 6), is one of the most famous rainbow and brown trout stretches of water in the state. It is an excellent fishery year round, and receives a lot of pressure.

Sevenmile Road

Dog Creek

Craig

Craig Access

Missouri River

Flow

Rock Creek

Wolf Creek Bridge
Access

Beartooth Road

Burke Creek

Wolf Creek

Little Prickly Pear Creek

Holter Dam
Campground

Holter Dam

Holter Dam
GPS

Holter Lake State
Recreation Area

Log Gulch
Recreation Area

Departure Point

Holter Lake

Rainbows of more than 3 pounds can be hooked from the docks and banks of Holter Lake for several weeks following ice out. Both flies and bait are productive.

Oxbow Bend

Cottonwood Creek

N
W E
S

GPS

Mid-Canon: Lat 47.125, Lng -111.885
Eagle Island: Lat 47.121, Lng -111.89
Dearborn: Lat 47.126, Lng -111.907
Spite Hill: Lat 47.121, Lng -111.937
Stickney Creek: Lat 47.116, Lng -111.946
Craig: Lat 47.073, Lng -111.963
Wolf Creek Bridge: Lat 47.02, Lng -112.011
Holter Dam Campground: Lat 46.994, Lng -112.010
Holter Dam: Lat 46.991, Lng -112.004
Holter Lake State Recreation Area: Lat 46.993, Lng -111.990
Log Gulch: Lat 46.961, Lng -111.942
Departure Point: Lat 46.955, Lng -111.938

Helena

National

Forest

Willow Creek

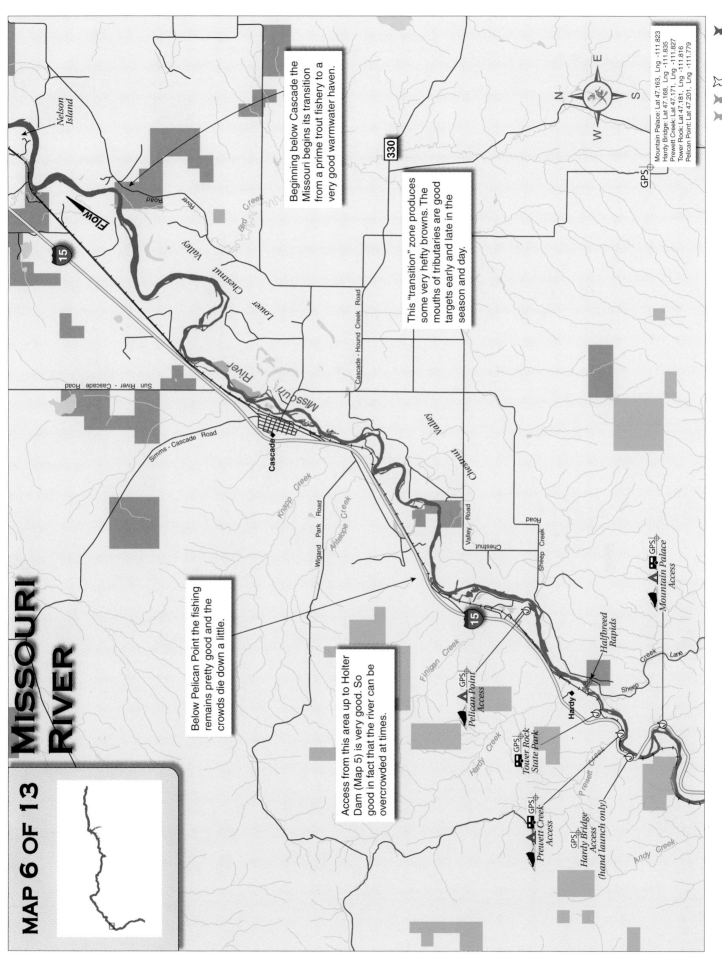

MAP 6 OF 13

MISSOURI RIVER

Beginning below Cascade the Missouri begins its transition from a prime trout fishery to a very good warmwater haven.

This "transition" zone produces some very hefty browns. The mouths of tributaries are good targets early and late in the season and day.

Below Pelican Point the fishing remains pretty good and the crowds die down a little.

Access from this area up to Holter Dam (Map 5) is very good. So good in fact that the river can be overcrowded at times.

Mountain Palace: Lat 47.163, Lng -111.823
Hardy Bridge: Lat 47.168, Lng -111.835
Prewett Creek: Lat 47.171, Lng -111.827
Tower Rock: Lat 47.181, Lng -111.816
Pelican Point: Lat 47.201, Lng -111.779

Nelson Island

Flow

Cascade

Lower Chestnut Valley

Bird Creek

River Road

Sun River - Cascade Road

Simms - Cascade Road

Missouri River

Knapp Creek

Wigand Park Road

Antelope Creek

Cascade - Hound Creek Road

Chestnut Valley

Valley Road

Chestnut Road

Sheep Creek

Finigan Creek

Pelican Point Access

Tower Rock State Park

Hardy Creek

Prewett Creek Access

Hardy Bridge Access (hand launch only)

Prewett Creek

Andy Creek

Hardy

Halfbreed Rapids

Sheep Creek

Lane

Mountain Palace Access

330

15

15

N E S W

GPS

© 2006 Wilderness Adventures Press, Inc.

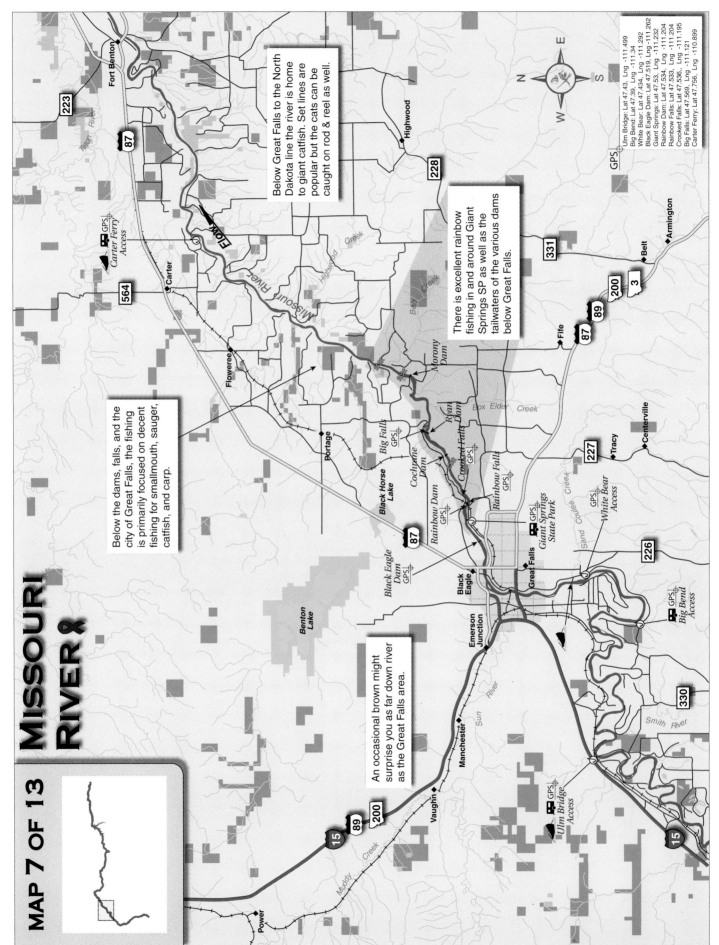

MAP 7 OF 13

MISSOURI RIVER 🐟

Below the dams, falls, and the city of Great Falls, the fishing is primarily focused on decent fishing for smallmouth, sauger, catfish, and carp.

Below Great Falls to the North Dakota line the river is home to giant catfish. Set lines are popular but the cats can be caught on rod & reel as well.

There is excellent rainbow fishing in and around Giant Springs SP as well as the tailwaters of the various dams below Great Falls.

An occasional brown might surprise you as far down river as the Great Falls area.

GPS
Ulm Bridge: Lat 47.43, Lng -111.499
Big Bend: Lat 47.39, Lng -111.34
White Bear: Lat 47.434, Lng -111.292
Black Eagle Dam: Lat 47.519, Lng -111.262
Giant Springs: Lat 47.53, Lng -111.232
Rainbow Dam: Lat 47.534, Lng -111.204
Rainbow Falls: Lat 47.533, Lng -111.204
Crooked Falls: Lat 47.536, Lng -111.195
Big Falls: Lat 47.569, Lng -111.121
Carter Ferry: Lat 47.756, Lng -110.899

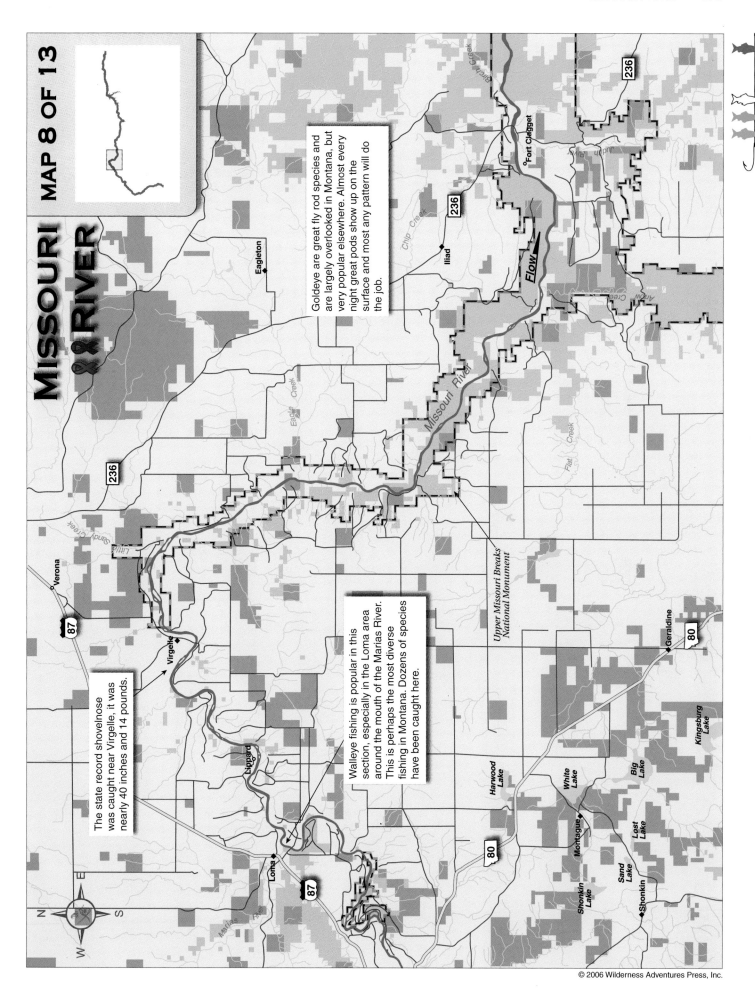

MAP 8 OF 13

MISSOURI RIVER

The state record shovelnose was caught near Virgelle, it was nearly 40 inches and 14 pounds.

Goldeye are great fly rod species and are largely overlooked in Montana, but very popular elsewhere. Almost every night great pods show up on the surface and most any pattern will do the job.

Walleye fishing is popular in this section, especially in the Loma area around the mouth of the Marias River. This is perhaps the most diverse fishing in Montana. Dozens of species have been caught here.

Upper Missouri Breaks National Monument

Missouri River

Flow

Eagleton

Iliad

Fort Clagget

Verona

Virgelle

Lippard

Loma

Geraldine

Montague

Shonkin

Harwood Lake

White Lake

Big Lake

Lost Lake

Sand Lake

Shonkin Lake

Kingsburg Lake

Eagle Creek

Sandy Creek

Little Sandy Creek

Chip Creek

Flat Creek

Arrow Creek

Birch Creek

Judith River

Marias River

236

87

80

N

S

E

W

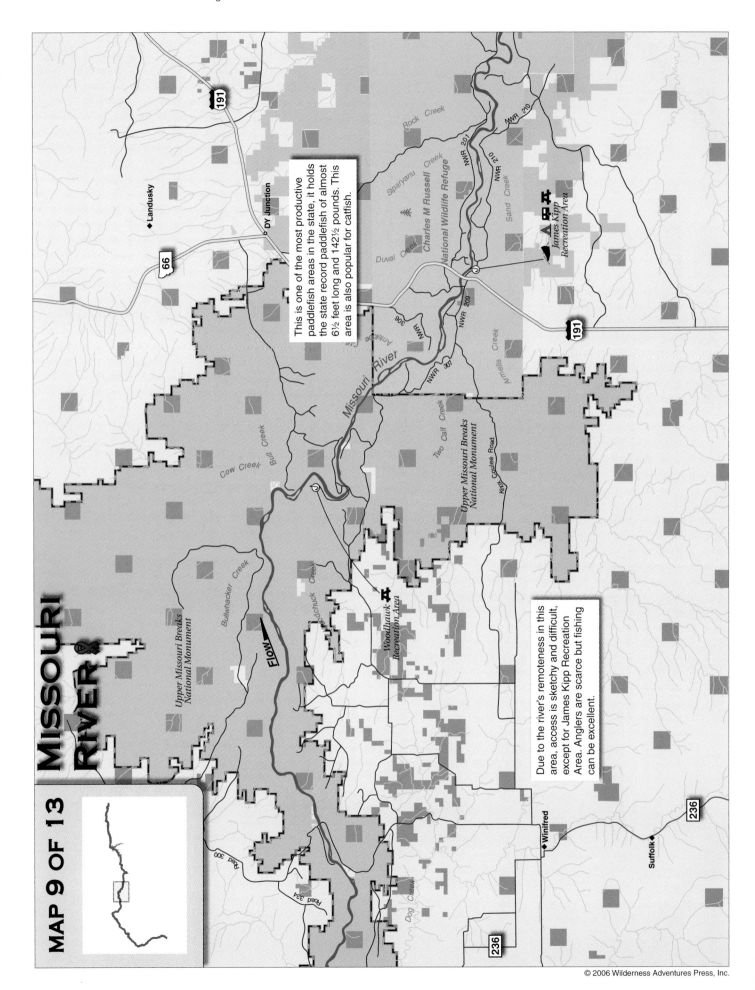

MAP 9 OF 13

MISSOURI RIVER

This is one of the most productive paddlefish areas in the state, it holds the state record paddlefish of almost 6½ feet long and 142½ pounds. This area is also popular for catfish.

Due to the river's remoteness in this area, access is sketchy and difficult, except for James Kipp Recreation Area. Anglers are scarce but fishing can be excellent.

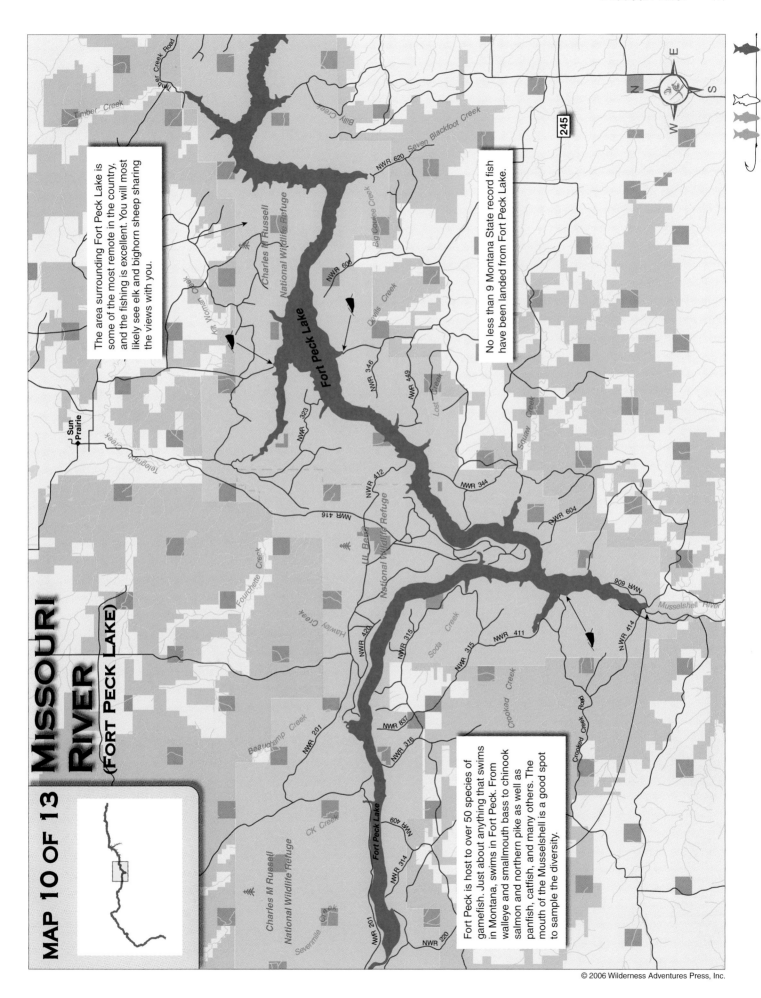

MAP 10 OF 13 MISSOURI RIVER (FORT PECK LAKE)

The area surrounding Fort Peck Lake is some of the most remote in the country, and the fishing is excellent. You will most likely see elk and bighorn sheep sharing the views with you.

No less than 9 Montana State record fish have been landed from Fort Peck Lake.

Fort Peck is host to over 50 species of gamefish. Just about anything that swims in Montana, swims in Fort Peck. From walleye and smallmouth bass to chinook salmon and northern pike as well as panfish, catfish, and many others. The mouth of the Musselshell is a good spot to sample the diversity.

245

Timber Creek

Billy Creek

Seven Blackfoot Creek

NWR 620

Big Coulee Creek

Charles M Russell National Wildlife Refuge

Kill Woman Creek

Fort Peck Lake

Devils Creek

NWR 606

NWR 346

NWR 549

Lost Creek

Squaw Creek

NWR 323

Sun Prairie

Telegram Creek

NWR 412

NWR 416

NWR 344

NWR 504

UL Bend National Wildlife Refuge

Fourchette Creek

Hawley Creek

NWR 420

Soda Creek

NWR 315

NWR 315

NWR 411

NWR 504

NWR 909

Musselshell River

NWR 414

Crooked Creek

Beauchamp Creek

NWR 201

NWR 887

NWR 316

Crooked Creek Road

CK Creek

Charles M Russell National Wildlife Refuge

Fort Peck Lake

NWR 409

NWR 314

NWR 201

Sevenmile Creek

NWR 220

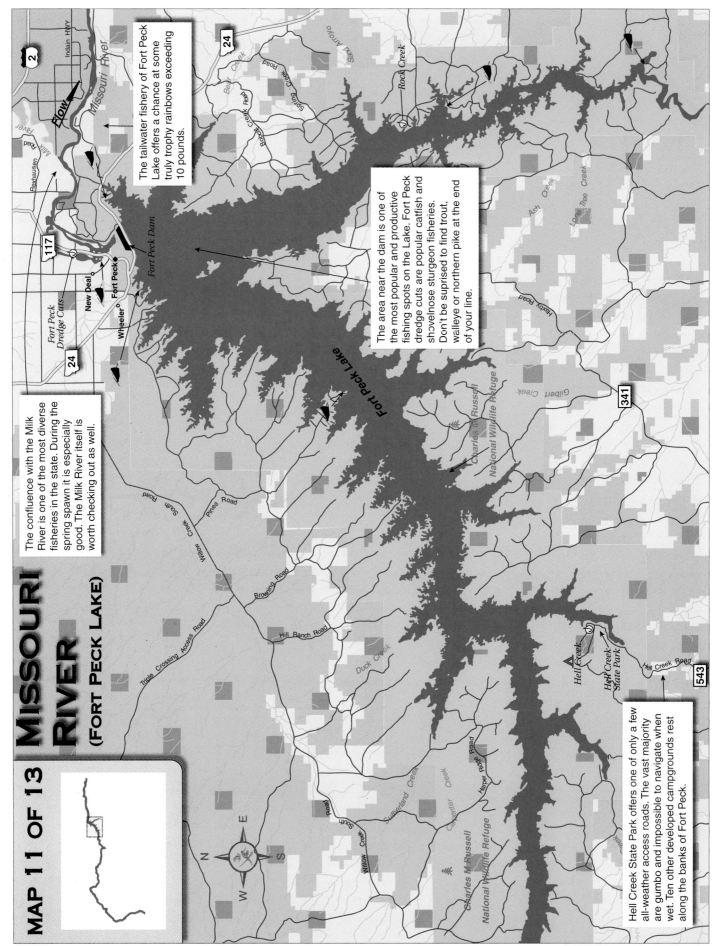

MAP 11 OF 13

MISSOURI RIVER
(FORT PECK LAKE)

The confluence with the Milk River is one of the most diverse fisheries in the state. During the spring spawn it is especially good. The Milk River itself is worth checking out as well.

The tailwater fishery of Fort Peck Lake offers a chance at some truly trophy rainbows exceeding 10 pounds.

The area near the dam is one of the most popular and productive fishing spots on the Lake. Fort Peck dredge cuts are popular catfish and shovelnose sturgeon fisheries. Don't be suprised to find trout, walleye or northern pike at the end of your line.

Hell Creek State Park offers one of only a few all-weather access roads. The vast majority are gumbo and impossible to navigate when wet. Ten other developed campgrounds rest along the banks of Fort Peck.

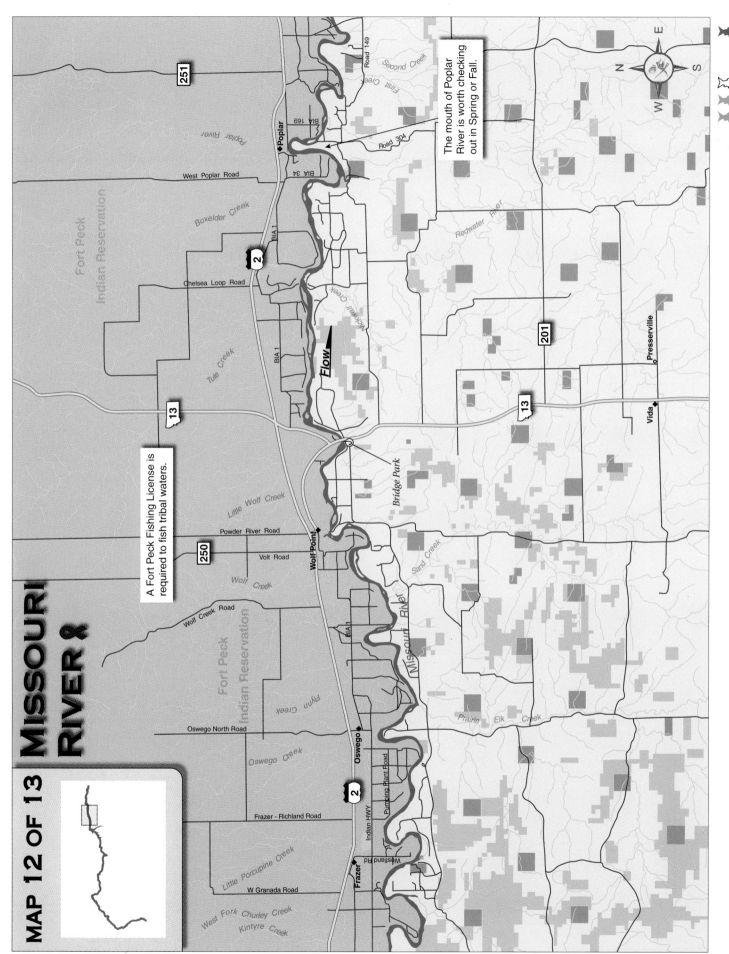

MAP 12 OF 13 MISSOURI RIVER 8

The mouth of Poplar River is worth checking out in Spring or Fall.

A Fort Peck Fishing License is required to fish tribal waters.

Fort Peck Indian Reservation

Fort Peck Indian Reservation

Poplar River

Poplar

West Poplar Road

Boxelder Creek

Chelsea Loop Road

Tule Creek

Little Wolf Creek

Powder River Road

Volt Road

Wolf Creek

Wolf Creek Road

Oswego North Road

Oswego Creek

Flynn Creek

Frazer - Richland Road

Little Porcupine Creek

W Granada Road

West Fork Churley Creek

Kintyre Creek

Second Creek

First Creek

Road 149

BIA 169

Road 304

Redwater River

BIA 34

BIA 1

BIA 1

Nickwall Creek

Flow

Bridge Park

Sand Creek

Missouri River

Prairie Elk Creek

Presserville

Vida

201

13

13

251

2

2

2

13

250

Wolf Point

Oswego

Frazer

Pumping Plant Road

Indian HWY

Westland Rd

© 2006 Wilderness Adventures Press, Inc.

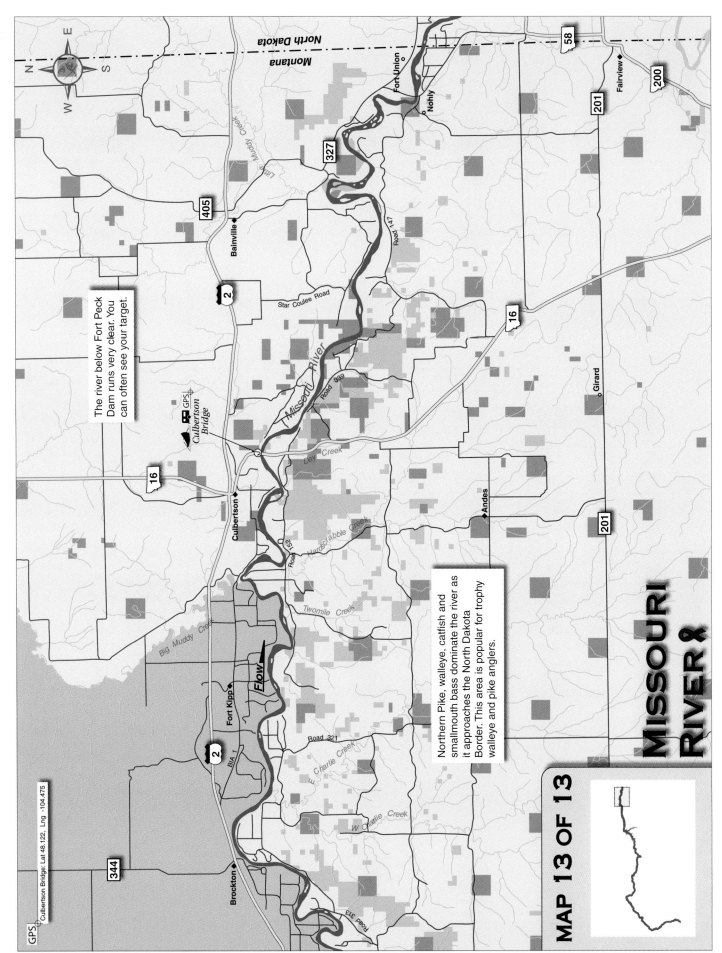

The river below Fort Peck Dam runs very clear. You can often see your target.

Northern Pike, walleye, catfish and smallmouth bass dominate the river as it approaches the North Dakota Border. This area is popular for trophy walleye and pike anglers.

MISSOURI RIVER

MAP 13 OF 13

GPS Culbertson Bridge: Lat 48.122; Lng -104.475

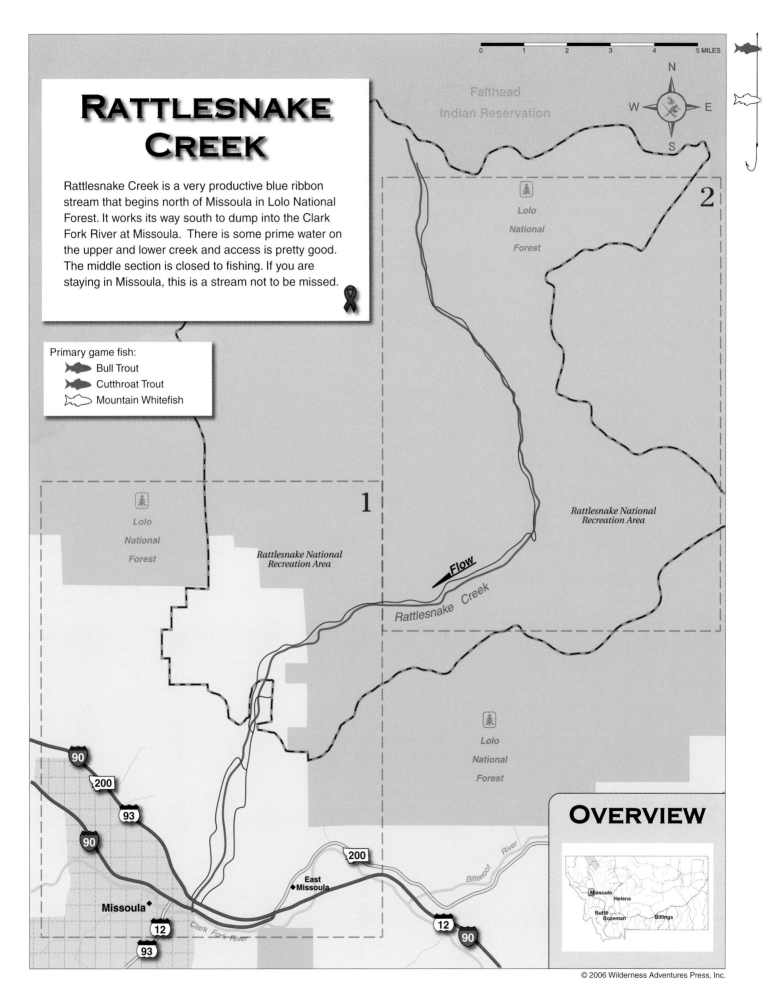

RATTLESNAKE CREEK

Rattlesnake Creek is a very productive blue ribbon stream that begins north of Missoula in Lolo National Forest. It works its way south to dump into the Clark Fork River at Missoula. There is some prime water on the upper and lower creek and access is pretty good. The middle section is closed to fishing. If you are staying in Missoula, this is a stream not to be missed.

Primary game fish:
Bull Trout
Cutthroat Trout
Mountain Whitefish

Flathead Indian Reservation

Lolo National Forest

2

1

Lolo National Forest

Rattlesnake National Recreation Area

Rattlesnake National Recreation Area

Flow

Rattlesnake Creek

Lolo National Forest

90
200
93
90
200
12
93

East Missoula

Missoula

Clark Fork River

Bitterroot River

12
90

OVERVIEW

Missoula Helena
Butte Bozeman Billings

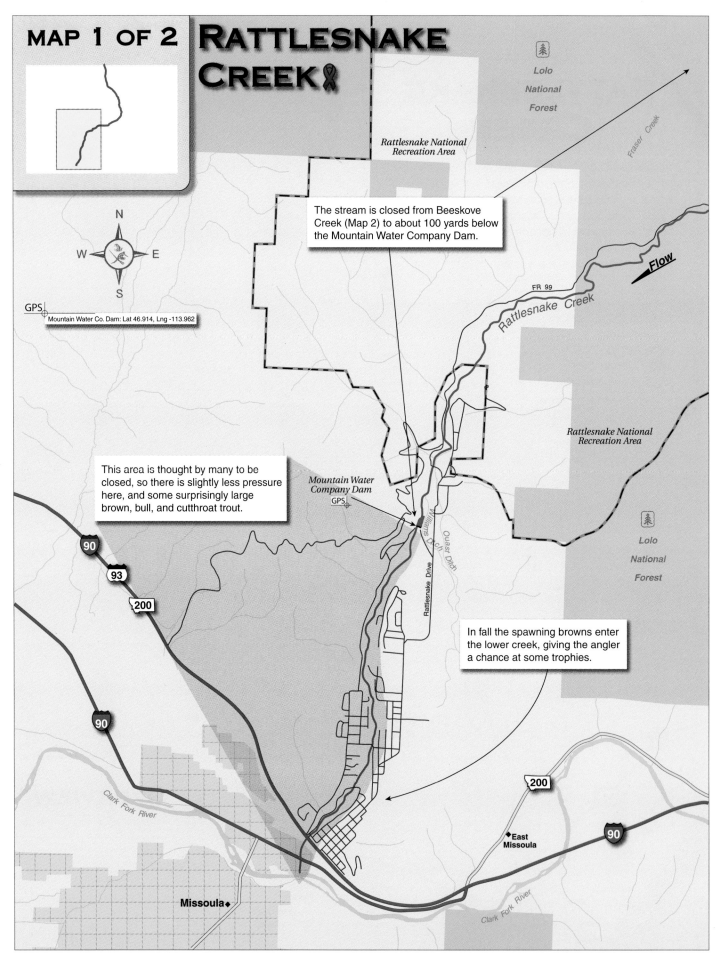

MAP 1 OF 2 RATTLESNAKE CREEK

Lolo National Forest

Rattlesnake National Recreation Area

Fraser Creek

The stream is closed from Beeskove Creek (Map 2) to about 100 yards below the Mountain Water Company Dam.

Flow

FR 99

Rattlesnake Creek

N
W E
S

GPS
Mountain Water Co. Dam: Lat 46.914, Lng -113.962

Rattlesnake National Recreation Area

This area is thought by many to be closed, so there is slightly less pressure here, and some surprisingly large brown, bull, and cutthroat trout.

Mountain Water Company Dam
GPS

Lolo National Forest

90
93
200

Williams Ditch

Ouast Ditch

Rattlesnake Drive

In fall the spawning browns enter the lower creek, giving the angler a chance at some trophies.

90

200

90

Clark Fork River

East Missoula

Missoula

Clark Fork River

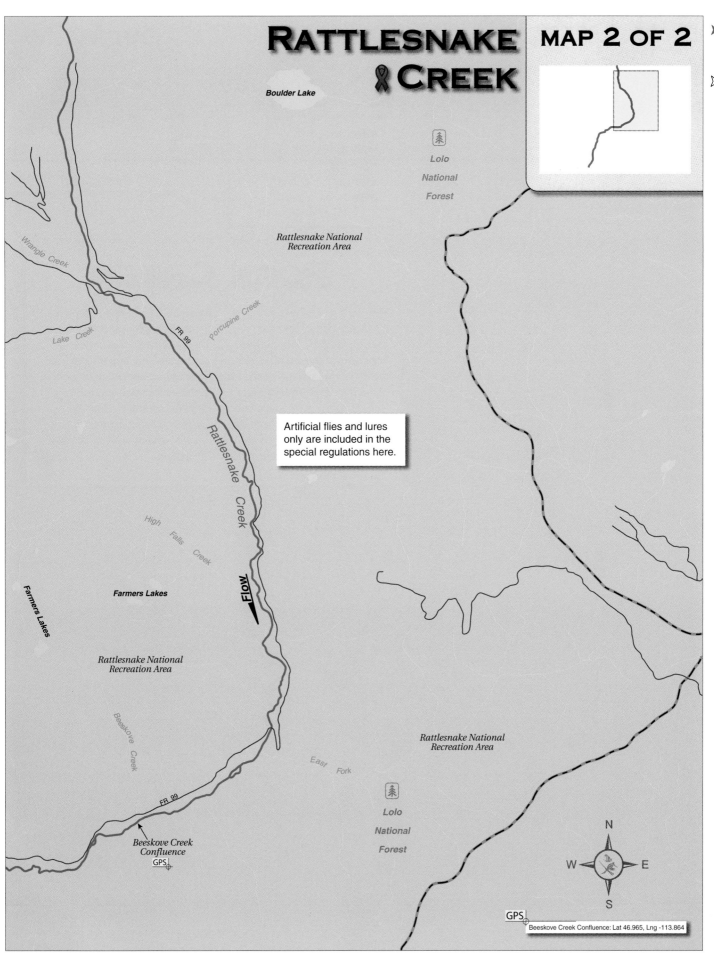

RATTLESNAKE CREEK

MAP 2 OF 2

Boulder Lake

Lolo

National

Forest

Rattlesnake National
Recreation Area

Wrangle Creek

Lake Creek

FR 99

Porcupine Creek

Rattlesnake Creek

Artificial flies and lures
only are included in the
special regulations here.

High Falls Creek

Farmers Lakes

Farmers Lakes

Flow

Rattlesnake National
Recreation Area

Beeskove Creek

Rattlesnake National
Recreation Area

East Fork

FR 99

Lolo

National

Forest

Beeskove Creek
Confluence
GPS

N

W   E

S

GPS

Beeskove Creek Confluence: Lat 46.965, Lng -113.864

© 2006 Wilderness Adventures Press, Inc.

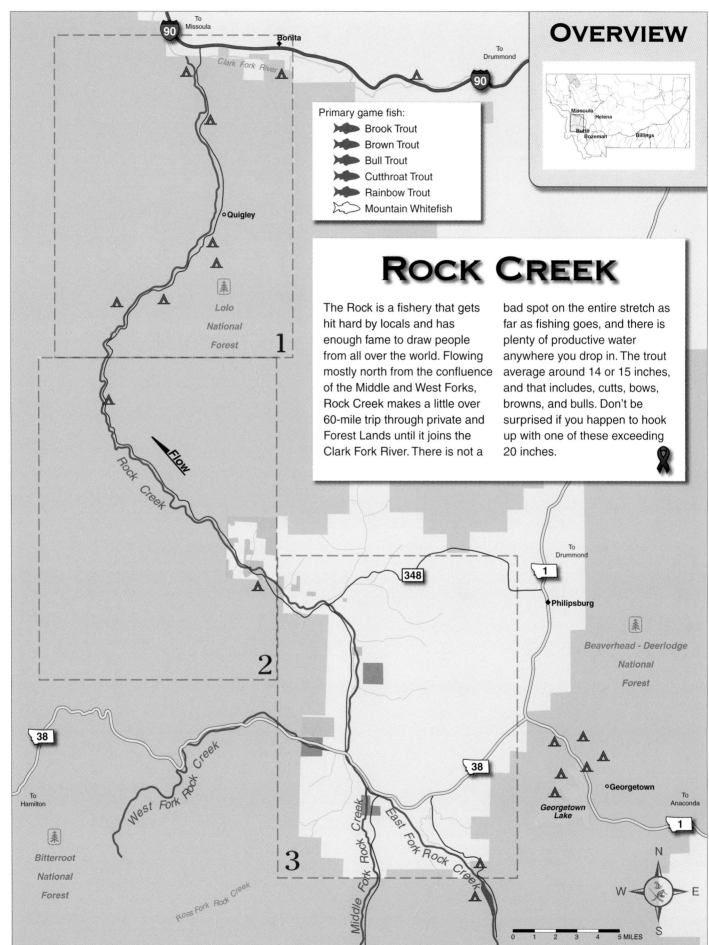

OVERVIEW

Primary game fish:
- Brook Trout
- Brown Trout
- Bull Trout
- Cutthroat Trout
- Rainbow Trout
- Mountain Whitefish

ROCK CREEK

The Rock is a fishery that gets hit hard by locals and has enough fame to draw people from all over the world. Flowing mostly north from the confluence of the Middle and West Forks, Rock Creek makes a little over 60-mile trip through private and Forest Lands until it joins the Clark Fork River. There is not a bad spot on the entire stretch as far as fishing goes, and there is plenty of productive water anywhere you drop in. The trout average around 14 or 15 inches, and that includes, cutts, bows, browns, and bulls. Don't be surprised if you happen to hook up with one of these exceeding 20 inches.

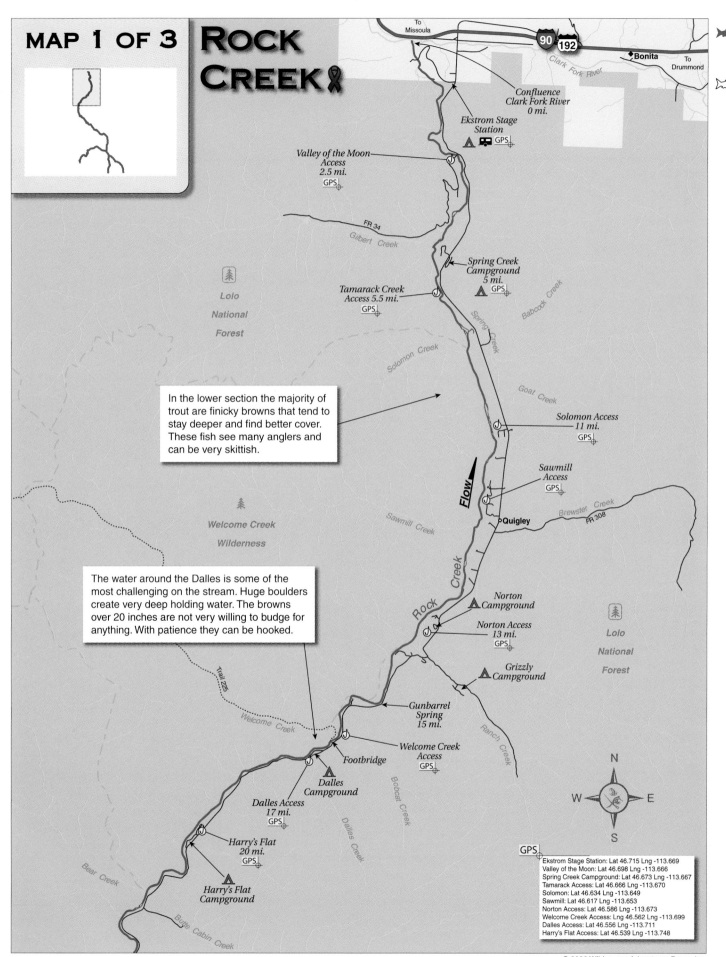

MAP 1 OF 3 ROCK CREEK

To Missoula

90 192

Clark Fork River

Bonita

To Drummond

Confluence
Clark Fork River
0 mi.

Ekstrom Stage
Station
GPS

Valley of the Moon
Access
2.5 mi.
GPS

FR 34

Gilbert Creek

Lolo

National

Forest

Spring Creek
Campground
5 mi.
GPS

Babcock Creek

Tamarack Creek
Access 5.5 mi.
GPS

Spring Creek

Solomon Creek

Goat Creek

Solomon Access
11 mi.
GPS

In the lower section the majority of
trout are finicky browns that tend to
stay deeper and find better cover.
These fish see many anglers and
can be very skittish.

Sawmill
Access
GPS

Flow

Brewster Creek

FR 308

Quigley

Welcome Creek

Wilderness

Sawmill Creek

Rock Creek

The water around the Dalles is some of the
most challenging on the stream. Huge boulders
create very deep holding water. The browns
over 20 inches are not very willing to budge for
anything. With patience they can be hooked.

Norton
Campground

Norton Access
13 mi.
GPS

Lolo

National

Forest

Grizzly
Campground

Trail 225

Welcome Creek

Gunbarrel
Spring
15 mi.

Welcome Creek
Access
GPS

Ranch Creek

Footbridge

Dalles
Campground

Dalles Access
17 mi.
GPS

Bobcat Creek

Dalles Creek

N

W   E

S

GPS

Bear Creek

Harry's Flat
20 mi.
GPS

Harry's Flat
Campground

Butte Cabin Creek

Ekstrom Stage Station: Lat 46.715 Lng -113.669
Valley of the Moon: Lat 46.698 Lng -113.666
Spring Creek Campground: Lat 46.673 Lng -113.667
Tamarack Access: Lat 46.666 Lng -113.670
Solomon: Lat 46.634 Lng -113.649
Sawmill: Lat 46.617 Lng -113.653
Norton Access: Lat 46.586 Lng -113.673
Welcome Creek Access: Lng 46.562 Lng -113.699
Dalles Access: Lat 46.556 Lng -113.711
Harry's Flat Access: Lat 46.539 Lng -113.748

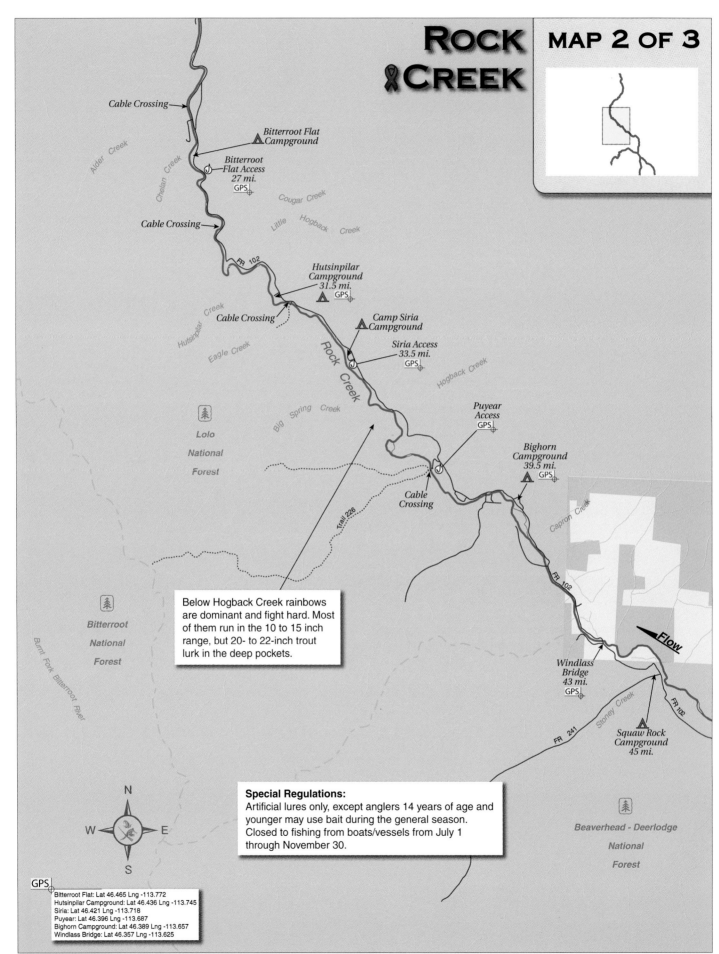

ROCK CREEK

MAP 2 OF 3

Cable Crossing

Bitterroot Flat Campground

Alder Creek

Chelan Creek

Bitterroot Flat Access 27 mi.
GPS

Cougar Creek

Little Hogback Creek

Cable Crossing

FR 102

Hutsinpilar Campground 31.5 mi.
GPS

Hutsinpilar Creek

Cable Crossing

Camp Siria Campground

Eagle Creek

Rock Creek

Siria Access 33.5 mi.
GPS

Hogback Creek

Lolo National Forest

Big Spring Creek

Puyear Access
GPS

Bighorn Campground 39.5 mi.
GPS

Capron Creek

Trail 226

Cable Crossing

FR 102

Bitterroot National Forest

Burnt Fork Bitterroot River

Flow

Below Hogback Creek rainbows are dominant and fight hard. Most of them run in the 10 to 15 inch range, but 20- to 22-inch trout lurk in the deep pockets.

Windlass Bridge 43 mi.
GPS

FR 102

FR 241

Stoney Creek

Squaw Rock Campground 45 mi.

N
W   E
S

Special Regulations:
Artificial lures only, except anglers 14 years of age and younger may use bait during the general season. Closed to fishing from boats/vessels from July 1 through November 30.

Beaverhead - Deerlodge National Forest

GPS

Bitterroot Flat: Lat 46.465 Lng -113.772
Hutsinpilar Campground: Lat 46.436 Lng -113.745
Siria: Lat 46.421 Lng -113.718
Puyear: Lat 46.396 Lng -113.687
Bighorn Campground: Lat 46.389 Lng -113.657
Windlass Bridge: Lat 46.357 Lng -113.625

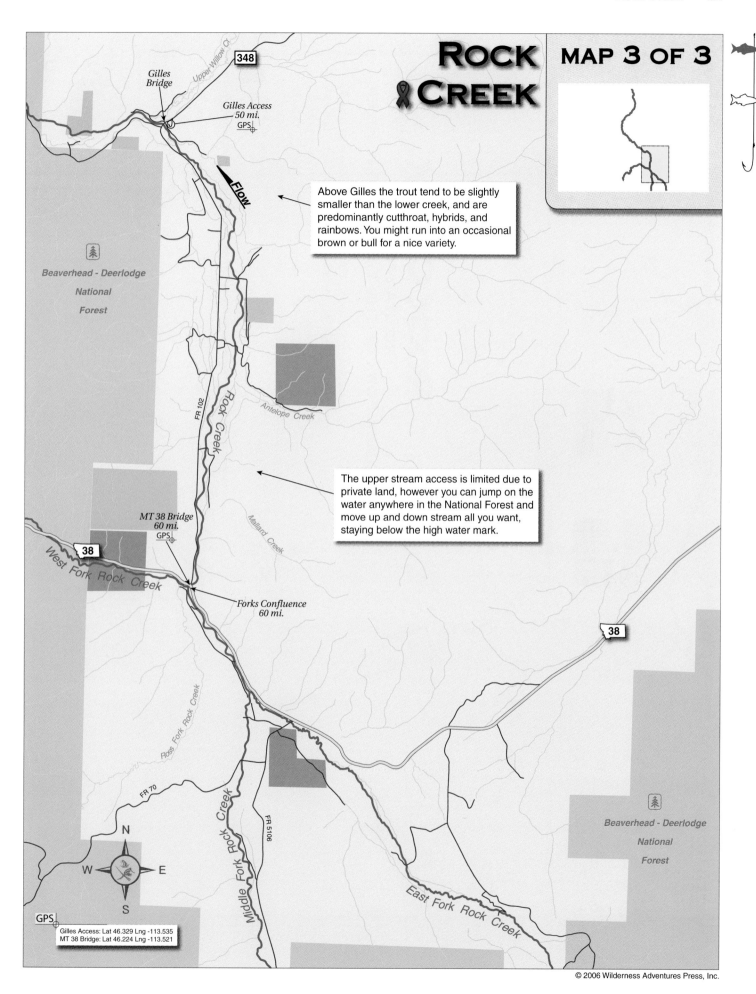

ROCK CREEK

MAP 3 OF 3

Above Gilles the trout tend to be slightly smaller than the lower creek, and are predominantly cutthroat, hybrids, and rainbows. You might run into an occasional brown or bull for a nice variety.

The upper stream access is limited due to private land, however you can jump on the water anywhere in the National Forest and move up and down stream all you want, staying below the high water mark.

Gilles Bridge

Gilles Access 50 mi. GPS

348

Upper Willow Cr.

Flow

Beaverhead - Deerlodge National Forest

FR 102

Rock Creek

Antelope Creek

Mallard Creek

MT 38 Bridge 60 mi. GPS

West Fork Rock Creek

38

Forks Confluence 60 mi.

Ross Fork Rock Creek

FR 70

Middle Fork Rock Creek

FR 5106

38

Beaverhead - Deerlodge National Forest

East Fork Rock Creek

N W E S

GPS

Gilles Access: Lat 46.329 Lng -113.535
MT 38 Bridge: Lat 46.224 Lng -113.521

© 2006 Wilderness Adventures Press, Inc.

ROCK CREEK

TRIBUTARY OF THE
CLARK FORK OF THE YELLOWSTONE RIVER

Flowing out of one of the most scenic places in the state, Rock Creek works its way out of the Absaroka-Beartooth Wilderness, through Red Lodge and out into the rolling plains of eastern Montana. It merges with the Clark Fork of the Yellowstone near Silesta, south of Laurel. The river fishes very well in its upper reaches, and in good years fishes well below too. There is very good access, and it's a drive that people come from all over to make.

Primary game fish:

Brook Trout
Brown Trout
Rainbow Trout

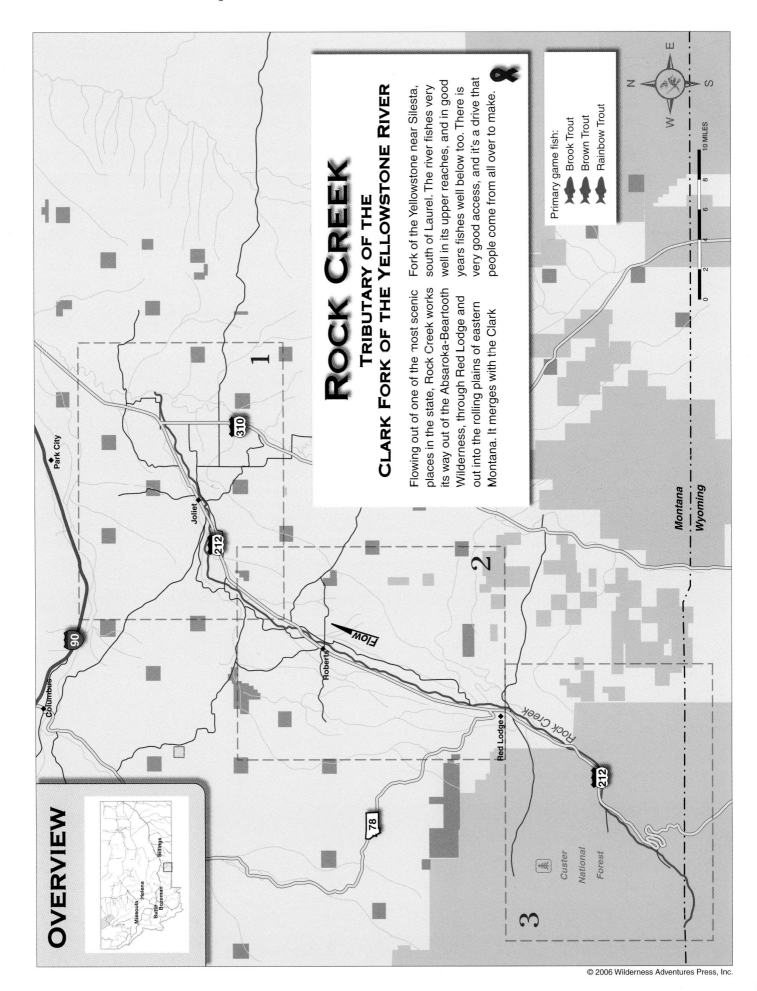

OVERVIEW

© 2006 Wilderness Adventures Press, Inc.

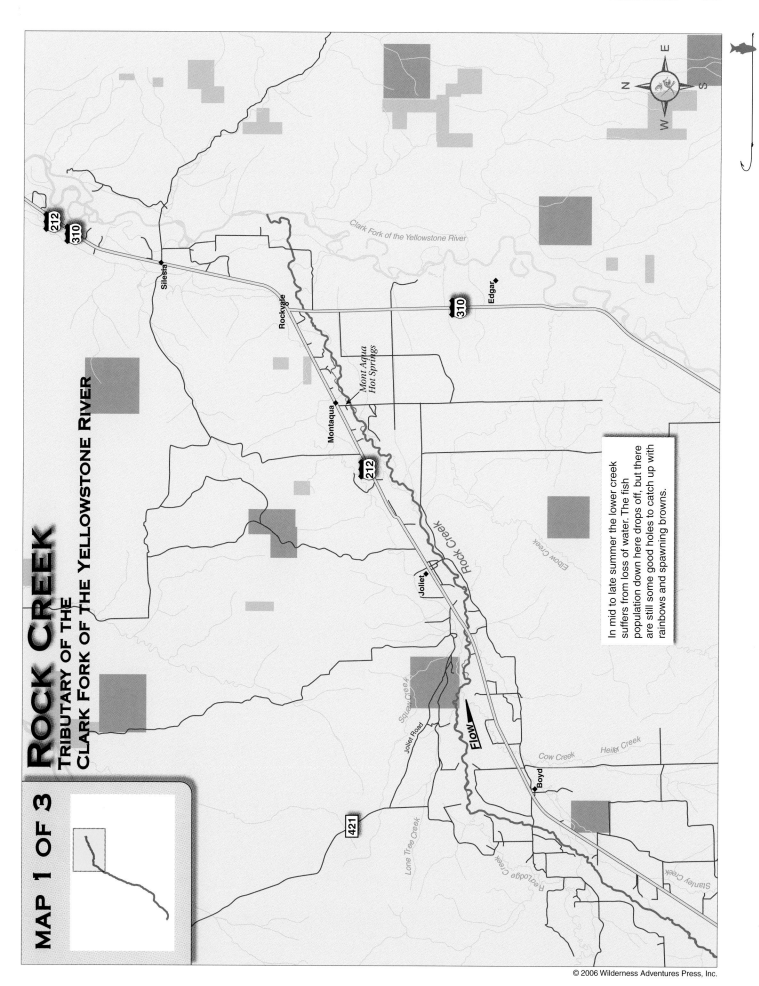

MAP 1 OF 3

ROCK CREEK

TRIBUTARY OF THE CLARK FORK OF THE YELLOWSTONE RIVER

In mid to late summer the lower creek suffers from loss of water. The fish population down here drops off, but there are still some good holes to catch up with rainbows and spawning browns.

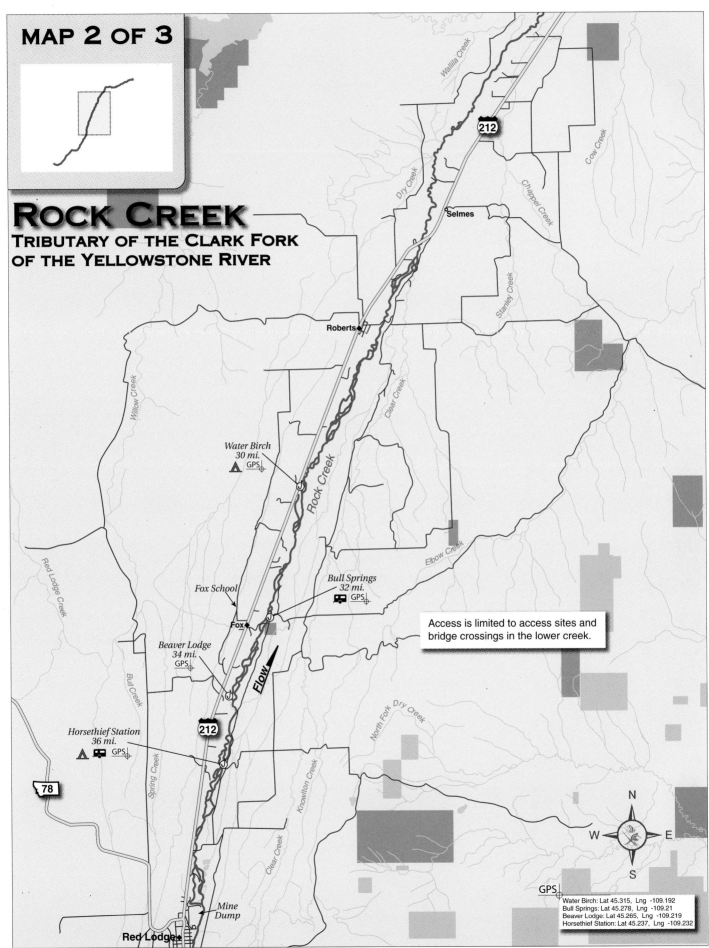

MAP 2 OF 3

ROCK CREEK
TRIBUTARY OF THE CLARK FORK
OF THE YELLOWSTONE RIVER

212

Walilla Creek

Cow Creek

Chappel Creek

Dry Creek

Selmes

Stanley Creek

Roberts

Clear Creek

Willow Creek

Rock Creek

Water Birch
30 mi.
GPS

Elbow Creek

Fox School

Bull Springs
32 mi.
GPS

Red Lodge Creek

Fox

Beaver Lodge
34 mi.
GPS

Flow

Access is limited to access sites and
bridge crossings in the lower creek.

Bull Creek

North Fork Dry Creek

212

Horsethief Station
36 mi.
GPS

78

Spring Creek

Clear Creek

Knowlton Creek

N
W   E
S

GPS

Water Birch: Lat 45.315, Lng -109.192
Bull Springs: Lat 45.278, Lng -109.21
Beaver Lodge: Lat 45.265, Lng -109.219
Horsethief Station: Lat 45.237, Lng -109.232

Mine
Dump

Red Lodge

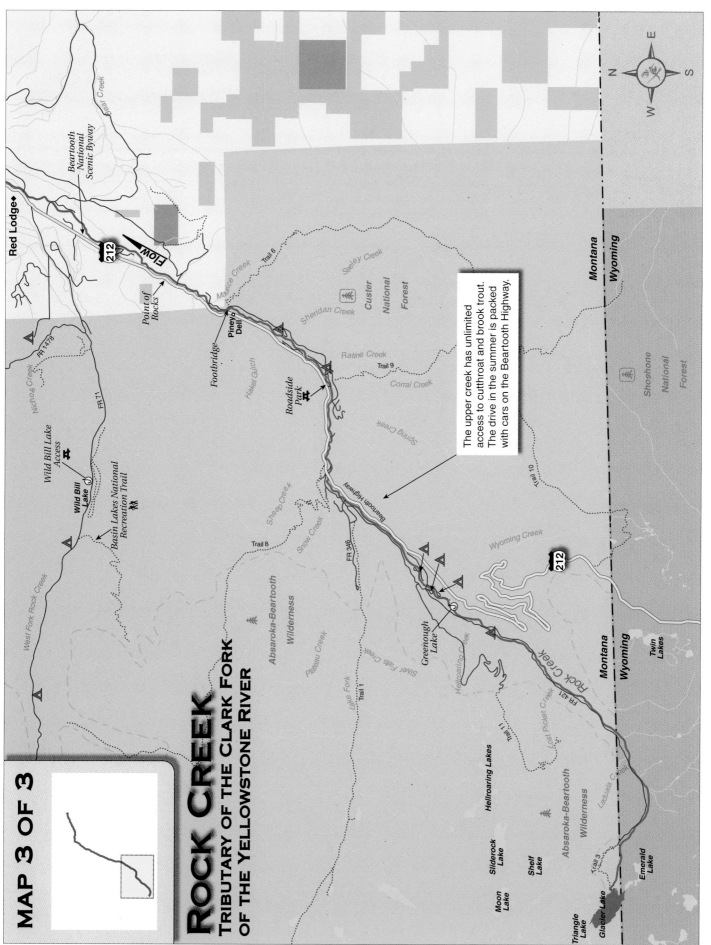

MAP 3 OF 3

ROCK CREEK
TRIBUTARY OF THE CLARK FORK
OF THE YELLOWSTONE RIVER

Red Lodge

Beartooth National Scenic Byway

212

FLOW

Point of Rocks

Bear Creek

FR 1478

Nichos Creek

FR 71

Wild Bill Lake Access

Wild Bill Lake

Basin Lakes National Recreation Trail

West Fork Rock Creek

Footbridge

Piney Dell

Malice Creek

Trail 6

Hakel Gulch

Roadside Park

Sheridan Creek

Seeley Creek

Custer National Forest

Ratine Creek

Trail 9

Corral Creek

Spring Creek

The upper creek has unlimited access to cutthroat and brook trout. The drive in the summer is packed with cars on the Beartooth Highway.

Beartooth Highway

Trail 10

Shoshone National Forest

Sheep Creek

Snow Creek

Trail 8

Absaroka-Beartooth Wilderness

FR 346

Plateau Creek

Lake Fork

Trail 1

Silver Falls Creek

Greenough Lake

Hellroaring Creek

Wyoming Creek

212

Montana

Wyoming

Rock Creek

Twin Lakes

FR 421

Lost Picket Creek

Trail 1

Hellroaring Lakes

Moon Lake

Sliderock Lake

Shelf Lake

Absaroka-Beartooth Wilderness

Labuala Creek

Trail 3

Triangle Lake

Glacier Lake

Emerald Lake

Montana
Wyoming

N E S W

OVERVIEW

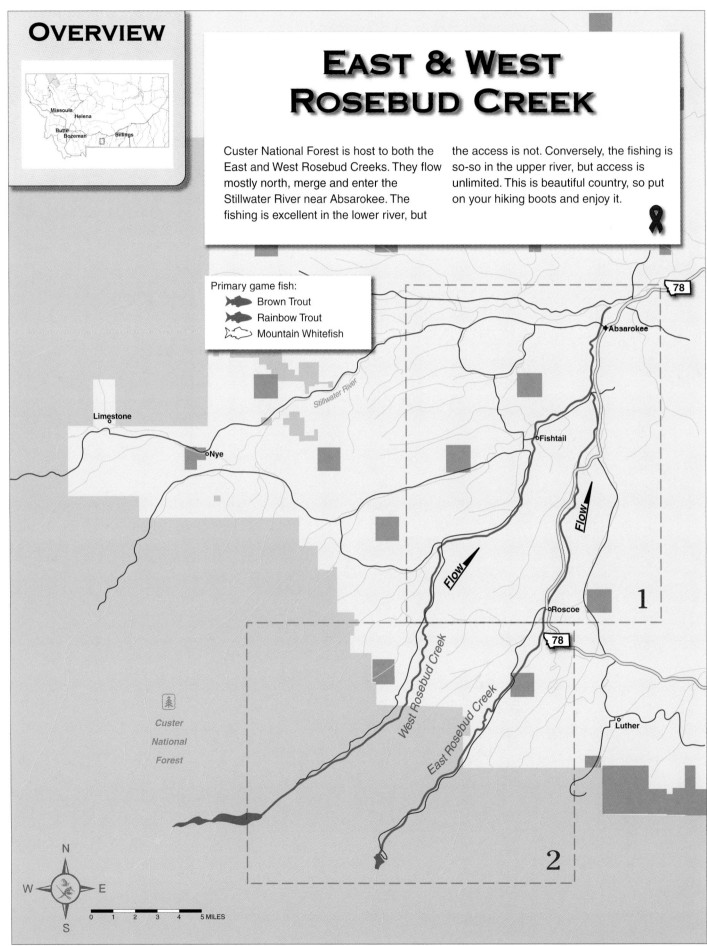

EAST & WEST ROSEBUD CREEK

Custer National Forest is host to both the East and West Rosebud Creeks. They flow mostly north, merge and enter the Stillwater River near Absarokee. The fishing is excellent in the lower river, but the access is not. Conversely, the fishing is so-so in the upper river, but access is unlimited. This is beautiful country, so put on your hiking boots and enjoy it.

Primary game fish:
- Brown Trout
- Rainbow Trout
- Mountain Whitefish

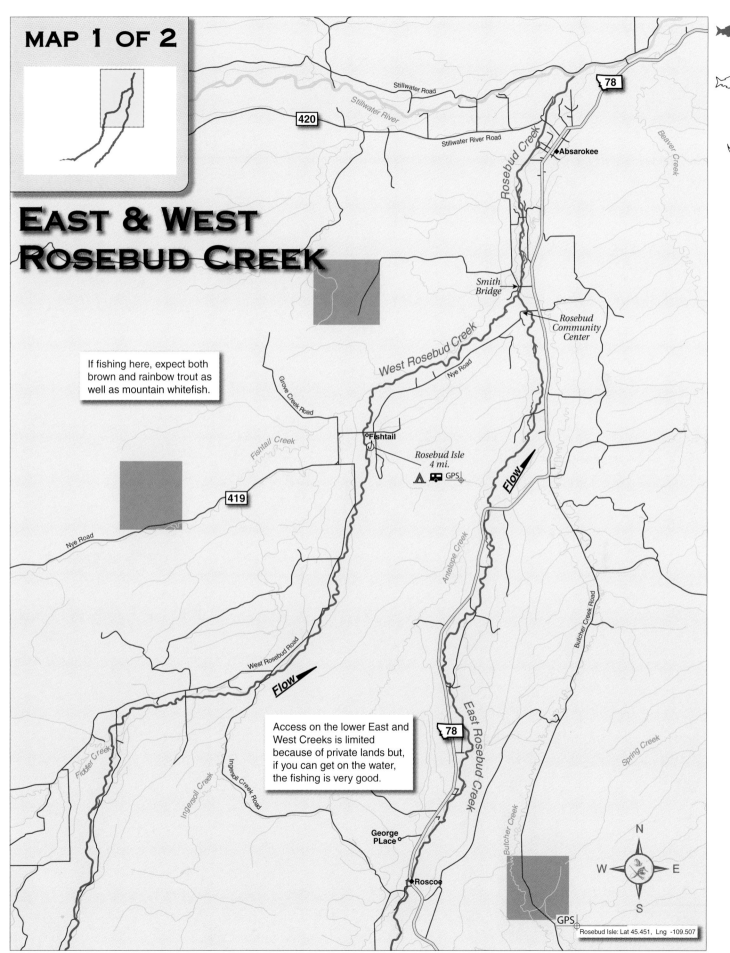

MAP 1 OF 2

EAST & WEST ROSEBUD CREEK

If fishing here, expect both brown and rainbow trout as well as mountain whitefish.

Access on the lower East and West Creeks is limited because of private lands but, if you can get on the water, the fishing is very good.

Stillwater Road

Stillwater River

420

Stillwater River Road

Rosebud Creek

78

Absarokee

Smith Bridge

Rosebud Community Center

West Rosebud Creek

Nye Road

Grove Creek Road

Fishtail Creek

Fishtail

Rosebud Isle 4 mi.

GPS

419

Nye Road

Antelope Creek

Beaver Creek

Flow

West Rosebud Road

Flow

Fiddler Creek

Ingersoll Creek

Ingersoll Creek Road

78

East Rosebud Creek

Butcher Creek Road

Spring Creek

Butcher Creek

George PLace

Roscoe

N

W   E

S

GPS

Rosebud Isle: Lat 45.451, Lng -109.507

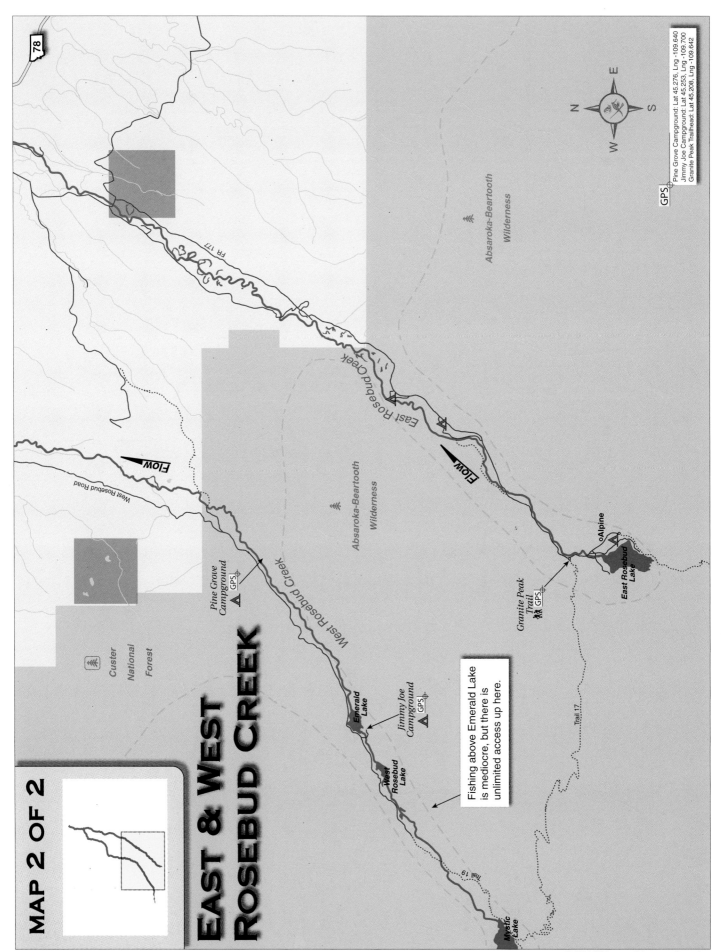

MAP 2 OF 2

EAST & WEST ROSEBUD CREEK

78

Flow

West Rosebud Road

FR 177

East Rosebud Creek

West Rosebud Creek

Flow

Custer National Forest

Absaroka-Beartooth Wilderness

Absaroka-Beartooth Wilderness

Pine Grove Campground GPS

Jimmy Joe Campground GPS

Emerald Lake

West Rosebud Lake

Mystic Lake

Trail 19

Trail 17

Granite Peak Trail GPS

oAlpine

East Rosebud Lake

Fishing above Emerald Lake is mediocre, but there is unlimited access up here.

N
W   E
S

Pine Grove Campground: Lat 45.276, Lng -109.640
Jimmy Joe Campground: Lat 45.253, Lng -109.700
Granite Peak Trailhead: Lat 45.208, Lng -109.642

GPS

© 2006 Wilderness Adventures Press, Inc.

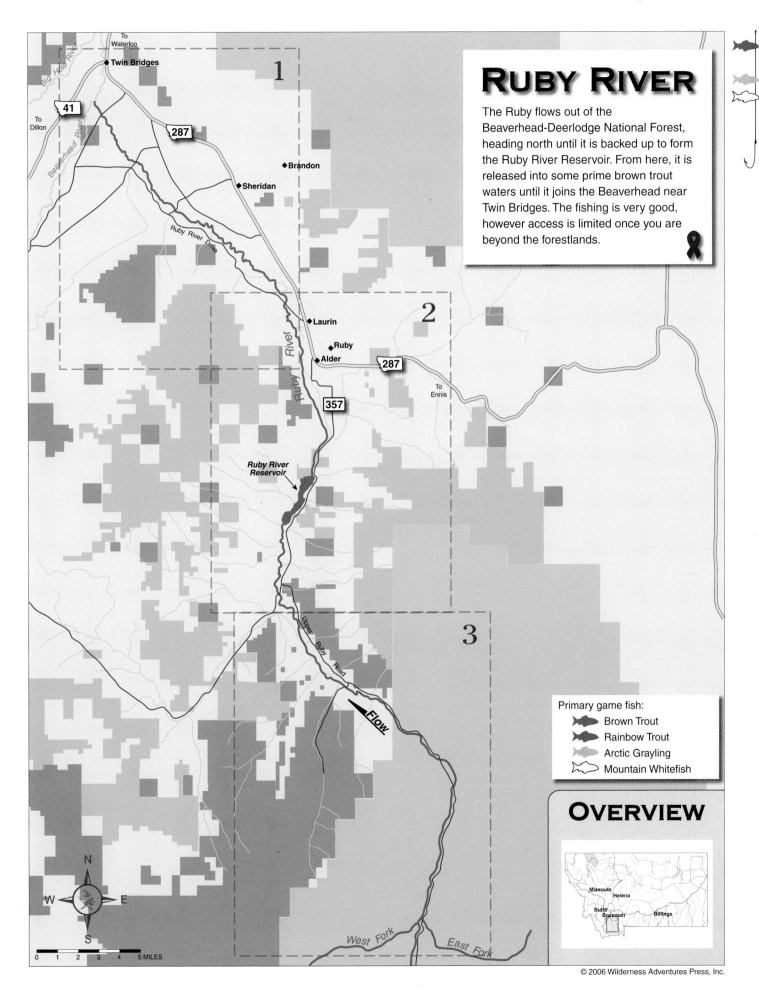

RUBY RIVER

The Ruby flows out of the Beaverhead-Deerlodge National Forest, heading north until it is backed up to form the Ruby River Reservoir. From here, it is released into some prime brown trout waters until it joins the Beaverhead near Twin Bridges. The fishing is very good, however access is limited once you are beyond the forestlands.

To Waterloo

Twin Bridges

To Dillon

41

287

Brandon

Sheridan

Ruby River Drive

1

Laurin

2

Ruby

Alder

287

To Ennis

357

Ruby River Reservoir

Upper Ruby Road

3

Flow

Primary game fish:
Brown Trout
Rainbow Trout
Arctic Grayling
Mountain Whitefish

OVERVIEW

Missoula
Helena
Butte
Bozeman
Billings

West Fork   East Fork

N
W   E
S

0 1 2 3 4 5 MILES

© 2006 Wilderness Adventures Press, Inc.

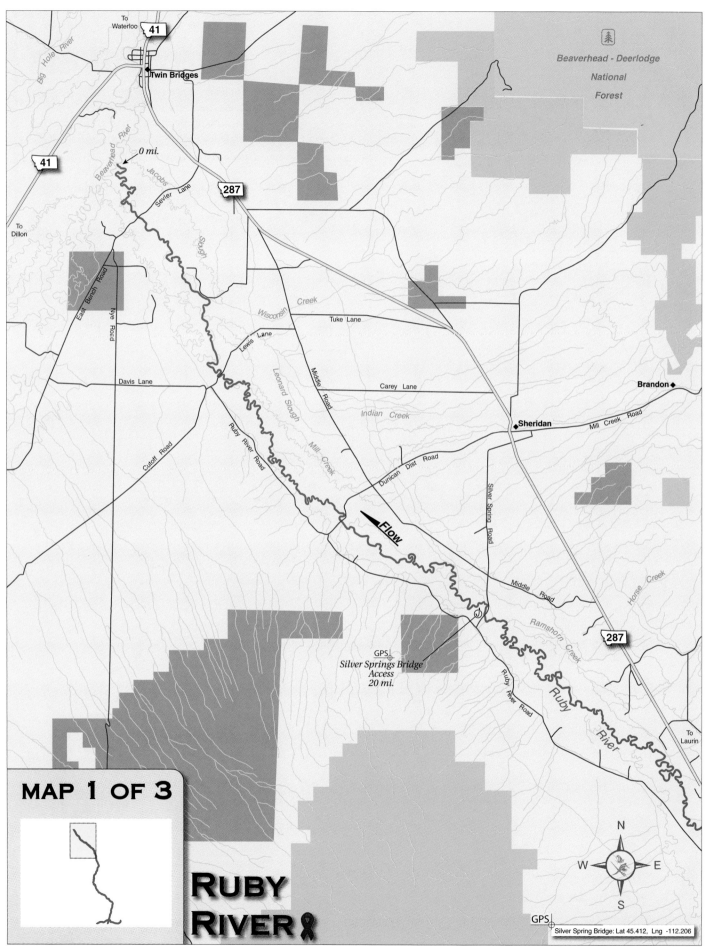

To Waterloo

41

To Dillon

Big Hole River

Twin Bridges

Beaverhead River

0 mi.

41

Jacobs

Sevler Lane

Slough

East Bench Road

Nye Road

Davis Lane

287

Wisconsin Creek

Tuke Lane

Lewis Lane

Middle Road

Leonard Slough

Carey Lane

Indian Creek

Ruby River Road

Mill Creek

Cutoff Road

Duncan Dist Road

Flow

Beaverhead - Deerlodge
National
Forest

Brandon

Sheridan

Mill Creek Road

Silver Spring Road

Middle Road

Horse Creek

287

GPS
Silver Springs Bridge
Access
20 mi.

Ramshorn Creek

Ruby River Road

Ruby River

To Laurin

N
W   E
S

MAP 1 OF 3

RUBY
RIVER

GPS
Silver Spring Bridge: Lat 45.412, Lng -112.206

© 2006 Wilderness Adventures Press, Inc.

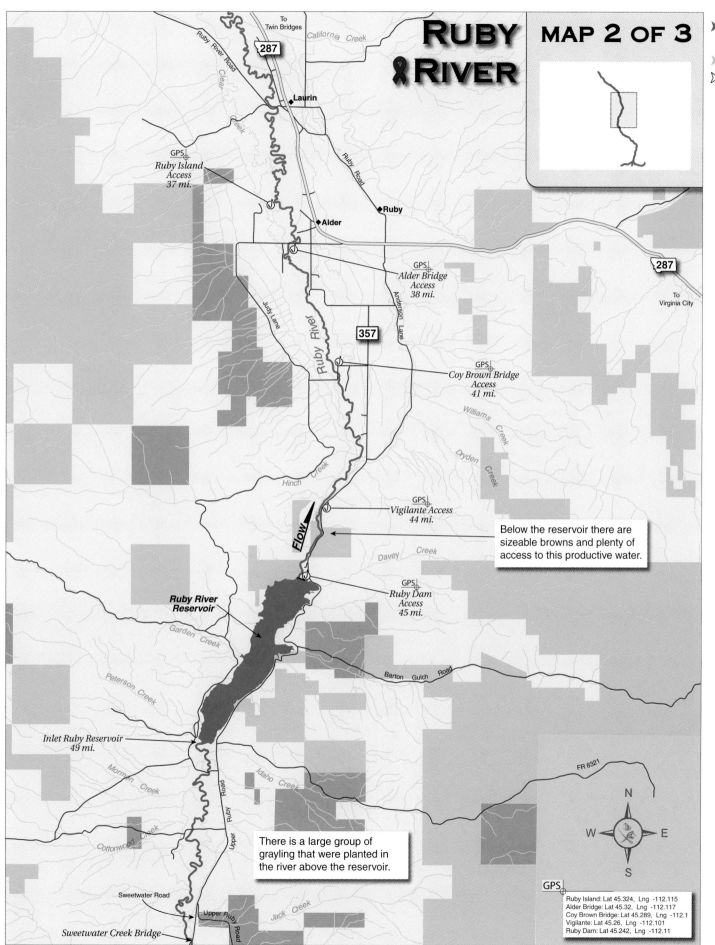

RUBY RIVER

MAP 2 OF 3

To Twin Bridges

California Creek

287

Ruby River Road

Clear Creek

Laurin

GPS
Ruby Island
Access
37 mi.

Ruby Road

Ruby

Alder

GPS
Alder Bridge
Access
38 mi.

Anderson Lane

Judy Lane

Ruby River

357

GPS
Coy Brown Bridge
Access
41 mi.

Williams Creek

Dryden Creek

Hinch Creek

Flow

GPS
Vigilante Access
44 mi.

Davey Creek

Below the reservoir there are sizeable browns and plenty of access to this productive water.

Ruby River Reservoir

GPS
Ruby Dam
Access
45 mi.

Garden Creek

Barton Gulch Road

Peterson Creek

Inlet Ruby Reservoir
49 mi.

Mormon Creek

Idaho Creek

Upper Ruby Road

FR 8321

There is a large group of grayling that were planted in the river above the reservoir.

Cottonwood Creek

N
W   E
S

Sweetwater Road

Jack Creek

Sweetwater Creek Bridge

287

To Virginia City

GPS
Ruby Island: Lat 45.324, Lng -112.115
Alder Bridge: Lat 45.32, Lng -112.117
Coy Brown Bridge: Lat 45.289, Lng -112.1
Vigilante: Lat 45.26, Lng -112.101
Ruby Dam: Lat 45.242, Lng -112.11

© 2006 Wilderness Adventures Press, Inc.

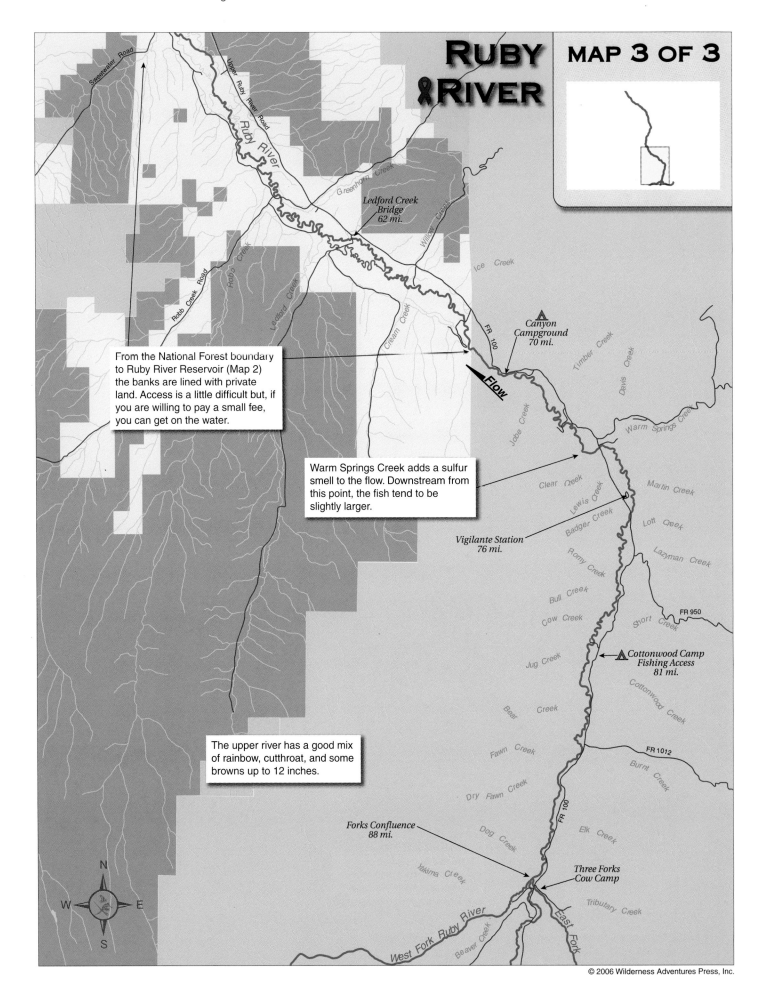

RUBY RIVER

MAP 3 OF 3

Ledford Creek
Bridge
62 mi.

Canyon
Campground
70 mi.

Flow

From the National Forest boundary
to Ruby River Reservoir (Map 2)
the banks are lined with private
land. Access is a little difficult but, if
you are willing to pay a small fee,
you can get on the water.

Warm Springs Creek adds a sulfur
smell to the flow. Downstream from
this point, the fish tend to be
slightly larger.

Vigilante Station
76 mi.

Cottonwood Camp
Fishing Access
81 mi.

The upper river has a good mix
of rainbow, cutthroat, and some
browns up to 12 inches.

Forks Confluence
88 mi.

Three Forks
Cow Camp

West Fork Ruby River

Beaver Creek

East Fork

Tributary Creek

N
W   E
S

OVERVIEW

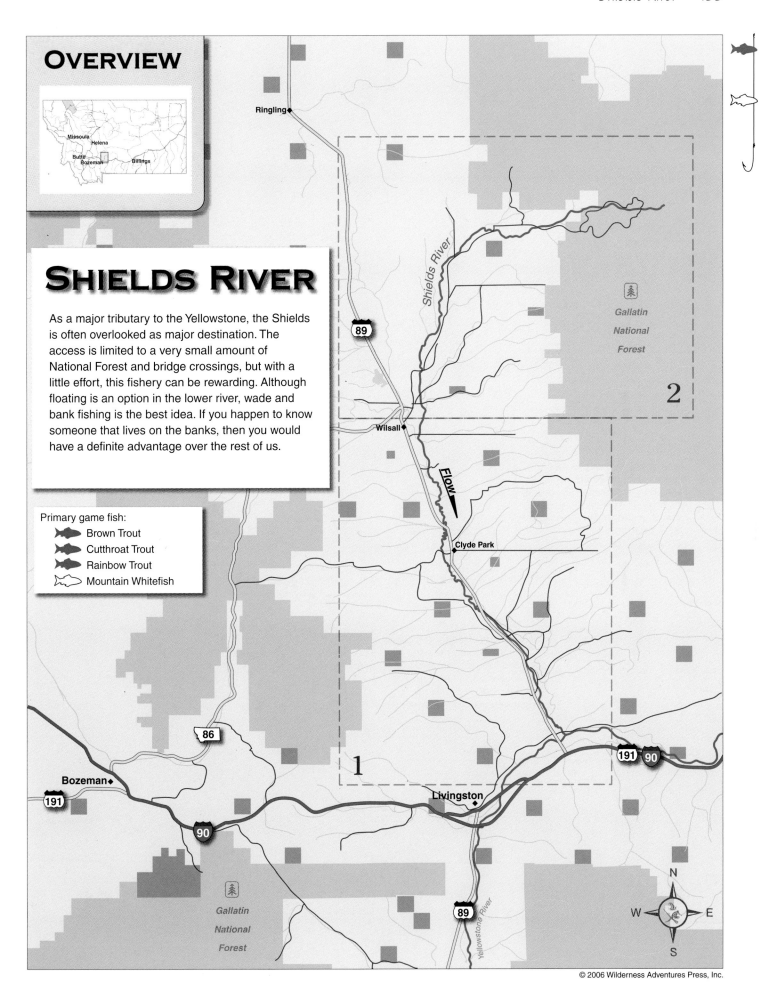

SHIELDS RIVER

As a major tributary to the Yellowstone, the Shields is often overlooked as major destination. The access is limited to a very small amount of National Forest and bridge crossings, but with a little effort, this fishery can be rewarding. Although floating is an option in the lower river, wade and bank fishing is the best idea. If you happen to know someone that lives on the banks, then you would have a definite advantage over the rest of us.

Primary game fish:
- Brown Trout
- Cutthroat Trout
- Rainbow Trout
- Mountain Whitefish

Ringling

Shields River

89

Gallatin National Forest

2

Wilsall

Flow

Clyde Park

86

1

Bozeman

191

90

Livingston

191 90

89

Yellowstone River

Gallatin National Forest

N
W E
S

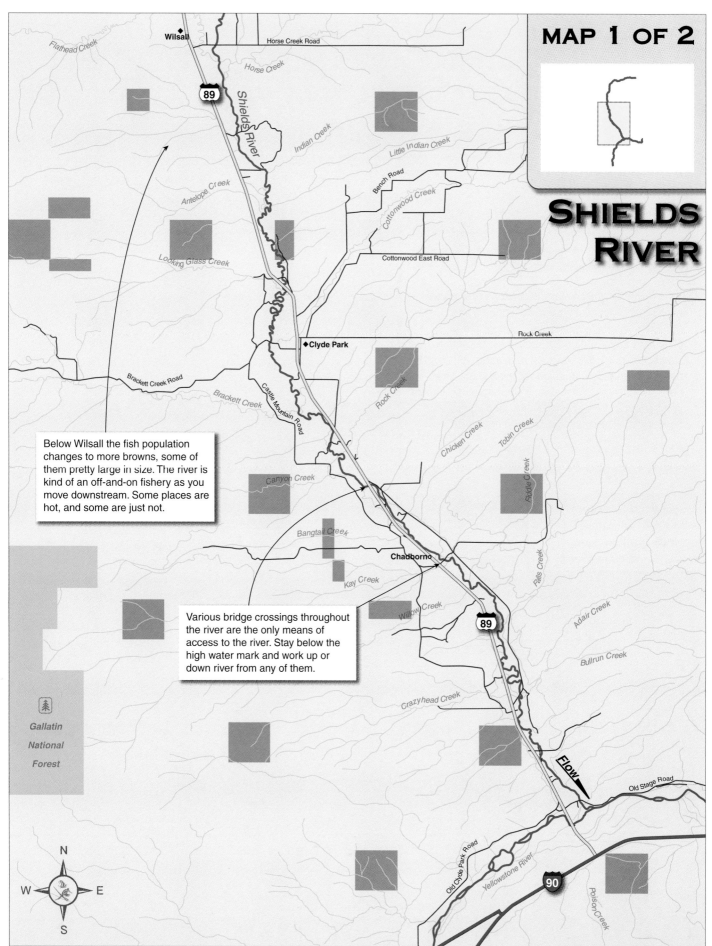

MAP 1 OF 2

SHIELDS RIVER

Wilsall

Horse Creek Road

Horse Creek

89

Shields River

Indian Creek

Little Indian Creek

Bench Road

Cottonwood Creek

Antelope Creek

Cottonwood East Road

Looking Glass Creek

Rock Creek

Clyde Park

Rock Creek

Brackett Creek Road

Chicken Creek

Tobin Creek

Brackett Creek

Castle Mountain Road

Fiddle Creek

Below Wilsall the fish population changes to more browns, some of them pretty large in size. The river is kind of an off-and-on fishery as you move downstream. Some places are hot, and some are just not.

Canyon Creek

Bangtail Creek

Chadborno

Falls Creek

Kay Creek

Various bridge crossings throughout the river are the only means of access to the river. Stay below the high water mark and work up or down river from any of them.

Willow Creek

89

Adair Creek

Bullrun Creek

Crazyhead Creek

Gallatin

National

Forest

Flow

Old Stage Road

N

W E

S

Old Clyde Park Road

Yellowstone River

90

Poison Creek

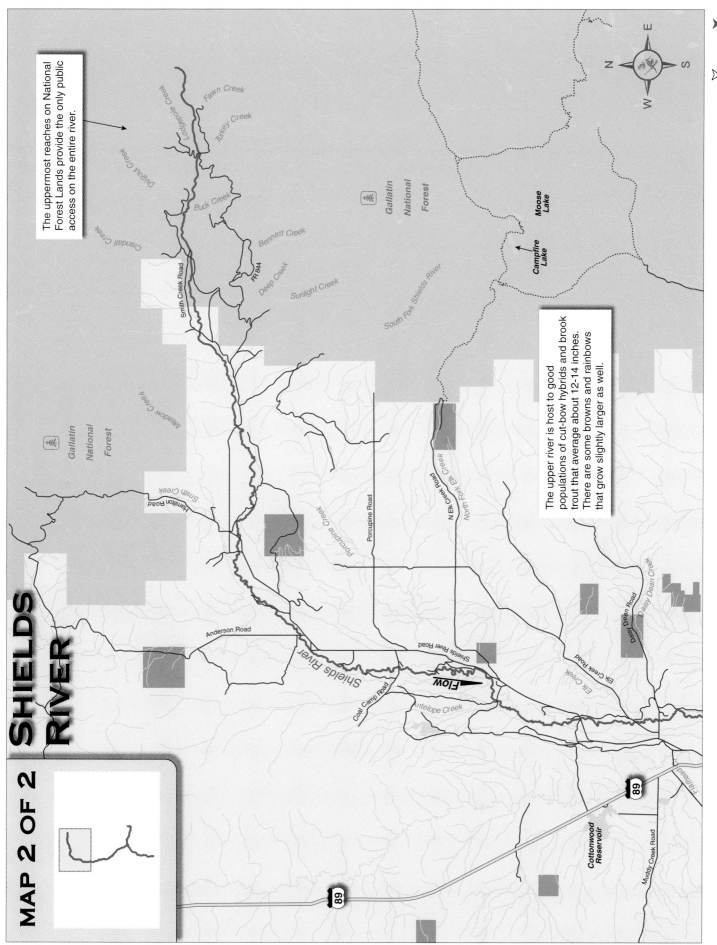

MAP 2 OF 2

SHIELDS RIVER

The uppermost reaches on National Forest Lands provide the only public access on the entire river.

The upper river is host to good populations of cut-bow hybrids and brook trout that average about 12-14 inches. There are some browns and rainbows that grow slightly larger as well.

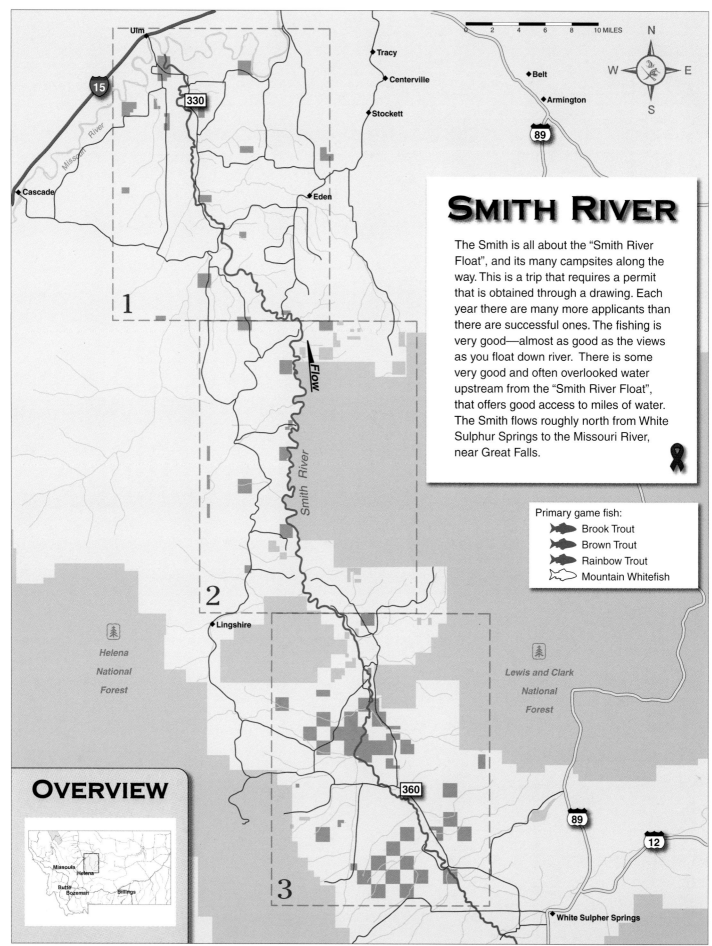

SMITH RIVER

The Smith is all about the "Smith River Float", and its many campsites along the way. This is a trip that requires a permit that is obtained through a drawing. Each year there are many more applicants than there are successful ones. The fishing is very good—almost as good as the views as you float down river. There is some very good and often overlooked water upstream from the "Smith River Float", that offers good access to miles of water. The Smith flows roughly north from White Sulphur Springs to the Missouri River, near Great Falls.

Primary game fish:
- Brook Trout
- Brown Trout
- Rainbow Trout
- Mountain Whitefish

Flow

Smith River

Ulm

Tracy

Centerville

Belt

Armington

Stockett

15

330

89

Cascade

Eden

1

2

Lingshire

Helena National Forest

Lewis and Clark National Forest

3

360

89

12

White Sulpher Springs

OVERVIEW

Missoula
Helena
Butte
Bozeman
Billings

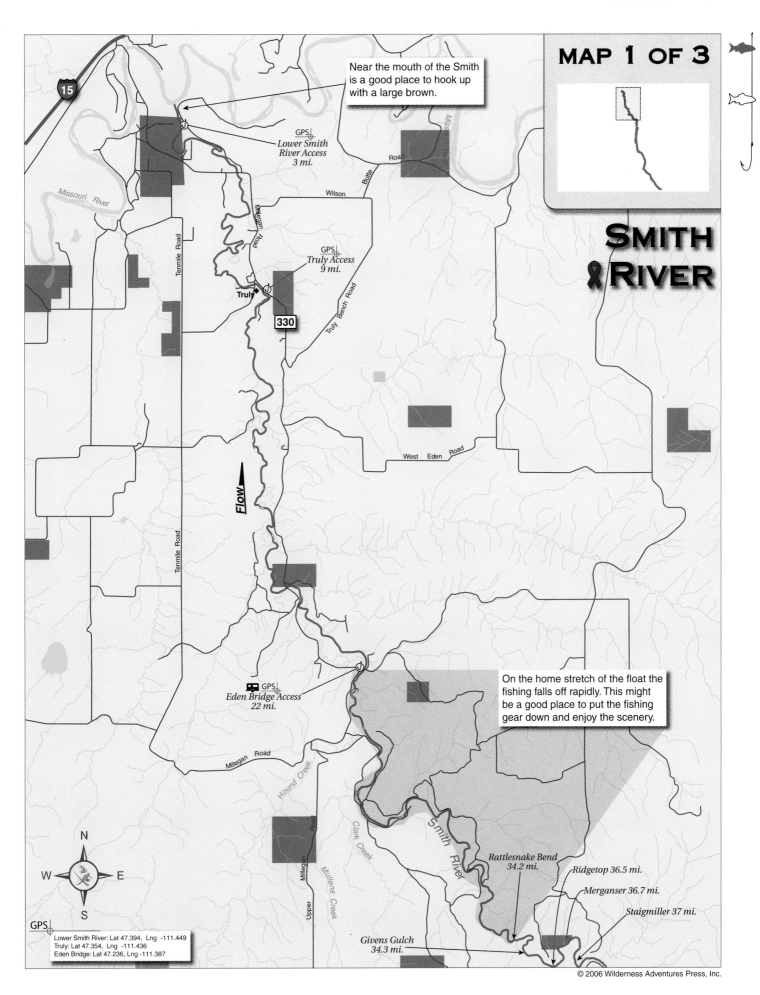

Near the mouth of the Smith is a good place to hook up with a large brown.

GPS
Lower Smith River Access 3 mi.

GPS
Truly Access 9 mi.

Truly

330

Flow

GPS
Eden Bridge Access 22 mi.

On the home stretch of the float the fishing falls off rapidly. This might be a good place to put the fishing gear down and enjoy the scenery.

MAP 1 OF 3

SMITH RIVER

Rattlesnake Bend 34.2 mi.

Ridgetop 36.5 mi.

Merganser 36.7 mi.

Staigmiller 37 mi.

Givens Gulch 34.3 mi.

Missouri River

Tenmile Road

Hound Creek

Clark Creek

Mullens Creek

Millegan Road

Smith River

N W E S

GPS

Lower Smith River: Lat 47.394, Lng -111.449
Truly: Lat 47.354, Lng -111.436
Eden Bridge: Lat 47.236, Lng -111.387

© 2006 Wilderness Adventures Press, Inc.

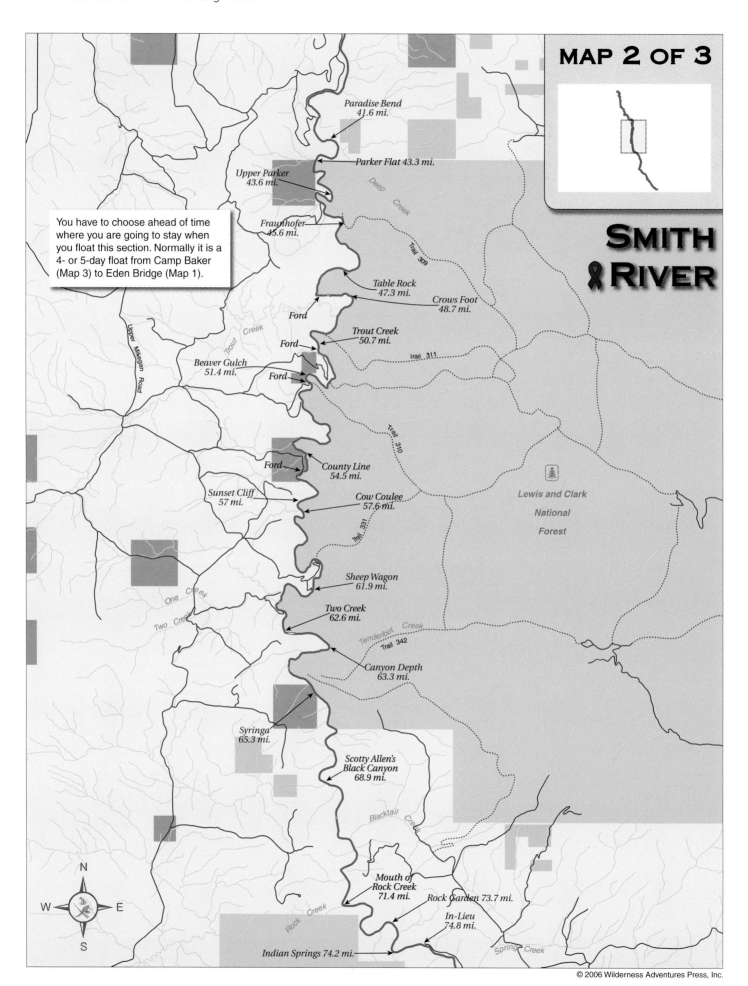

MAP 2 OF 3

SMITH
RIVER

You have to choose ahead of time where you are going to stay when you float this section. Normally it is a 4- or 5-day float from Camp Baker (Map 3) to Eden Bridge (Map 1).

Paradise Bend
41.6 mi.

Parker Flat 43.3 mi.

Upper Parker
43.6 mi.

Deep Creek

Fraunhofer
45.6 mi.

Trail 309

Table Rock
47.3 mi.

Crows Foot
48.7 mi.

Ford

Trout Creek
50.7 mi.

Creek

Ford

Trail 311

Beaver Gulch
51.4 mi.

Ford

Upper Millegan Road

Trail 310

Ford

County Line
54.5 mi.

Sunset Cliff
57 mi.

Cow Coulee
57.6 mi.

Lewis and Clark

National

Forest

Trail 331

One Creek

Sheep Wagon
61.9 mi.

Two Creek

Two Creek
62.6 mi.

Tenderfoot Creek

Trail 342

Canyon Depth
63.3 mi.

Syringa
65.3 mi.

Scotty Allen's
Black Canyon
68.9 mi.

Blacktail Creek

Mouth of
Rock Creek
71.4 mi.

Rock Garden 73.7 mi.

In-Lieu
74.8 mi.

N
W   E
S

Indian Springs 74.2 mi.

Rock Creek

Spring Creek

© 2006 Wilderness Adventures Press, Inc.

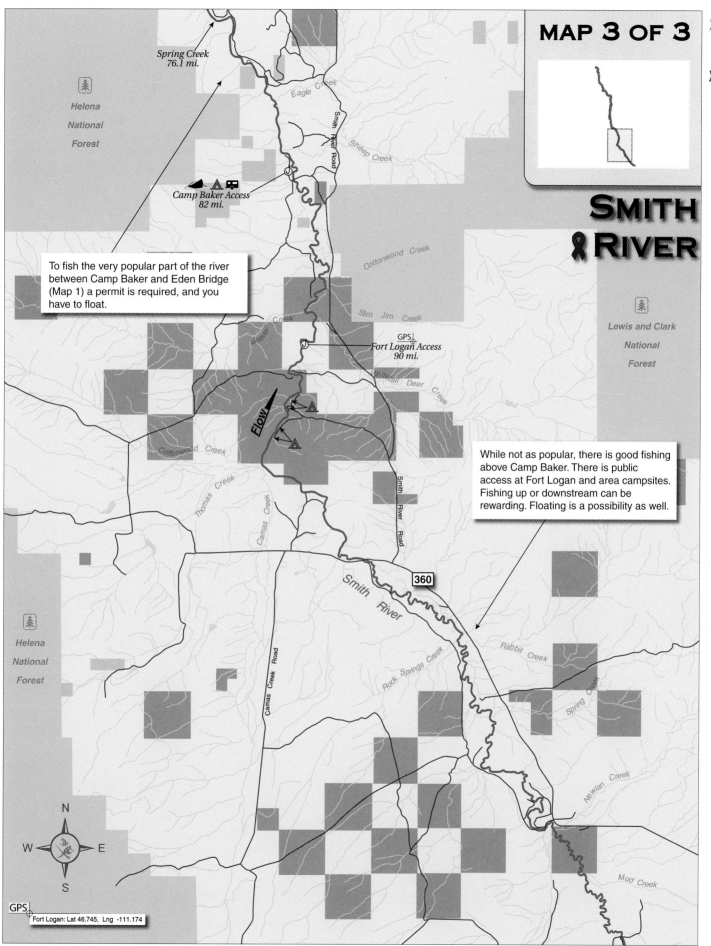

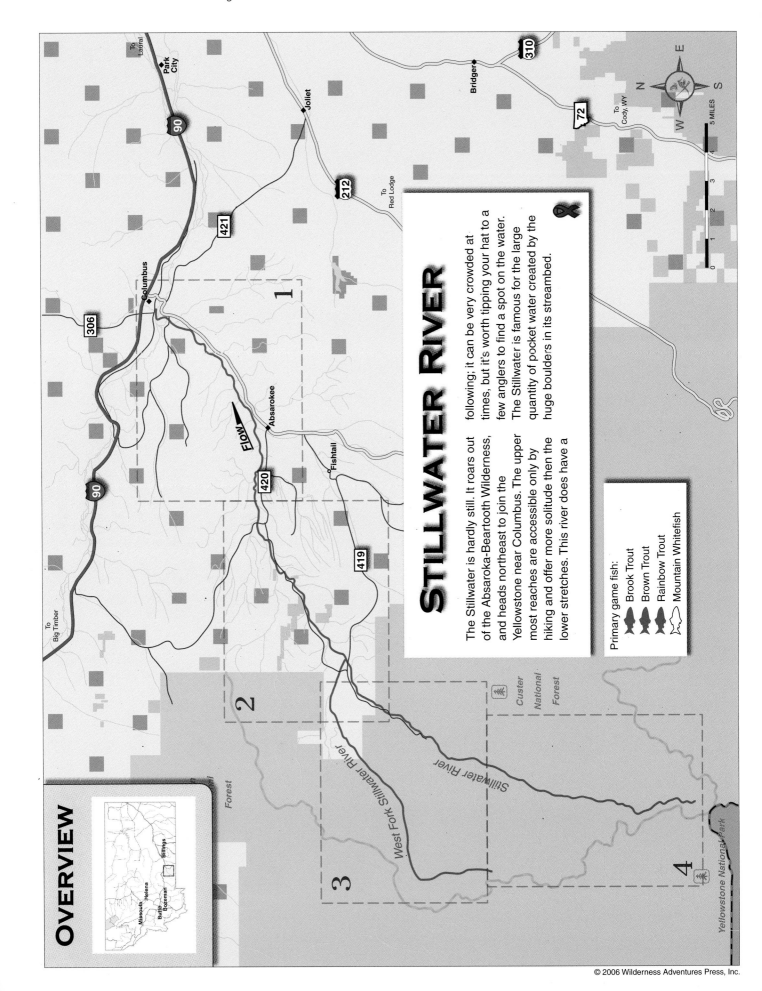

STILLWATER RIVER

The Stillwater is hardly still. It roars out of the Absaroka-Beartooth Wilderness, and heads northeast to join the Yellowstone near Columbus. The upper most reaches are accessible only by hiking and offer more solitude then the lower stretches. This river does have a following; it can be very crowded at times, but it's worth tipping your hat to a few anglers to find a spot on the water. The Stillwater is famous for the large quantity of pocket water created by the huge boulders in its streambed.

Primary game fish:
Brook Trout
Brown Trout
Rainbow Trout
Mountain Whitefish

OVERVIEW

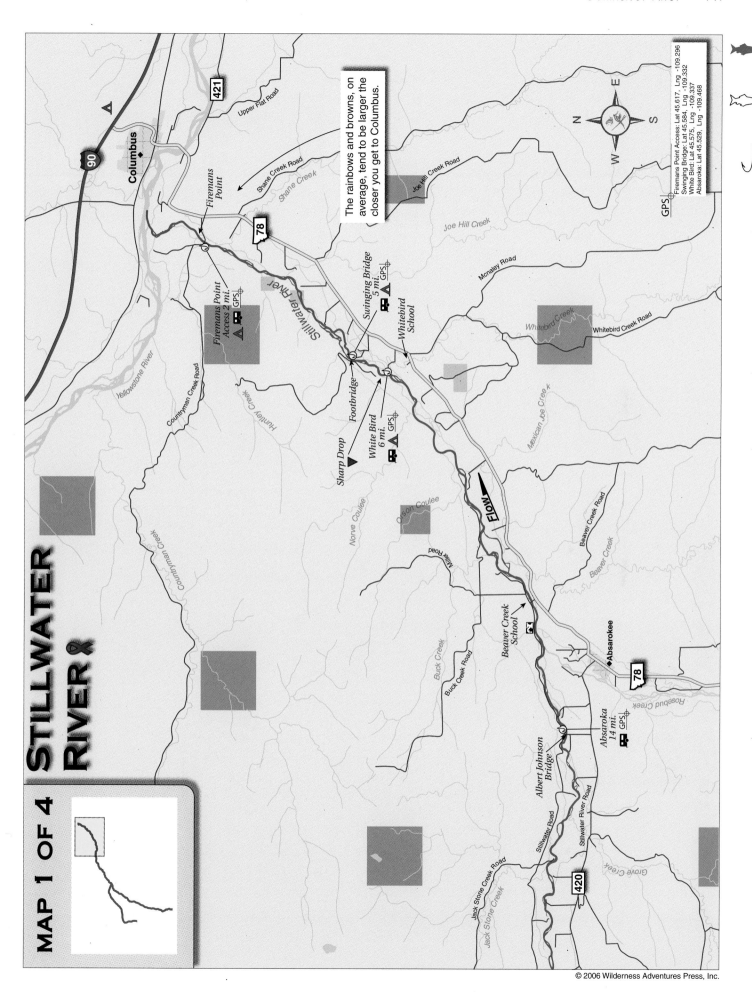

MAP 1 OF 4

STILLWATER RIVER

The rainbows and browns, on average, tend to be larger the closer you get to Columbus.

Firemans Point Access: Lat 45.617, Lng -109.296
Swinging Bridge: Lat 45.584, Lng -109.332
White Bird: Lat 45.575, Lng -109.337
Absaroka: Lat 45.529, Lng -109.468

N E S W

GPS

Columbus

Upper Flat Road

Shane Creek Road

Shane Creek

Firemans Point

Firemans Point Access 2 mi. GPS

Stillwater River

Yellowstone River

Countryman Creek Road

Countryman Creek

Huntley Creek

Joe Hill Creek Road

Joe Hill Creek

Mcnaley Road

Whitebird Creek

Whitebird Creek Road

Swinging Bridge 5 mi. GPS

Whitebird School

Footbridge

White Bird 6 mi. GPS

Sharp Drop

Norve Coulee

Olson Coulee

Mexican Joe Creek

FLOW

Miller Road

Buck Creek

Buck Creek Road

Beaver Creek Road

Beaver Creek

Beaver Creek School

Absarokee

Rosebud Creek

Albert Johnson Bridge

Absaroka 14 mi. GPS

Stillwater Road

Stillwater River Road

Jack Stone Creek Road

Jack Stone Creek

Grove Creek

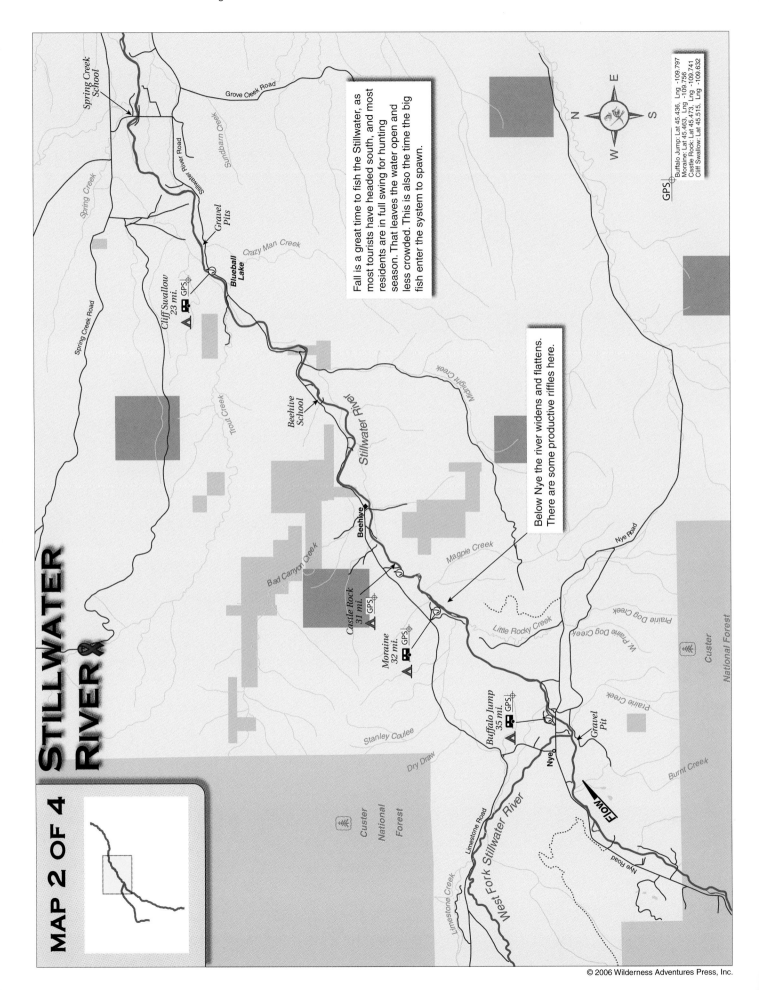

MAP 2 OF 4

STILLWATER RIVER

Grove Creek Road

Spring Creek School

Spring Creek

Spring Creek Road

Sundbarn Creek

Stillwater River Road

Gravel Pits

Crazy Man Creek

Blueball Lake

Cliff Swallow
23 mi. GPS

Trout Creek

Beehive School

Stillwater River

Midnight Creek

Fall is a great time to fish the Stillwater, as most tourists have headed south, and most residents are in full swing for hunting season. That leaves the water open and less crowded. This is also the time the big fish enter the system to spawn.

Bad Canyon Creek

Beehive

Magpie Creek

Below Nye the river widens and flattens. There are some productive riffles here.

Castle Rock
31 mi. GPS

Moraine
32 mi. GPS

Little Rocky Creek

Prairie Dog Creek

W Prairie Dog Creek

Custer National Forest

Stanley Coulee

Dry Draw

Prairie Creek

Custer National Forest

Buffalo Jump
35 mi. GPS

Gravel Pit

Nye

Burnt Creek

Limestone Creek

Limestone Road

FLOW

West Fork Stillwater River

Nye Road

Nye Road

N E S W

GPS

Buffalo Jump: Lat 45.436, Lng -109.797
Moraine: Lat 45.463, Lng -109.756
Castle Rock: Lat 45.473, Lng -109.741
Cliff Swallow: Lat 45.515, Lng -109.632

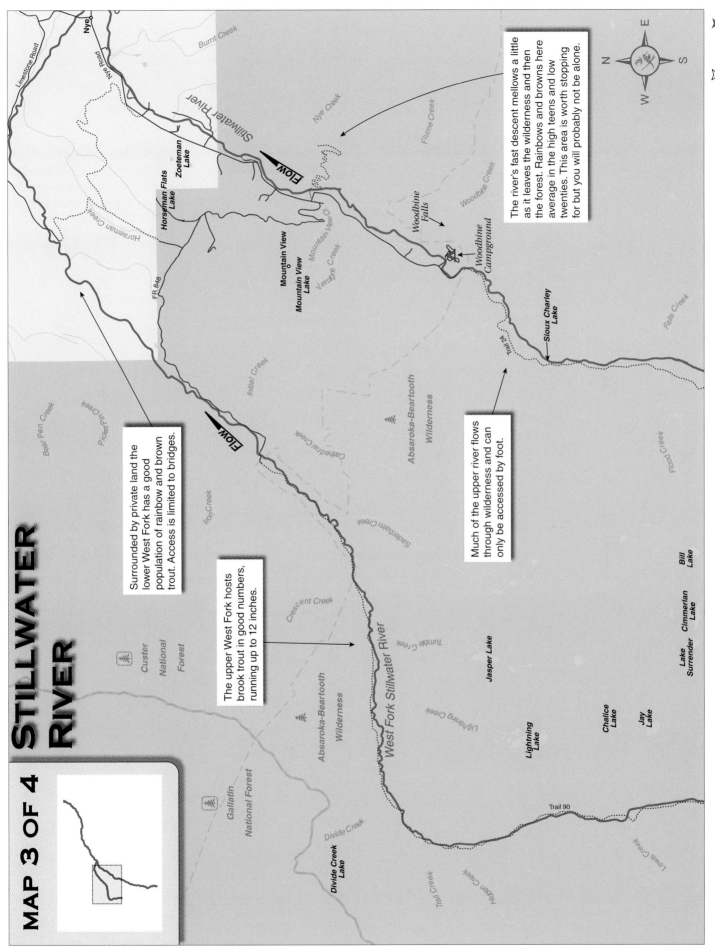

MAP **3** OF **4**

STILLWATER RIVER

Surrounded by private land the lower West Fork has a good population of rainbow and brown trout. Access is limited to bridges.

The upper West Fork hosts brook trout in good numbers, running up to 12 inches.

Much of the upper river flows through wilderness and can only be accessed by foot.

The river's fast descent mellows a little as it leaves the wilderness and then the forest. Rainbows and browns here average in the high teens and low twenties. This area is worth stopping for but you will probably not be alone.

Woodbine Campground

Woodbine Falls

Sioux Charley Lake

Custer National Forest

Gallatin National Forest

Absaroka-Beartooth Wilderness

Absaroka-Beartooth Wilderness

West Fork Stillwater River

Divide Creek Lake

Lightning Lake

Chalice Lake

Jay Lake

Lake Surrender

Cimmerian Lake

Bill Lake

Jasper Lake

Trail 90

Trail 24

Mountain View Lake

Horseman Flats Lake

Zoeteman Lake

Nye

FR 848

FLOW

FLOW

Linestone Road

Nye Road

Stillwater River

Burnt Creek

Nye Creek

Flume Creek

Woodbine Creek

Falls Creek

Flood Creek

Horseman Creek

Bear Pen Creek

Picket Pin Creek

Iron Creek

Crescent Creek

Initial Creek

Cathedral Creek

Verdigris Creek

Mountain View Ck.

Sadelbath Creek

Tumble Creek

Lightning Creek

Divide Creek

Trail Creek

Hidden Creek

Lewis Creek

N E S W

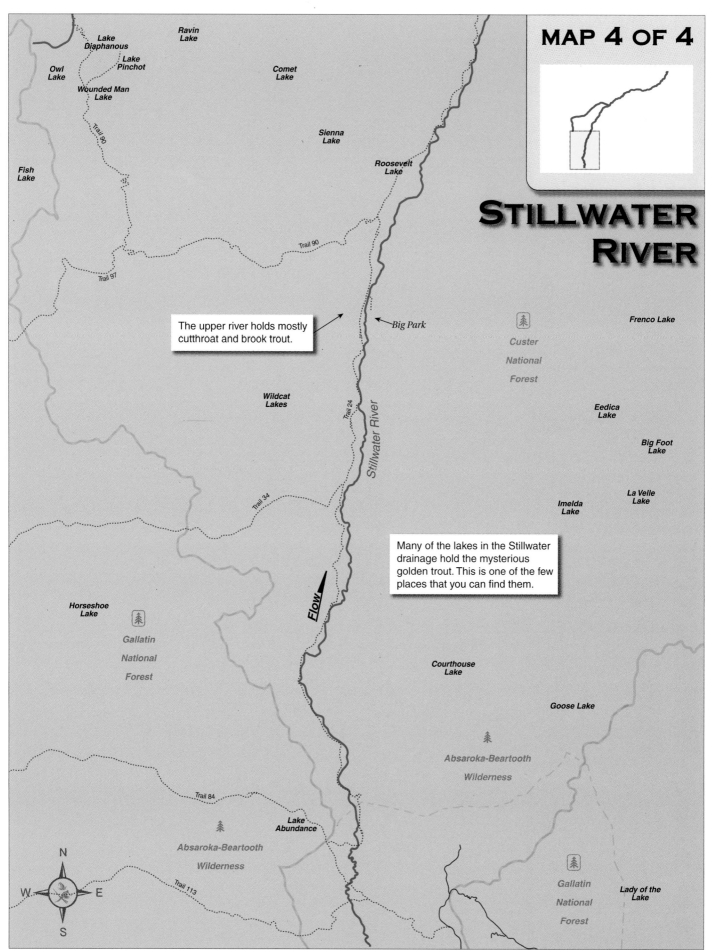

MAP **4** OF **4**

STILLWATER RIVER

The upper river holds mostly cutthroat and brook trout.

Big Park

Many of the lakes in the Stillwater drainage hold the mysterious golden trout. This is one of the few places that you can find them.

Lake Diaphanous

Ravin Lake

Lake Pinchot

Owl Lake

Comet Lake

Wounded Man Lake

Trail 90

Sienna Lake

Fish Lake

Roosevelt Lake

Trail 90

Trail 97

Frenco Lake

Custer National Forest

Wildcat Lakes

Trail 24

Eedica Lake

Stillwater River

Big Foot Lake

La Velle Lake

Trail 34

Imelda Lake

Flow

Horseshoe Lake

Gallatin National Forest

Courthouse Lake

Goose Lake

Absaroka-Beartooth Wilderness

Trail 84

Lake Abundance

N

W   E

S

Absaroka-Beartooth Wilderness

Trail 113

Gallatin National Forest

Lady of the Lake

OVERVIEW

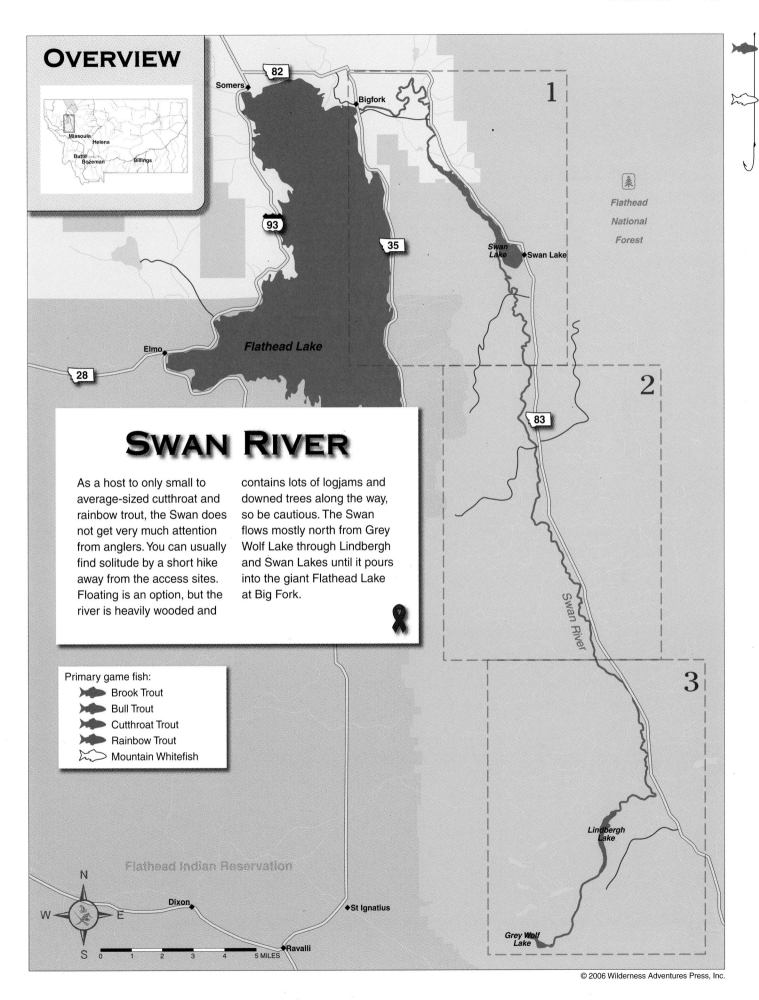

82
Somers
Bigfork
93
35
Flathead National Forest
Swan Lake
Swan Lake
Elmo
28
Flathead Lake
83

SWAN RIVER

As a host to only small to average-sized cutthroat and rainbow trout, the Swan does not get very much attention from anglers. You can usually find solitude by a short hike away from the access sites. Floating is an option, but the river is heavily wooded and contains lots of logjams and downed trees along the way, so be cautious. The Swan flows mostly north from Grey Wolf Lake through Lindbergh and Swan Lakes until it pours into the giant Flathead Lake at Big Fork.

Swan River

Primary game fish:
Brook Trout
Bull Trout
Cutthroat Trout
Rainbow Trout
Mountain Whitefish

1

2

3

Lindbergh Lake

Flathead Indian Reservation

N
W   E
S

Dixon
St Ignatius
Ravalli

0   1   2   3   4   5 MILES

Grey Wolf Lake

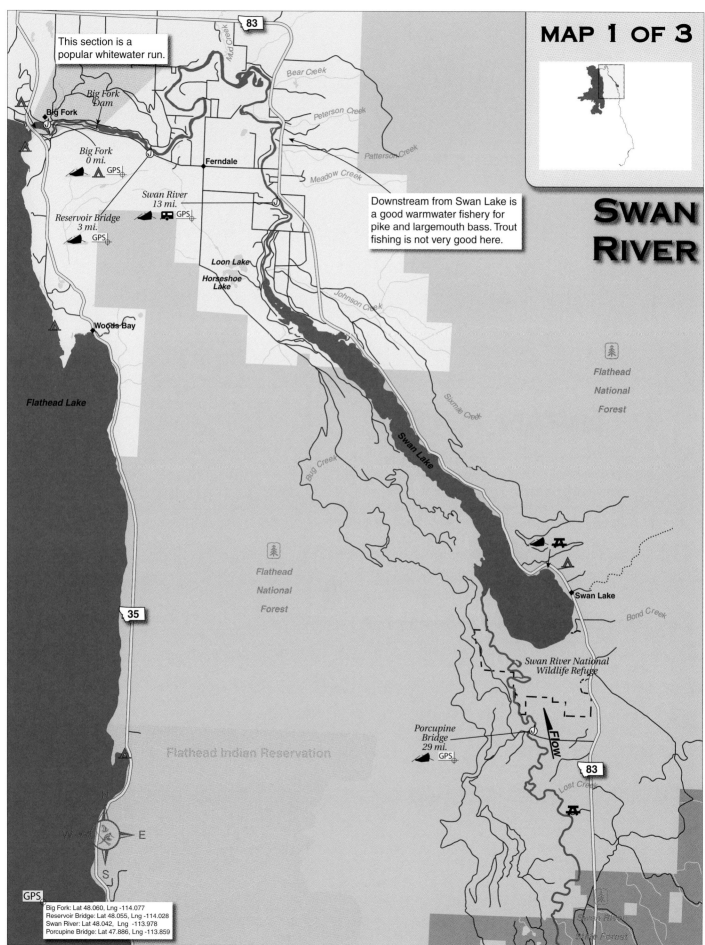

This section is a popular whitewater run.

83

Mud Creek

Bear Creek

Peterson Creek

Patterson Creek

Big Fork Dam

Big Fork

Big Fork 0 mi.

GPS

Ferndale

Meadow Creek

Swan River 13 mi.

GPS

Reservoir Bridge 3 mi.

GPS

Loon Lake

Horseshoe Lake

Downstream from Swan Lake is a good warmwater fishery for pike and largemouth bass. Trout fishing is not very good here.

Johnson Creek

Woods Bay

Flathead Lake

Sixmile Creek

Flathead National Forest

Big Creek

Swan Lake

35

Flathead National Forest

Swan Lake

Bond Creek

Swan River National Wildlife Refuge

Flathead Indian Reservation

Porcupine Bridge 29 mi.

GPS

FLOW

83

Lost Creek

N
W   E
S

GPS
Big Fork: Lat 48.060, Lng -114.077
Reservoir Bridge: Lat 48.055, Lng -114.028
Swan River: Lat 48.042, Lng -113.978
Porcupine Bridge: Lat 47.886, Lng -113.859

MAP 1 OF 3

SWAN RIVER

© 2006 Wilderness Adventures Press, Inc.

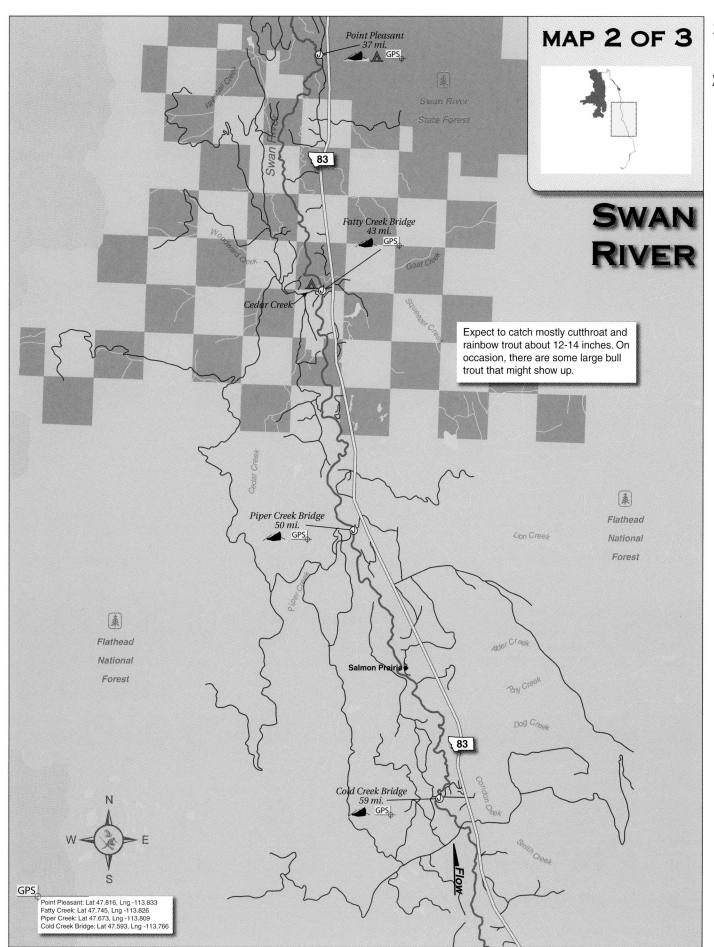

MAP **2** OF **3**

SWAN
RIVER

Point Pleasant
37 mi.
GPS

*Swan River
State Forest*

83

Fatty Creek Bridge
43 mi.
GPS

Goat Creek

Woodward Creek

Squeezer Creek

Cedar Creek

Expect to catch mostly cutthroat and rainbow trout about 12-14 inches. On occasion, there are some large bull trout that might show up.

Cedar Creek

Piper Creek Bridge
50 mi.
GPS

Lion Creek

Flathead

National

Forest

Piper Creek

Alder Creek

Flathead

National

Forest

Salmon Prairie

Pony Creek

Dog Creek

83

Condon Creek

Cold Creek Bridge
59 mi.
GPS

Smith Creek

Flow

N
W E
S

GPS

Point Pleasant: Lat 47.816, Lng -113.833
Fatty Creek: Lat 47.745, Lng -113.826
Piper Creek: Lat 47.673, Lng -113.809
Cold Creek Bridge: Lat 47.593, Lng -113.766

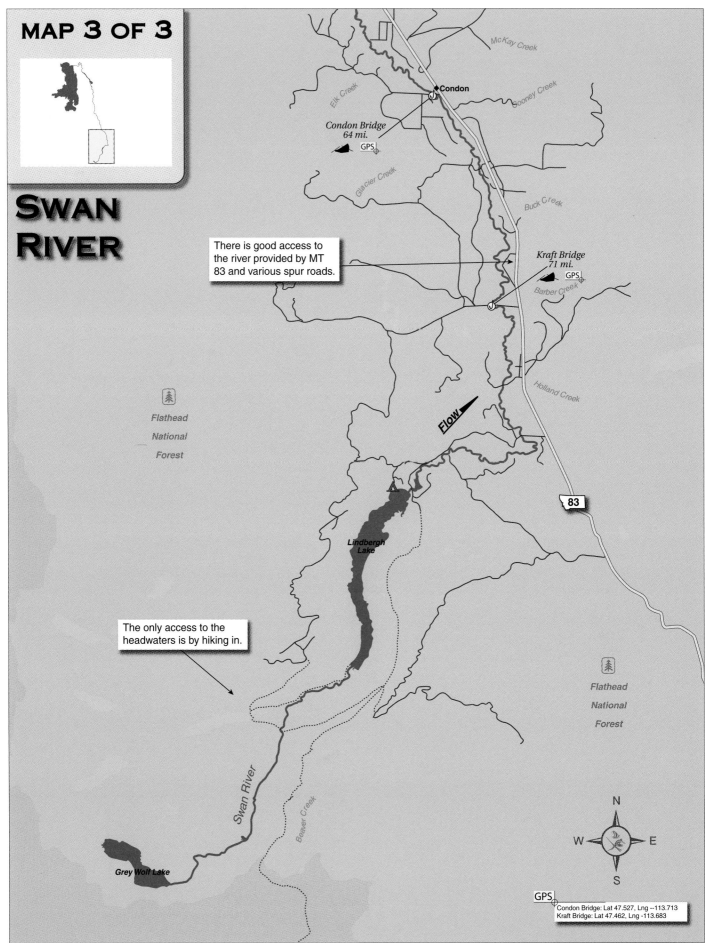

MAP 3 OF 3

SWAN RIVER

Condon

McKay Creek

Sooney Creek

Elk Creek

Condon Bridge
64 mi.
GPS

Glacier Creek

Buck Creek

There is good access to
the river provided by MT
83 and various spur roads.

Kraft Bridge
71 mi.
GPS

Barber Creek

Holland Creek

Flow

Flathead

National

Forest

83

Lindbergh
Lake

The only access to the
headwaters is by hiking in.

Flathead

National

Forest

Swan River

Beaver Creek

N
W   E
S

Grey Wolf Lake

GPS

Condon Bridge: Lat 47.527, Lng --113.713
Kraft Bridge: Lat 47.462, Lng -113.683

OVERVIEW

TONGUE RIVER

The Tongue is a target for warmwater anglers, and is fairly productive, both in the lower river and in the reservoir. The trout fishing is mostly limited to the area immediately below the dam. The reservoir sits near the Wyoming border releasing water into the short trout section to the north. Then the Tongue flows northeast until it joins forces with the Yellowstone River at Miles City. The reservoir receives by far the most pressure. In mid to late summer it can be hard to find a spot without rubbing elbows with a few hundred people.

Missoula
Helena
Butte
Bozeman
Billings

Primary game fish:

Rainbow Trout
Smallmouth Bass
Channel Catfish
Crappie
Yellow Perch
Northern Pike
Sauger
Sturgeon
Walleye

Northern Cheyenne Indian Reservation

1

To Miles City

566

Birney

Custer

National

Forest

Tongue River Road

Tongue River

566

2

Flow

Tongue River
State Park

Tongue River
Reservoir

314

Decker

To
Wyoming

N

W   E

S

0   1   2   3   4   5 MILES

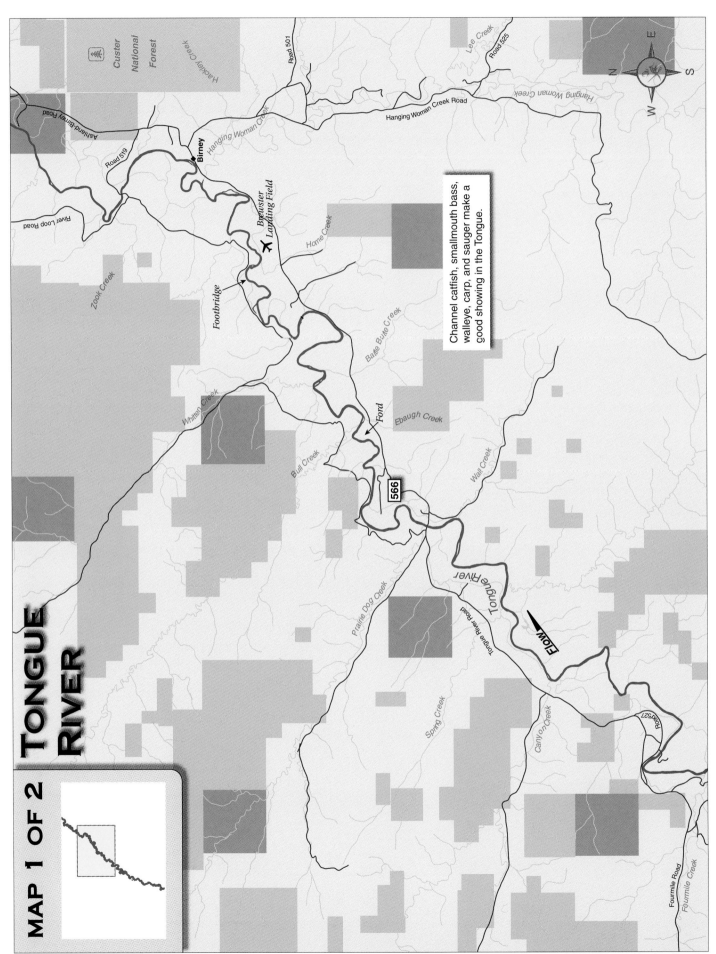

MAP 1 OF 2

TONGUE RIVER

Custer National Forest

Ashland-Birney Road

Road 519

River Loop Road

Hackley Creek

Road 501

Lee Creek

Road 525

Hanging Woman Creek Road

Hanging Woman Creek

Birney

Hanging Woman Creek

Brewster Landing Field

Home Creek

Footbridge

Zook Creek

Battle Butte Creek

Whitten Creek

Ebaugh Creek

Ford

Bull Creek

Wall Creek

566

Prairie Dog Creek

Tongue River

Tongue River Road

FLOW

Spring Creek

Canyon Creek

Road 527

Fourmile Road

Fourmile Creek

Channel catfish, smallmouth bass, walleye, carp, and sauger make a good showing in the Tongue.

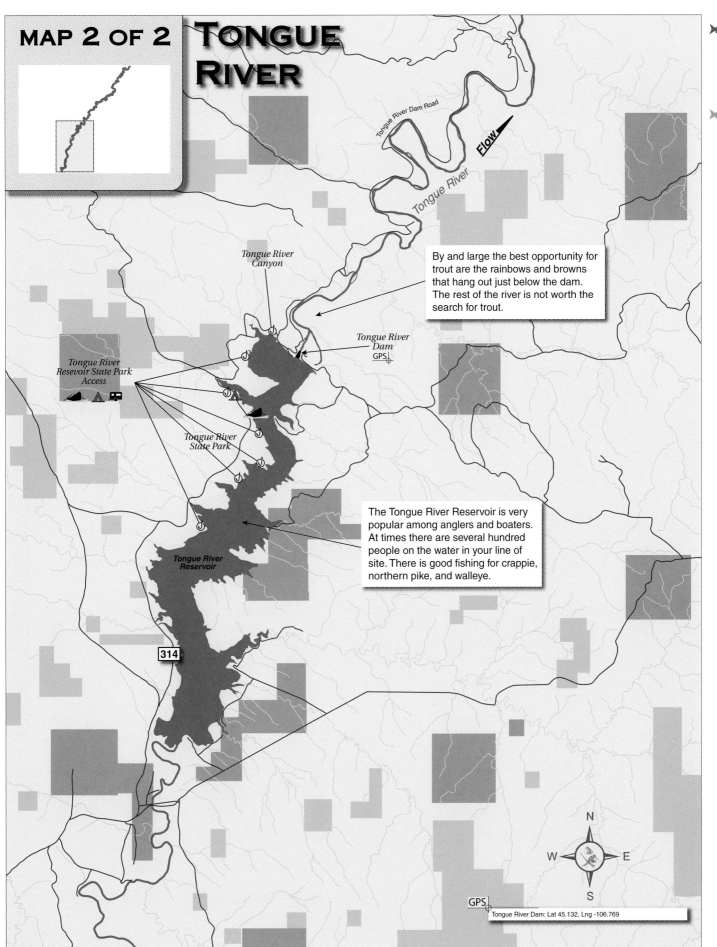

MAP 2 OF 2

TONGUE RIVER

Tongue River Dam Road

Tongue River

Flow

Tongue River
Canyon

By and large the best opportunity for trout are the rainbows and browns that hang out just below the dam. The rest of the river is not worth the search for trout.

Tongue River
Dam
GPS

Tongue River
Resevoir State Park
Access

Tongue River
State Park

The Tongue River Reservoir is very popular among anglers and boaters. At times there are several hundred people on the water in your line of site. There is good fishing for crappie, northern pike, and walleye.

Tongue River
Reservoir

314

N
W   E
S

GPS

Tongue River Dam: Lat 45.132, Lng -106.769

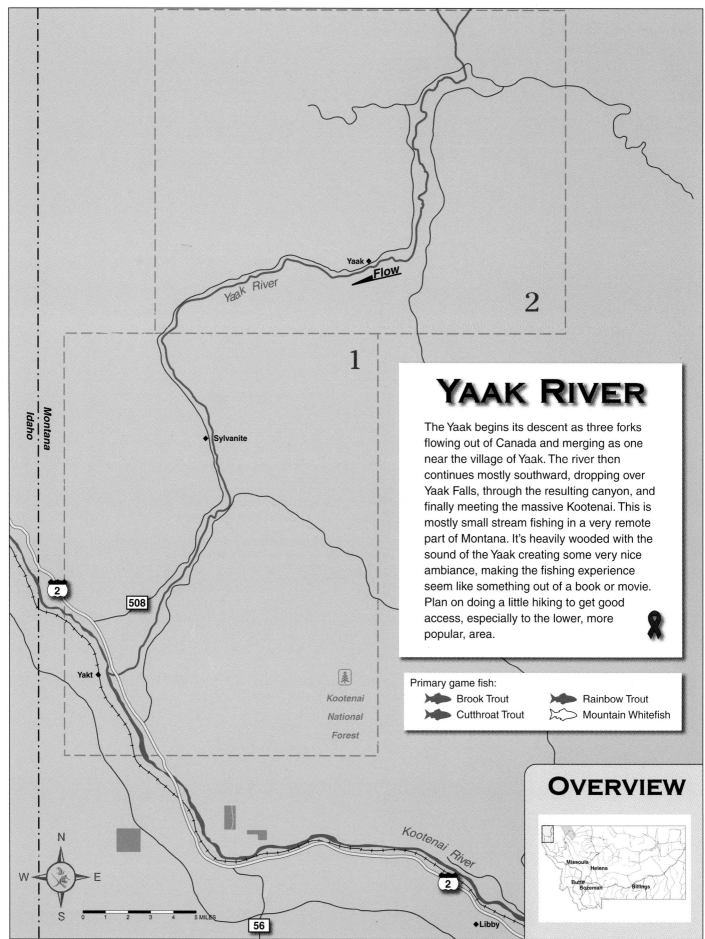

Flow

Yaak ◆

Yaak River

Montana
Idaho

1

2

◆ Sylvanite

2

508

Yakt ◆

Kootenai
National
Forest

YAAK RIVER

The Yaak begins its descent as three forks flowing out of Canada and merging as one near the village of Yaak. The river then continues mostly southward, dropping over Yaak Falls, through the resulting canyon, and finally meeting the massive Kootenai. This is mostly small stream fishing in a very remote part of Montana. It's heavily wooded with the sound of the Yaak creating some very nice ambiance, making the fishing experience seem like something out of a book or movie. Plan on doing a little hiking to get good access, especially to the lower, more popular, area.

Primary game fish:

Brook Trout   Rainbow Trout

Cutthroat Trout   Mountain Whitefish

Kootenai River

2

OVERVIEW

Missoula
Helena
Butte
Bozeman   Billings

N
W   E
S

0   1   2   3   4   5 MILES

56

◆ Libby

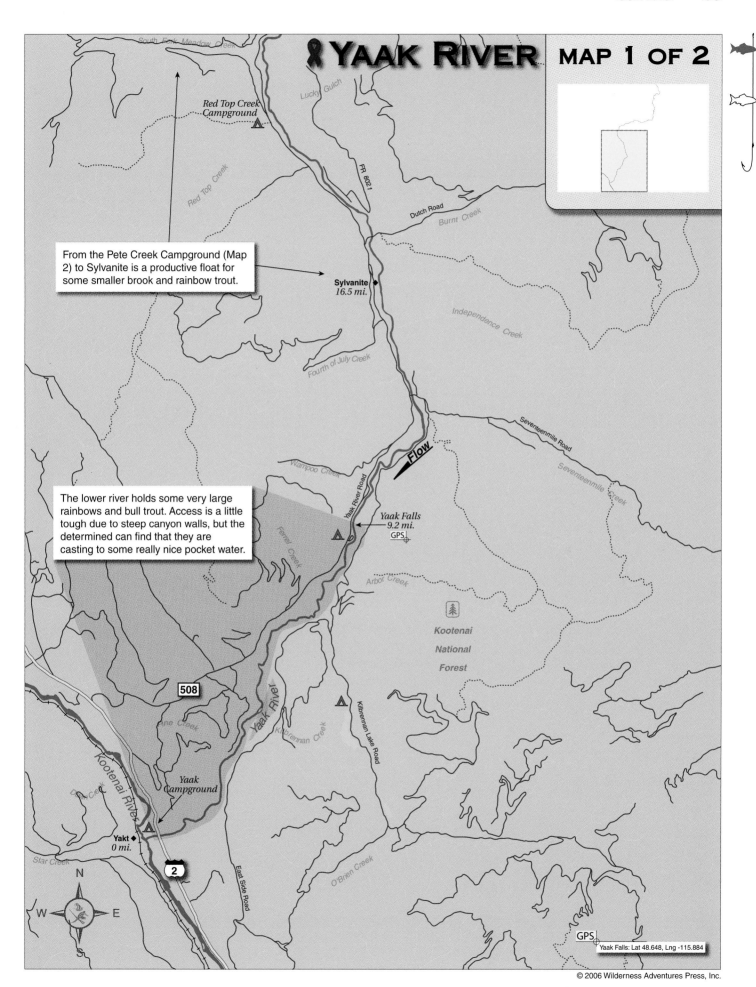

YAAK RIVER MAP 1 OF 2

Red Top Creek Campground

South Fork Meadow Creek

Lucky Gulch

FR 8021

Dutch Road

Burnt Creek

From the Pete Creek Campground (Map 2) to Sylvanite is a productive float for some smaller brook and rainbow trout.

Sylvanite
16.5 mi.

Independence Creek

Fourth of July Creek

Seventeenmile Road

Wampoo Creek

Yaak River Road

Flow

The lower river holds some very large rainbows and bull trout. Access is a little tough due to steep canyon walls, but the determined can find that they are casting to some really nice pocket water.

Ferrel Creek

Yaak Falls
9.2 mi.
GPS

Arbor Creek

Seventeenmile Creek

Kootenai

National

Forest

508

Kilbrennan Lake Road

Lane Creek

Kilbrennan Creek

Yaak River

Deep Creek

Kootenai River

Yaak Campground

Yakt ◆
0 mi.

Star Creek

O'Brien Creek

East Side Road

2

N
W   E
S

GPS

Yaak Falls: Lat 48.648, Lng -115.884

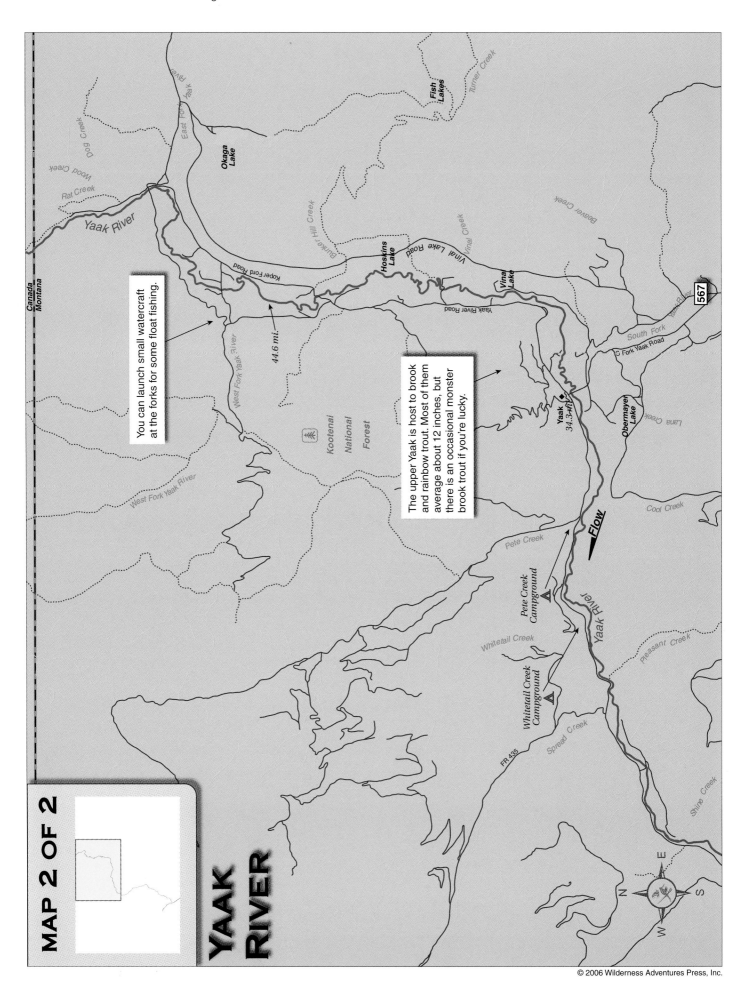

You can launch small watercraft at the forks for some float fishing.

The upper Yaak is host to brook and rainbow trout. Most of them average about 12 inches, but there is an occasional monster brook trout if you're lucky.

MAP 2 OF 2

YAAK RIVER

© 2006 Wilderness Adventures Press, Inc.

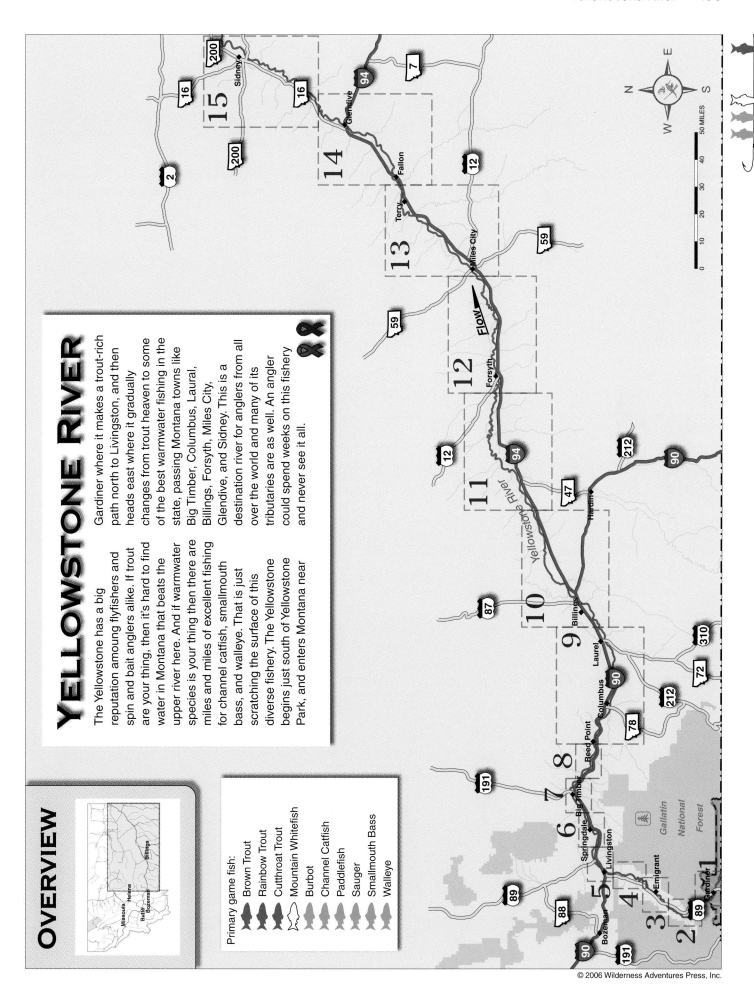

Overview

Yellowstone River

The Yellowstone has a big reputation among flyfishers and spin and bait anglers alike. If trout are your thing, then it's hard to find water in Montana that beats the upper river here. And if warmwater species is your thing then there are miles and miles of excellent fishing for channel catfish, smallmouth bass, and walleye. That is just scratching the surface of this diverse fishery. The Yellowstone begins just south of Yellowstone Park, and enters Montana near

Gardiner where it makes a trout-rich path north to Livingston, and then heads east where it gradually changes from trout heaven to some of the best warmwater fishing in the state, passing Montana towns like Big Timber, Columbus, Laural, Billings, Forsyth, Miles City, Glendive, and Sidney. This is a destination river for anglers from all over the world and many of its tributaries are as well. An angler could spend weeks on this fishery and never see it all.

Primary game fish:
Brown Trout
Rainbow Trout
Cutthroat Trout
Mountain Whitefish
Burbot
Channel Catfish
Paddlefish
Sauger
Smallmouth Bass
Walleye

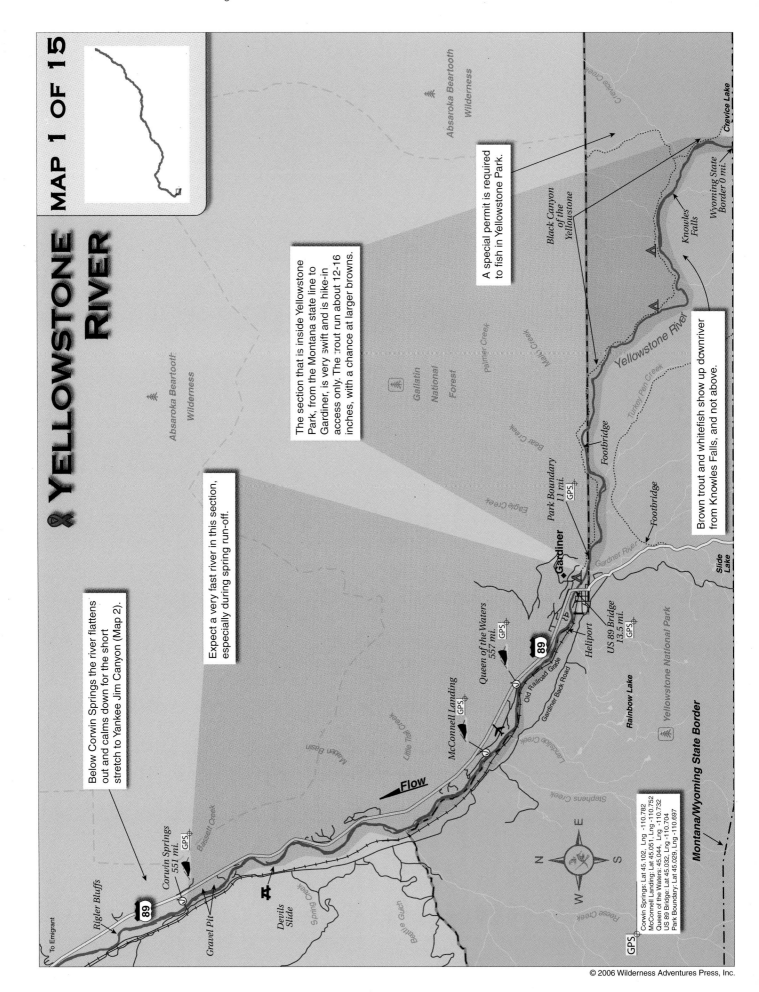

MAP 1 OF 15

YELLOWSTONE RIVER

Below Corwin Springs the river flattens out and calms down for the short stretch to Yankee Jim Canyon (Map 2).

Expect a very fast river in this section, especially during spring run-off.

The section that is inside Yellowstone Park, from the Montana state line to Gardiner, is very swift and is hike-in access only. The trout run about 12-16 inches, with a chance at larger browns.

A special permit is required to fish in Yellowstone Park.

Brown trout and whitefish show up downriver from Knowles Falls, and not above.

Absaroka Beartooth Wilderness

Absaroka Beartooth Wilderness

Crevice Creek

Crevice Lake

Wyoming State Border 0 mi.

Knowles Falls

Black Canyon of the Yellowstone

Yellowstone River

Palmer Creek

Mol Creek

Gallatin National Forest

Bear Creek

Footbridge

Turkey Pen Creek

Footbridge

Eagle Creek

Park Boundary 11 mi. GPS

Gardiner

Gardner River

Slide Lake

Heliport

US 89 Bridge 13.5 mi. GPS

Yellowstone National Park

Rainbow Lake

Old Railroad Grade

Gardiner Back Road

Queen of the Waters 557 mi. GPS

McConnell Landing GPS

Landslide Creek

Little Trail Creek

Maiden Basin

Flow

Stephens Creek

Reese Creek

Rigler Bluffs

To Emigrant

Corwin Springs 551 mi. GPS

Bassett Creek

Gravel Pit

Devils Slide

Spring Creek

Battle Gulch

Montana/Wyoming State Border

GPS Corwin Springs: Lat 45.102, Lng -110.782
McConnell Landing: Lat 45.051, Lng -110.752
Queen of the Waters: Lat 45.044, Lng -110.732
US 89 Bridge: Lat 45.032, Lng -110.704
Park Boundary: Lat 45.029, Lng -110.697

N E S W

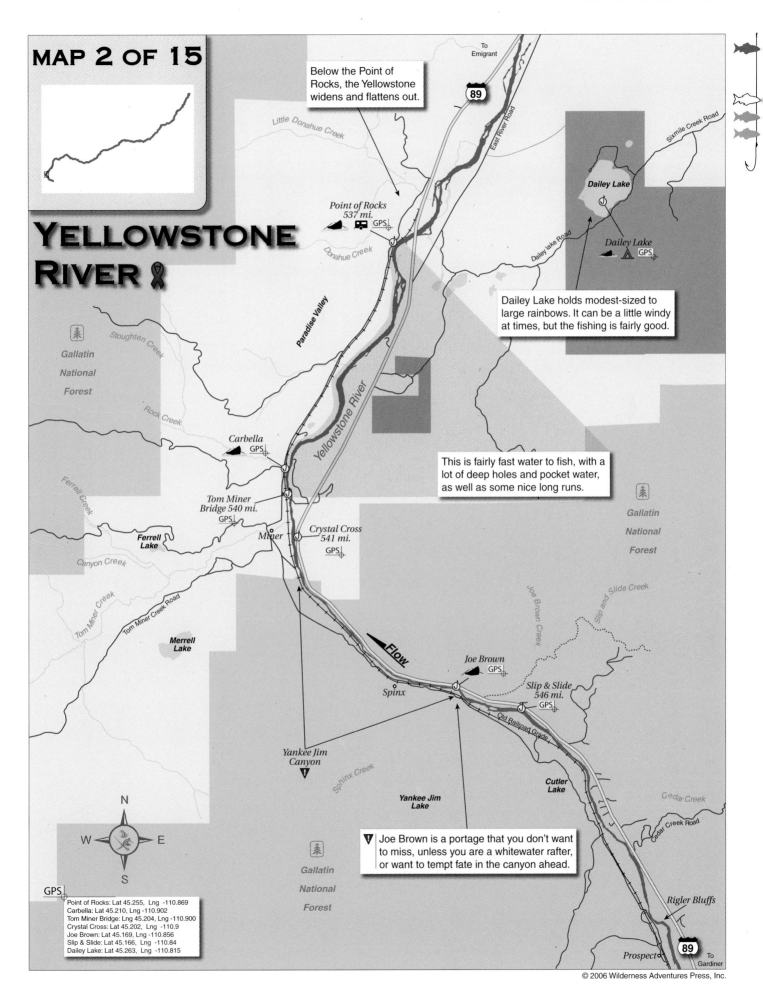

MAP 2 OF 15

YELLOWSTONE RIVER

Below the Point of Rocks, the Yellowstone widens and flattens out.

Point of Rocks 537 mi. GPS

Dailey Lake GPS

Dailey Lake holds modest-sized to large rainbows. It can be a little windy at times, but the fishing is fairly good.

Paradise Valley

Little Donahue Creek

Donahue Creek

Stoughten Creek

Gallatin National Forest

Rock Creek

Carbella GPS

Ferrell Creek

Tom Miner Bridge 540 mi. GPS

Ferrell Lake

Miner

Canyon Creek

Crystal Cross 541 mi. GPS

This is fairly fast water to fish, with a lot of deep holes and pocket water, as well as some nice long runs.

Gallatin National Forest

Tom Miner Creek

Merrell Lake

Flow

Joe Brown GPS

Slip and Slide Creek

Joe Brown Creek

Slip & Slide 546 mi. GPS

Spinx

Old Railroad Grade

Cutler Lake

Cedar Creek

Yankee Jim Canyon

Sphinx Creek

Yankee Jim Lake

Joe Brown is a portage that you don't want to miss, unless you are a whitewater rafter, or want to tempt fate in the canyon ahead.

Gallatin National Forest

N W E S

GPS

Cedar Creek Road

Rigler Bluffs

Prospect

To Gardiner

Point of Rocks: Lat 45.255, Lng -110.869
Carbella: Lat 45.210, Lng -110.902
Tom Miner Bridge: Lng 45.204, Lng -110.900
Crystal Cross: Lat 45.202, Lng -110.9
Joe Brown: Lat 45.169, Lng -110.856
Slip & Slide: Lat 45.166, Lng -110.84
Dailey Lake: Lat 45.263, Lng -110.815

© 2006 Wilderness Adventures Press, Inc.

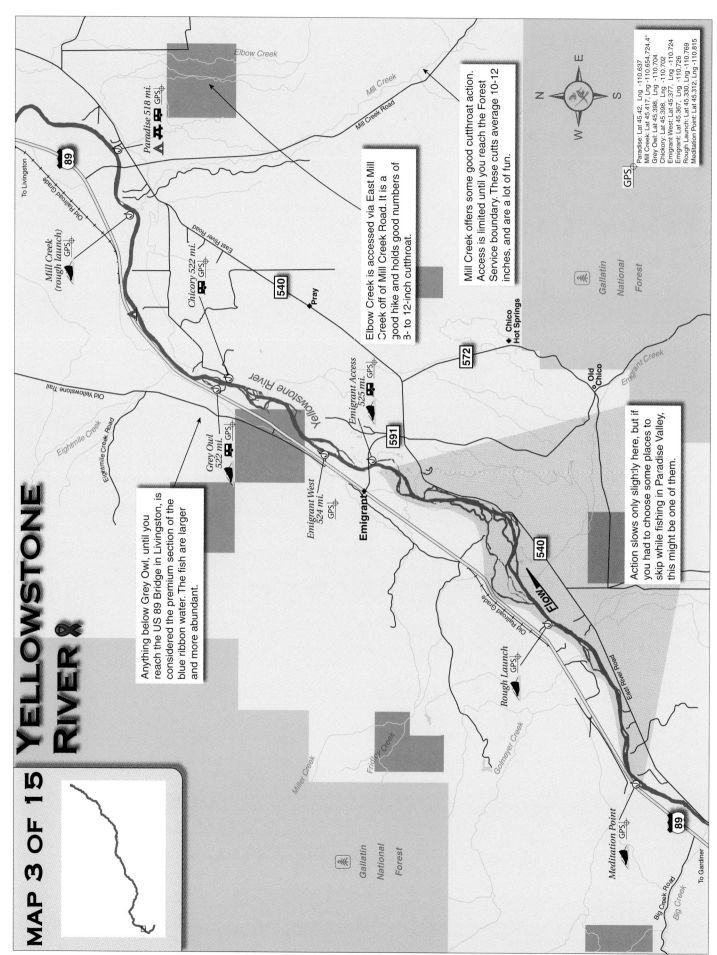

MAP 3 OF 15
YELLOWSTONE RIVER ✕

Anything below Grey Owl, until you reach the US 89 Bridge in Livingston, is considered the premium section of the blue ribbon water. The fish are larger and more abundant.

Elbow Creek is accessed via East Mill Creek off of Mill Creek Road. It is a good hike and holds good numbers of 3- to 12-inch cutthroat.

Mill Creek offers some good cutthroat action. Access is limited until you reach the Forest Service boundary. These cutts average 10-12 inches, and are a lot of fun.

Action slows only slightly here, but if you had to choose some places to skip while fishing in Paradise Valley, this might be one of them.

Paradise: Lat 45.42, Lng -110.637
Mill Creek: Lat 45.417, Lng -110.654,724,4°
Grey Owl: Lat 45.398, Lng -110.704
Chickory: Lat 45.398, Lng -110.702
Emigrant West: Lat 45.377, Lng -110.724
Emigrant: Lat 45.367, Lng -110.726
Rough Launch: Lat 45.330, Lng -110.769
Meditation Point: Lat 45.312, Lng -110.815

Elbow Creek

Mill Creek

Mill Creek Road

To Livingston

Old Railroad Grade

89

Mill Creek
(rough launch)
GPS

Paradise 518 mi.
GPS

East River Road

Chicory 522 mi.
GPS

540

Pray

Chico
Hot Springs

572

Old Chico

Emigrant Creek

Eightmile Creek

Eightmile Creek Road

Old Yellowstone Trail

Yellowstone River

Grey Owl
522 mi.
GPS

Emigrant Access
525 mi.
GPS

591

Emigrant West
524 mi.
GPS

Emigrant

Gallatin
National
Forest

540

FLOW

Old Railroad Grade

Rough Launch
GPS

Golmeyer Creek

East River Road

Fridley Creek

Miller Creek

Gallatin
National
Forest

Meditation Point
GPS

89

Big Creek Road

Big Creek

To Gardiner

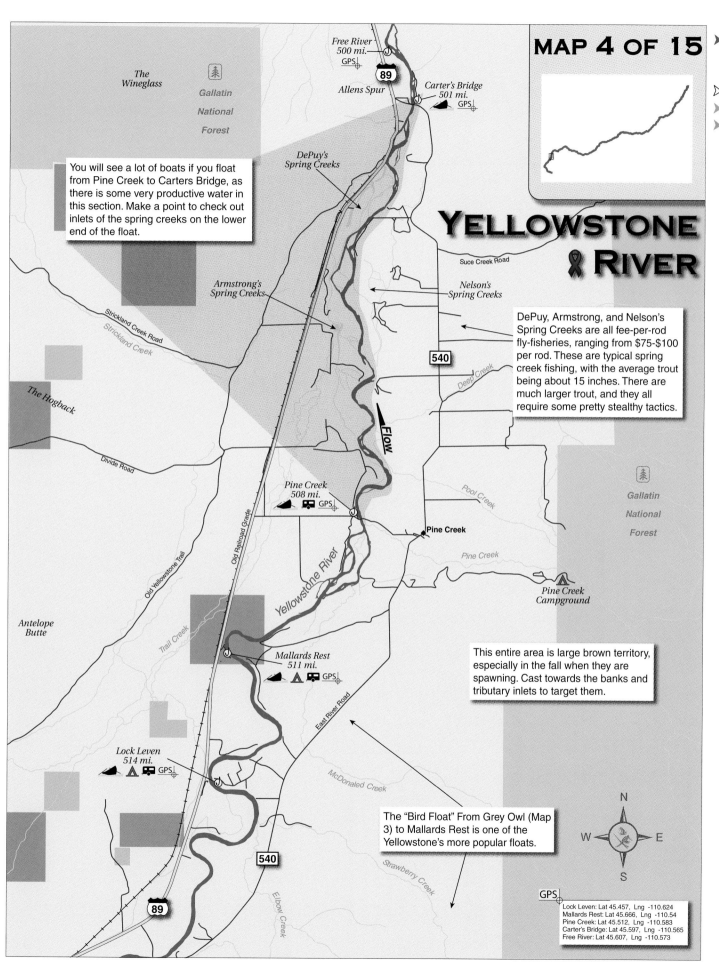

MAP **4** OF **15**

You will see a lot of boats if you float from Pine Creek to Carters Bridge, as there is some very productive water in this section. Make a point to check out inlets of the spring creeks on the lower end of the float.

The Wineglass

Gallatin

National

Forest

Free River 500 mi.
GPS

89

Allens Spur

Carter's Bridge 501 mi.
GPS

DePuy's Spring Creeks

Suce Creek Road

YELLOWSTONE
RIVER

Armstrong's Spring Creeks

Nelson's Spring Creeks

Strickland Creek Road

Strickland Creek

540

Deep Creek

DePuy, Armstrong, and Nelson's Spring Creeks are all fee-per-rod fly-fisheries, ranging from $75-$100 per rod. These are typical spring creek fishing, with the average trout being about 15 inches. There are much larger trout, and they all require some pretty stealthy tactics.

The Hogback

Flow

Divide Road

Pine Creek 508 mi.
GPS

Pool Creek

Gallatin

National

Forest

Pine Creek

Old Railroad Grade

Old Yellowstone Trail

Yellowstone River

Pine Creek

Pine Creek Campground

Antelope Butte

Trail Creek

Mallards Rest 511 mi.
GPS

This entire area is large brown territory, especially in the fall when they are spawning. Cast towards the banks and tributary inlets to target them.

East River Road

Lock Leven 514 mi.
GPS

McDonaled Creek

The "Bird Float" From Grey Owl (Map 3) to Mallards Rest is one of the Yellowstone's more popular floats.

540

N

W   E

S

Strawberry Creek

89

Elbow Creek

GPS

Lock Leven: Lat 45.457, Lng -110.624
Mallards Rest: Lat 45.666, Lng -110.54
Pine Creek: Lat 45.512, Lng -110.583
Carter's Bridge: Lat 45.597, Lng -110.565
Free River: Lat 45.607, Lng -110.573

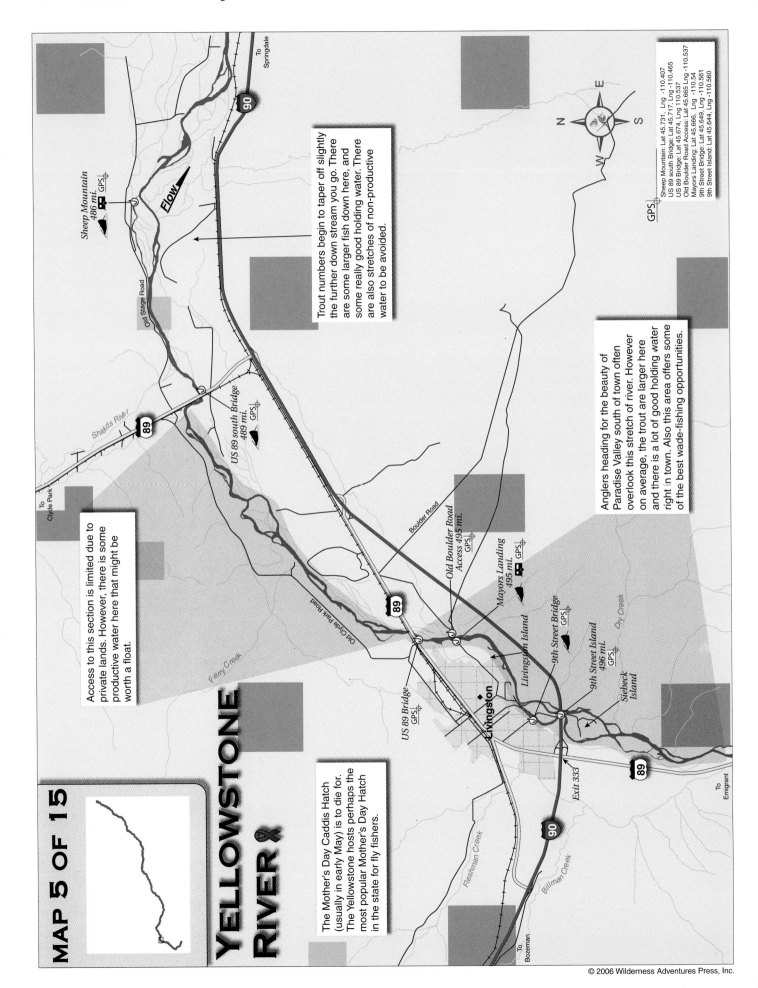

MAP 5 OF 15

YELLOWSTONE RIVER

Sheep Mountain: Lat 45.731, Lng -110.407
US 89 south Bridge: Lat 45.717, Lng -110.465
US 89 Bridge: Lat 45.674, Lng 110.537
Old Boulder Road Access: Lat 45.665 Lng -110.537
Mayors Landing: Lat 45.666, Lng -110.54
9th Street Bridge: Lat 45.649, Lng -110.561
9th Street Island: Lat 45.644, Lng -110.560

GPS

Trout numbers begin to taper off slightly the further down stream you go. There are some larger fish down here, and some really good holding water. There are also stretches of non-productive water to be avoided.

Anglers heading for the beauty of Paradise Valley south of town often overlook this stretch of river. However on average, the trout are larger here and there is a lot of good holding water right in town. Also this area offers some of the best wade-fishing opportunities.

Access to this section is limited due to private lands. However, there is some productive water here that might be worth a float.

The Mother's Day Caddis Hatch (usually in early May) is to die for. The Yellowstone hosts perhaps the most popular Mother's Day Hatch in the state for fly fishers.

Sheep Mountain
486 mi.   GPS

Flow

US 89 south Bridge
489 mi.   GPS

Shields River

Old Stage Road

To Springdale

To Clyde Park

Old Clyde Park Road

Ferry Creek

Boulder Road

Old Boulder Road
Access 495 mi.   GPS

Mayors Landing
495 mi.   GPS

Livingston Island

9th Street Bridge   GPS

9th Street Island
496 mi.   GPS

Siebeck Island

Dry Creek

US 89 Bridge   GPS

Livingston

Exit 333

Fleshman Creek

Billman Creek

To Bozeman

To Emigrant

© 2006 Wilderness Adventures Press, Inc.

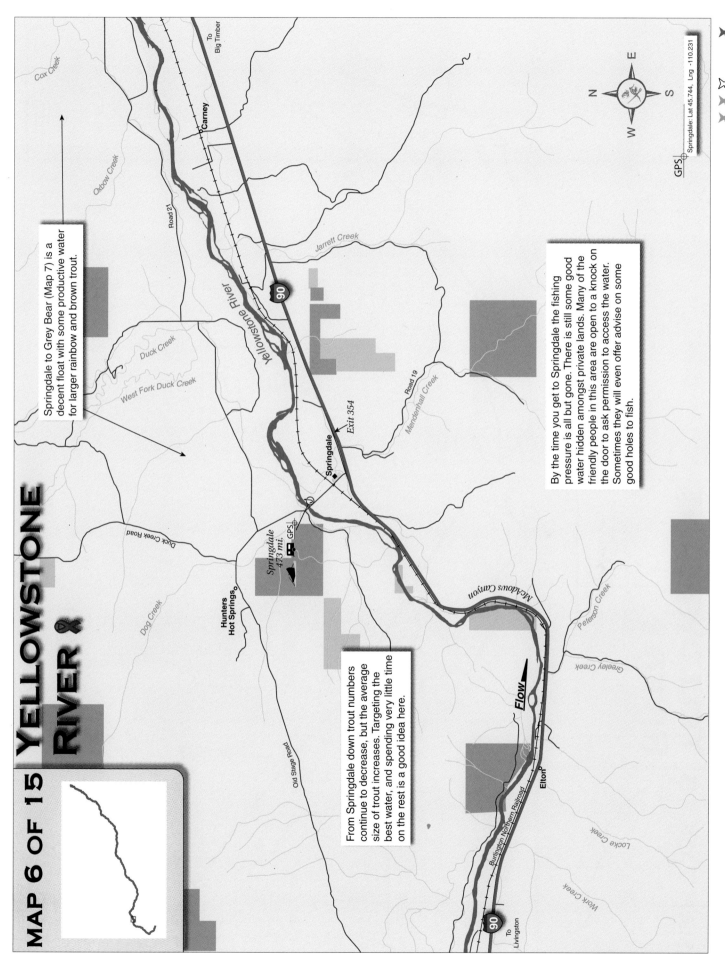

MAP 6 OF 15 YELLOWSTONE RIVER 8

Springdale to Grey Bear (Map 7) is a decent float with some productive water for larger rainbow and brown trout.

By the time you get to Springdale the fishing pressure is all but gone. There is still some good water hidden amongst private lands. Many of the friendly people in this area are open to a knock on the door to ask permission to access the water. Sometimes they will even offer advise on some good holes to fish.

From Springdale down trout numbers continue to decrease, but the average size of trout increases. Targeting the best water, and spending very little time on the rest is a good idea here.

Springdale: Lat 45.744, Lng -110.231

Cox Creek
Oxbow Creek
To Big Timber
Carney
Road 21
Yellowstone River
Jarrett Creek
90
Exit 354
Road 19
Mendenhall Creek
Springdale
Duck Creek
West Fork Duck Creek
Duck Creek Road
Hunters Hot Springs
Dog Creek
GPS
Springdale 473 mi.
Old Stage Road
Meadows Canyon
Peterson Creek
Greeley Creek
Flow
Elton
Burlington Northern Railroad
Locke Creek
Work Creek
90
To Livingston

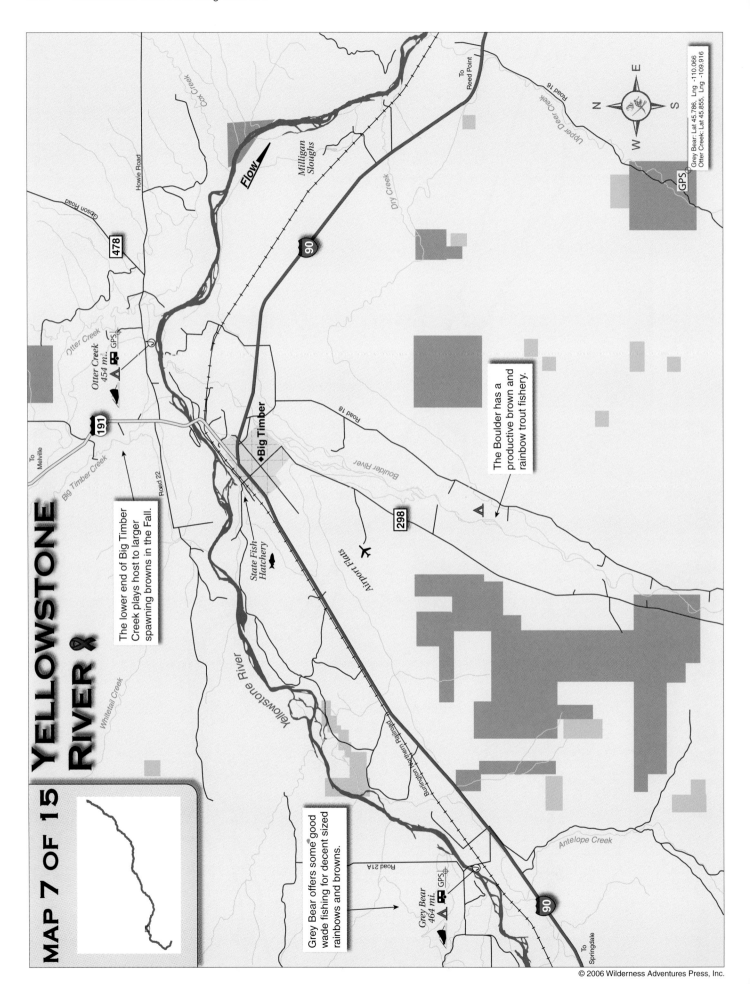

MAP 7 OF 15

YELLOWSTONE
RIVER

The lower end of Big Timber Creek plays host to larger spawning browns in the Fall.

Grey Bear offers some good wade fishing for decent sized rainbows and browns.

The Boulder has a productive brown and rainbow trout fishery.

Flow

Milligan Sloughs

Cox Creek

Howie Road

Gibson Road

478

Otter Creek

Otter Creek
454 mi.

GPS

191

To Melville

Big Timber Creek

Road 22

Whitetail Creek

Yellowstone River

State Fish Hatchery

Big Timber

Road 18

Boulder River

Airport Flats

298

Dry Creek

90

To Reed Point

Upper Deer Creek

Road 16

GPS

N
W E
S

Grey Bear: Lat 45.786, Lng -110.066
Otter Creek: Lat 45.855, Lng -109.916

Burlington Northern Railroad

Road 21A

Grey Bear
464 mi.

GPS

Antelope Creek

90

To Springdale

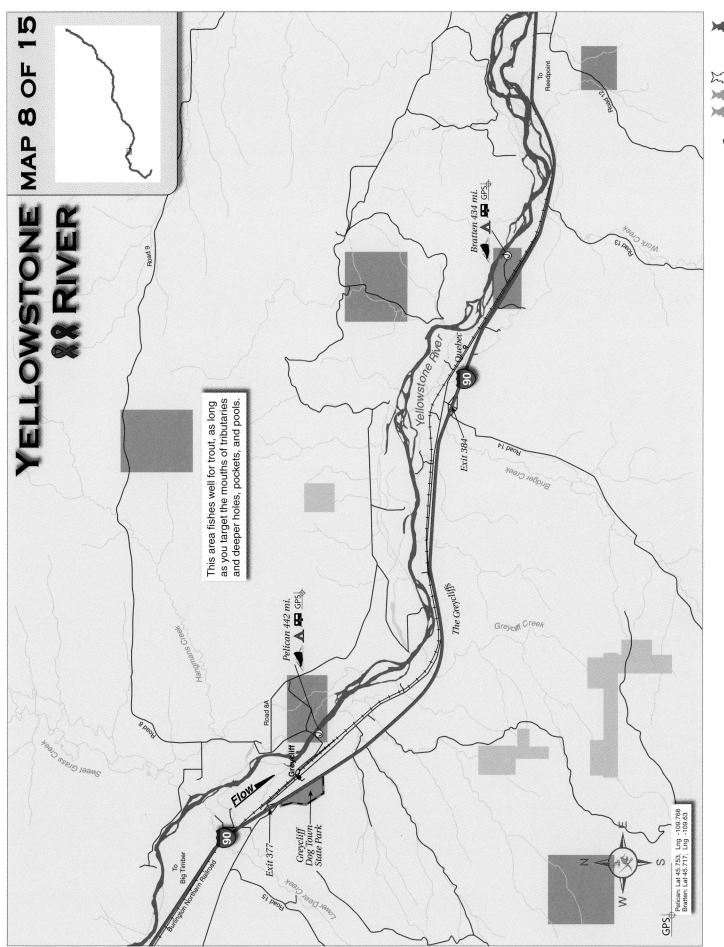

YELLOWSTONE
MAP 8 OF 15
RIVER

This area fishes well for trout, as long as you target the mouths of tributaries and deeper holes, pockets, and pools.

Road 9

To Reedpoint

Road 12

Work Creek

Road 13

Bratten 434 mi.

GPS

Yellowstone River

Quebec

90

Exit 384

Road 14

Bridger Creek

The Greycliffs

Greycliff Creek

Hangmans Creek

Road 8

Road 8A

Pelican 442 mi.

GPS

Greycliff

Flow

90

To Big Timber

Burlington Northern Railroad

Exit 377

Greycliff Dog Town State Park

Sweet Grass Creek

Lower Deer Creek

Road 15

N
W   E
S

GPS

Pelican: Lat 45.753, Lng -109.768
Bratten: Lat 45.717, Lng -109.63

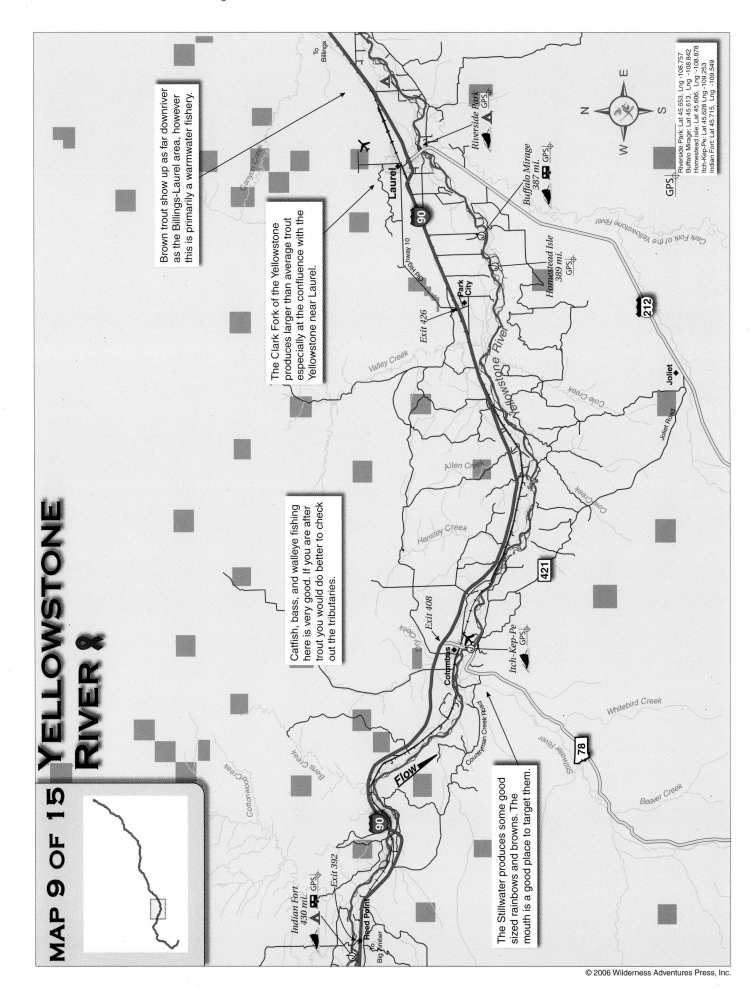

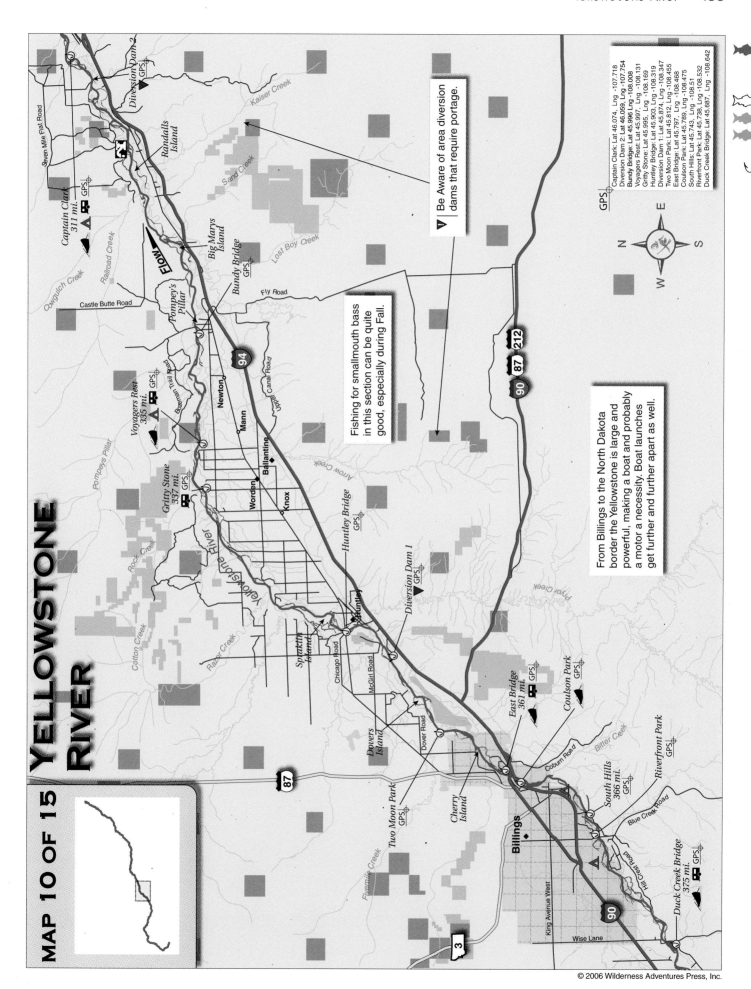

MAP 10 OF 15

YELLOWSTONE RIVER

FLOW

Fishing for smallmouth bass in this section can be quite good, especially during Fall.

Be Aware of area diversion dams that require portage.

From Billings to the North Dakota border the Yellowstone is large and powerful, making a boat and probably a motor a necessity. Boat launches get further and further apart as well.

Captain Clark: Lat 46.074, Lng -107.718
Diversion Dam 2: Lat 46.059, Lng -107.754
Bundy Bridge: Lat 45.996 Lng -108.008
Voyagers Rest: Lat 45.997, Lng -108.131
Gritty Stone: Lat 45.995, Lng -108.169
Huntley Bridge: Lat 45.903, Lng -108.319
Diversion Dam 1: Lat 45.874, Lng -108.347
Two Moon Park: Lat 45.797, Lng -108.455
East Bridge: Lat 45.812, Lng -108.468
Coulson Park: Lat 45.789, Lng -108.475
South Hills: Lat 45.743, Lng -108.51
Riverfront Park: Lat 45.738, Lng -108.532
Duck Creek Bridge: Lat 45.687, Lng -108.642

Captain Clark 311 mi.
Voyagers Rest 335 mi.
Gritty Stone 337 mi.
East Bridge 361 mi.
South Hills 366 mi.
Duck Creek Bridge 375 mi.

Randalls Island
Big Marys Island
Pompey's Pillar
Spratlin Island
Dovers Island
Cherry Island

Diversion Dam 2
Diversion Dam 1
Bundy Bridge
Huntley Bridge
Two Moon Park
Coulson Park
Riverfront Park

Seven Mile Flat Road
Kaiser Creek
Sand Creek
Lost Boy Creek
Cowgulch Creek
Railroad Creek
Castle Butte Road
Fly Road
Bozeman Trail Road
Upper Canal Road
Pompeys pillar
Rock Creek
Cotton Creek
Razer Creek
Chicago Road
McGirl Road
Dover Road
Coburn Road
Bitter Creek
Pryor Creek
Arrow Creek
Blue Creek Road
Cliff Road
King Avenue West
Wise Lane
Fivemile Creek

Newton
Mann
Ballantine
Worden
Knox
Huntley
Billings

Yellowstone River

94
87
90
87
212
90
3

GPS
N E W S

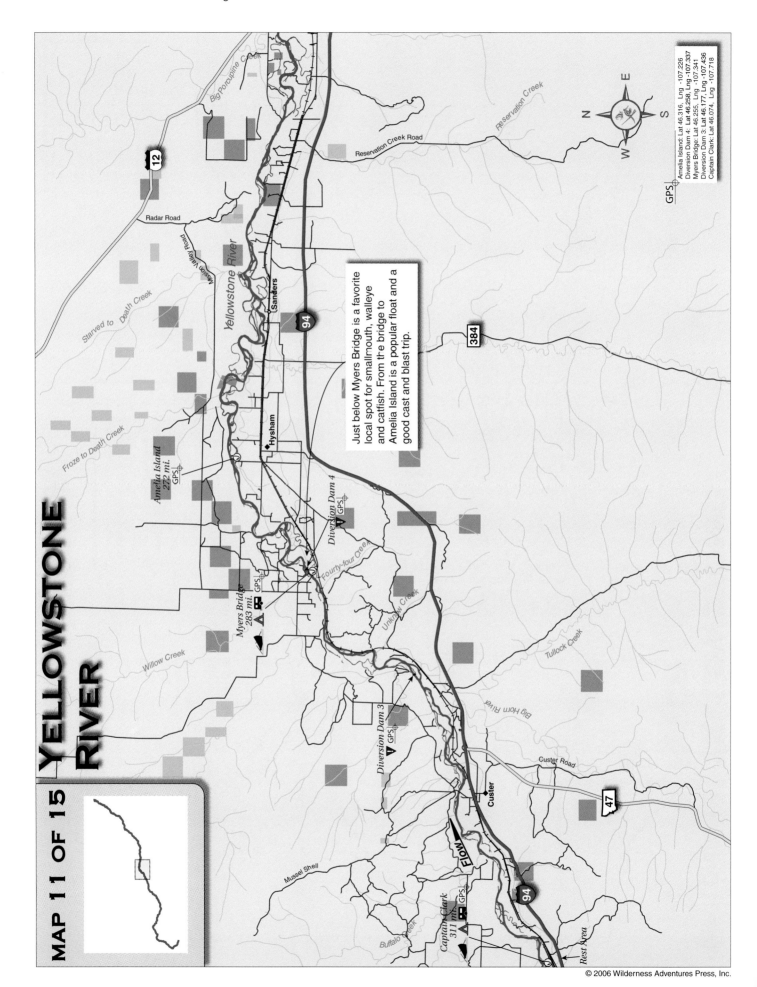

MAP 11 OF 15

YELLOWSTONE RIVER

Just below Myers Bridge is a favorite local spot for smallmouth, walleye and catfish. From the bridge to Amelia Island is a popular float and a good cast and blast trip.

GPS

Amelia Island: Lat 46.316, Lng -107.226
Diversion Dam 4: Lat 46.258, Lng -107.337
Myers Bridge: Lat 46.255, Lng -107.341
Diversion Dam 3: Lat 46.177, Lng -107.436
Captain Clark: Lat 46.074, Lng -107.718

Amelia Island 272 mi.

Myers Bridge 283 mi.

Diversion Dam 4

Diversion Dam 3

Captain Clark 311 mi.

© 2006 Wilderness Adventures Press, Inc.

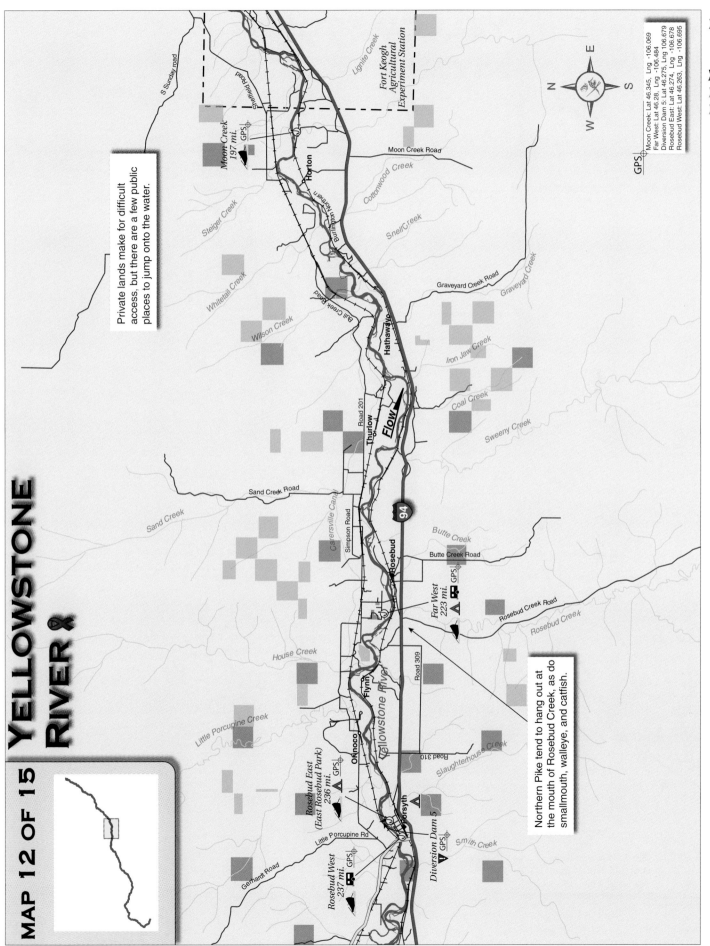

MAP 12 OF 15

YELLOWSTONE
RIVER

Private lands make for difficult access, but there are a few public places to jump onto the water.

Northern Pike tend to hang out at the mouth of Rosebud Creek, as do smallmouth, walleye, and catfish.

GPS
Moon Creek: Lat 46.345, Lng -106.069
Far West: Lat 46.28, Lng -106.484
Diversion Dam 5: Lat 46.275, Lng 106.679
Rosebud East: Lat 46.274, Lng -106.678
Rosebud West: Lat 46.263, Lng -106.695

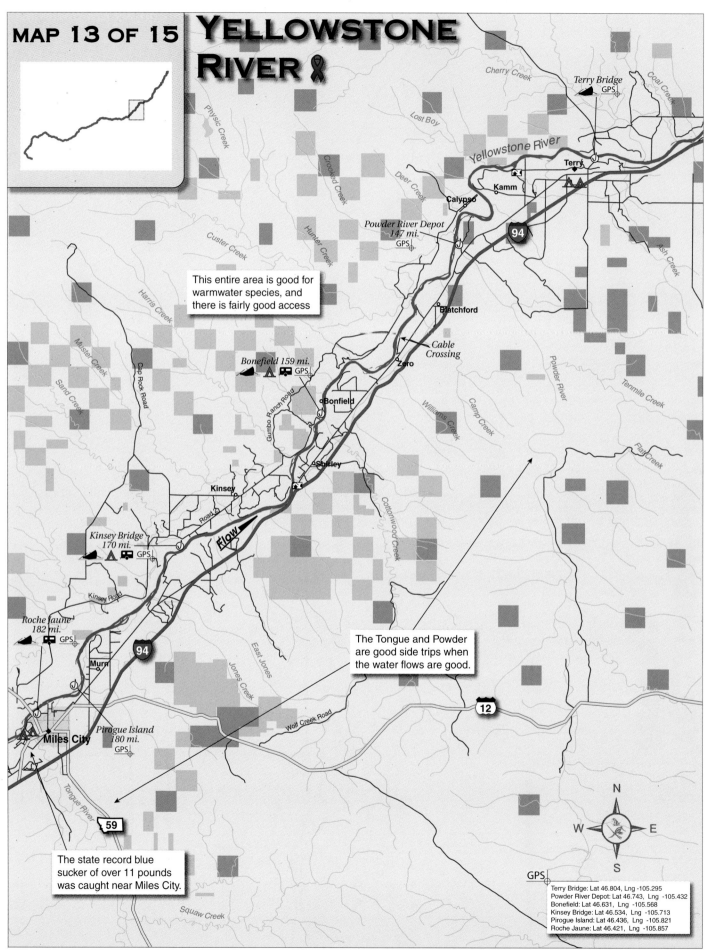

MAP 13 OF 15

YELLOWSTONE RIVER

This entire area is good for warmwater species, and there is fairly good access

Terry Bridge GPS

Cherry Creek

Coal Creek

Lost Boy

Yellowstone River

Terry

Physic Creek

Kamm

Deer Creek

Calypso

Ash Creek

94

Powder River Depot 147 mi. GPS

Crooked Creek

Hunter Creek

Custer Creek

Blatchford

Bonefield 159 mi. GPS

Cable Crossing

Zero

Bonefield

Powder River

Tenmile Creek

Harris Creek

Muster Creek

Cap Rock Road

Gumbo Ranch Road

Williams Creek

Camp Creek

Flat Creek

Sand Creek

Shirley

Kinsey

Cottonwood Creek

Road 2

FLOW

Kinsey Bridge 170 mi. GPS

The Tongue and Powder are good side trips when the water flows are good.

Kinsey Road

East Jones

Roche Jaune 182 mi. GPS

Jones Creek

94

Murn

12

Pirogue Island 180 mi. GPS

Wolf Creek Road

Miles City

N

W E

S

59

Tongue River

The state record blue sucker of over 11 pounds was caught near Miles City.

GPS

Squaw Creek

Terry Bridge: Lat 46.804, Lng -105.295
Powder River Depot: Lat 46.743, Lng -105.432
Bonefield: Lat 46.631, Lng -105.568
Kinsey Bridge: Lat 46.534, Lng -105.713
Pirogue Island: Lat 46.436, Lng -105.821
Roche Jaune: Lat 46.421, Lng -105.857

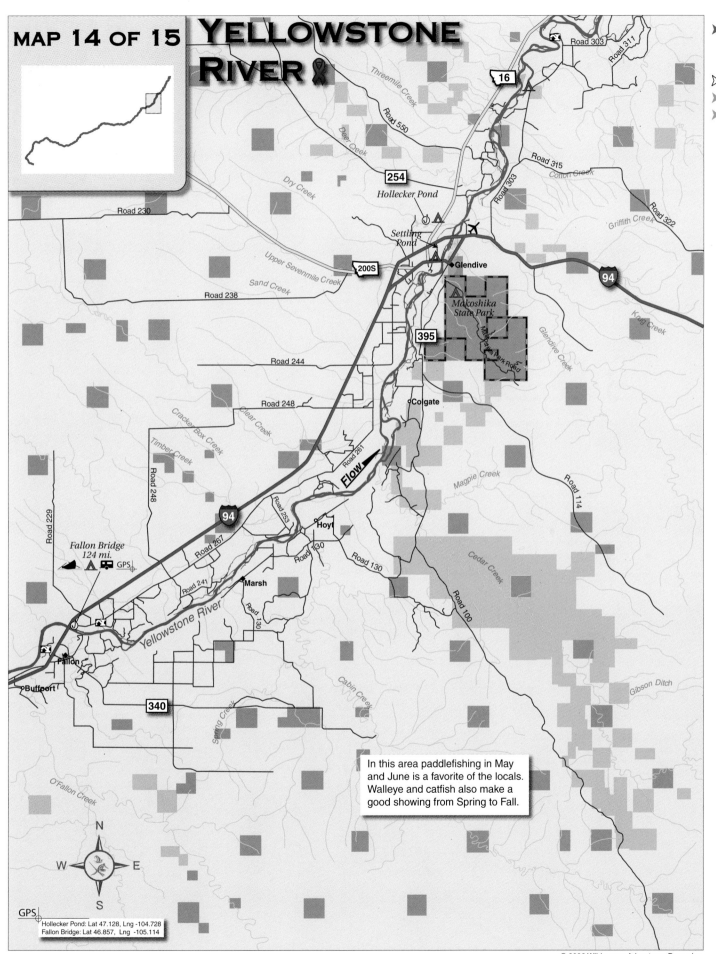

MAP 14 OF 15

YELLOWSTONE RIVER

In this area paddlefishing in May and June is a favorite of the locals. Walleye and catfish also make a good showing from Spring to Fall.

Hollecker Pond: Lat 47.128, Lng -104.728
Fallon Bridge: Lat 46.857, Lng -105.114

© 2006 Wilderness Adventures Press, Inc.

MAP 15 OF 15 YELLOWSTONE RIVER

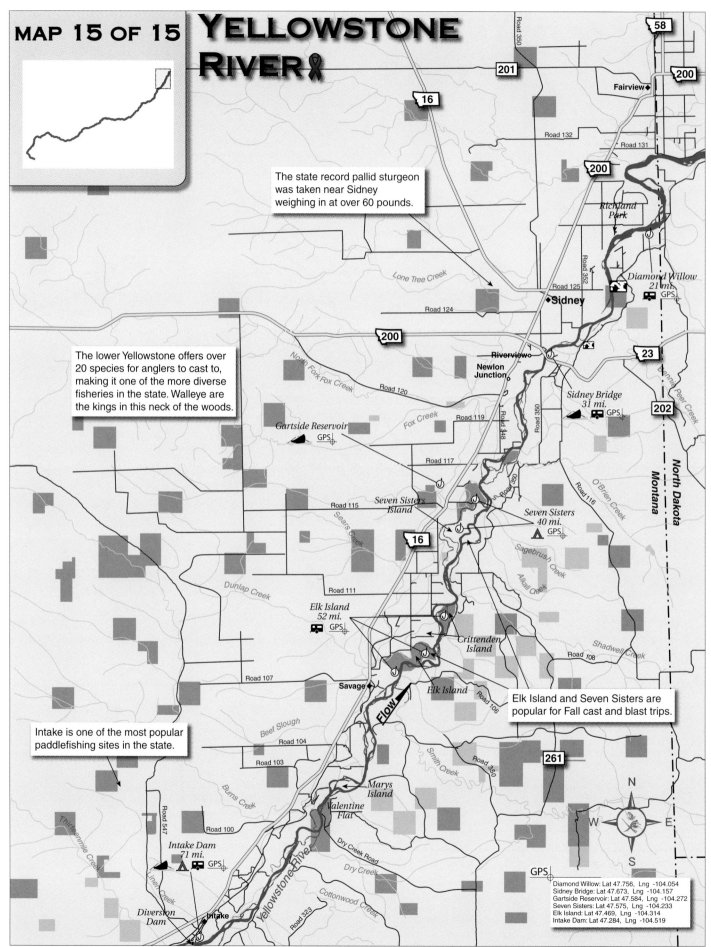

The state record pallid sturgeon was taken near Sidney weighing in at over 60 pounds.

The lower Yellowstone offers over 20 species for anglers to cast to, making it one of the more diverse fisheries in the state. Walleye are the kings in this neck of the woods.

Elk Island and Seven Sisters are popular for Fall cast and blast trips.

Intake is one of the most popular paddlefishing sites in the state.

Fairview

201

58

200

16

Road 132

Road 131

200

Richland Park

Road 352

Diamond Willow 21 mi. GPS

Road 125

Lone Tree Creek

Sidney

Road 124

Riverview

Newlon Junction

23

Sidney Bridge 31 mi. GPS

202

North Fork Fox Creek

Road 120

Road 119

Road 118

Road 350

Fox Creek

Gartside Reservoir GPS

Road 117

Sears Road

O'Brien Creek

Road 116

Bennie Peer Creek

Montana

North Dakota

Road 115

Seven Sisters Island

Seven Sisters 40 mi. GPS

Sagebrush Creek

Dunlap Creek

Road 111

Sears Creek

Alkali Creek

Elk Island 52 mi. GPS

Crittenden Island

Shadwell Creek

Road 108

Road 107

Savage

Elk Island

Road 106

Road 350

Beef Slough

Road 104

Flow

Smith Creek

261

Road 103

Marys Island

Burns Creek

Valentine Flat

N

W E

S

Road 547

Road 100

Thirteenmile Creek

Intake Dam 71 mi. GPS

Dry Creek Road

Dry Creek

GPS

Diversion Dam

Intake

Yellowstone River

Road 323

Cottonwood Creek

Liner Creek

Diamond Willow: Lat 47.756, Lng -104.054
Sidney Bridge: Lat 47.673, Lng -104.157
Gartside Reservoir: Lat 47.584, Lng -104.272
Seven Sisters: Lat 47.575, Lng -104.233
Elk Island: Lat 47.469, Lng -104.314
Intake Dam: Lat 47.284, Lng -104.519

NOTES

NOTES

NOTES

NOTES

NOTES

NOTES

NOTES

Other Fising Titles Available From Wilderness Adventures Press™

California's Best Fishing Waters

Colorado's Best Fishing Waters

Washington's Best Fishing Waters

Flyfisher's Guide to Alaska

Flyfisher's Guide to Chesapeake Bay

Flyfisher's Guide to Colorado

Flyfisher's Guide to the Florida Keys

Flyfisher's Guide to Freshwater Florida

Flyfisher's Guide to Saltwater Florida: Includes Light Tackle

Flyfisher's Guide to Idaho

Flyfisher's Guide to Montana

Flyfisher's Guide to Michigan

Flyfisher's Guide to Minnesota

Flyfisher's Guide to Missouri and Arkansas

Flyfisher's Guide to New Mexico

Flyfisher's Guide to New York

Flyfisher's Guide to Northern California

Flyfisher's Guide to Northern New England

Flyfisher's Guide to Oregon

Flyfisher's Guide to Pennsylvania

Flyfisher's Guide to Texas

Flyfisher's Guide to Utah

Flyfisher's Guide to Virginia

Flyfisher's Guide to Washington

Flyfisher's Guide to Wisconsin

Flyfisher's Guide to Wyoming

On the Fly Guide to the Northwest

On the Fly Guide to the Northern Rockies

Saltwater Angler's Guide to the Southeast

Saltwater Angler's Guide to Southern California

Field Guide to Fishing Knots

Go-To Flies: 101 Patterns the Pros Use When All Else Fails